AF214015

Language Intelligence

IEEE Press
445 Hoes Lane
Piscataway, NJ 08854

IEEE Press Editorial Board
Sarah Spurgeon, *Editor-in-Chief*

Moeness Amin
Jón Atli Benediktsson
Adam Drobot
James Duncan
Ekram Hossain
Brian Johnson
Hai Li
James Lyke
Joydeep Mitra
Desineni Subbaram Naidu
Tony Q. S. Quek
Behzad Razavi
Thomas Robertazzi
Diomidis Spinellis

Language Intelligence

Expanding Frontiers in Natural Language Processing

Akshi Kumar
Department of Computing
Goldsmiths, University of London
United Kingdom

IEEE Press
WILEY

Copyright © 2025 by The Institute of Electrical and Electronics Engineers, Inc. All rights reserved.

Published by John Wiley & Sons, Inc., Hoboken, New Jersey.
Published simultaneously in Canada.

No part of this publication may be reproduced, stored in a retrieval system, or transmitted in any form or by any means, electronic, mechanical, photocopying, recording, scanning, or otherwise, except as permitted under Section 107 or 108 of the 1976 United States Copyright Act, without either the prior written permission of the Publisher, or authorization through payment of the appropriate per-copy fee to the Copyright Clearance Center, Inc., 222 Rosewood Drive, Danvers, MA 01923, (978) 750-8400, fax (978) 750-4470, or on the web at www.copyright.com. Requests to the Publisher for permission should be addressed to the Permissions Department, John Wiley & Sons, Inc., 111 River Street, Hoboken, NJ 07030, (201) 748-6011, fax (201) 748-6008, or online at http://www.wiley.com/go/permission.

Trademarks: Wiley and the Wiley logo are trademarks or registered trademarks of John Wiley & Sons, Inc. and/or its affiliates in the United States and other countries and may not be used without written permission. All other trademarks are the property of their respective owners. John Wiley & Sons, Inc. is not associated with any product or vendor mentioned in this book.

Limit of Liability/Disclaimer of Warranty: While the publisher and author have used their best efforts in preparing this book, they make no representations or warranties with respect to the accuracy or completeness of the contents of this book and specifically disclaim any implied warranties of merchantability or fitness for a particular purpose. Certain AI systems have been used in the creation of this work. No warranty may be created or extended by sales representatives or written sales materials. The advice and strategies contained herein may not be suitable for your situation. You should consult with a professional where appropriate. Further, readers should be aware that websites listed in this work may have changed or disappeared between when this work was written and when it is read. Neither the publisher nor authors shall be liable for any loss of profit or any other commercial damages, including but not limited to special, incidental, consequential, or other damages.

For general information on our other products and services or for technical support, please contact our Customer Care Department within the United States at (800) 762-2974, outside the United States at (317) 572-3993 or fax (317) 572-4002.

Wiley also publishes its books in a variety of electronic formats. Some content that appears in print may not be available in electronic formats. For more information about Wiley products, visit our web site at www.wiley.com.

Library of Congress Cataloging-in-Publication Data Applied for:

Hardback ISBN: 9781394297269

Cover Design: Wiley
Cover Image: © John Lund/Getty Images

Set in 9.5/12.5pt STIXTwoText by Straive, Chennai, India

Contents

List of Figures

List of Tables

About the Author

Dr. Akshi Kumar is a Senior Lecturer (Associate Professor) and Director of Post-Graduate Research in the Department of Computing at Goldsmiths, University of London, United Kingdom. She is a Post-doc from Federal Institute of Education, Science and Technology of Ceará, Fortaleza, Brazil and a PhD from Faculty of Technology, University of Delhi, India. Dr. Kumar has been endorsed by the Royal Academy of Engineering, United Kingdom as an Exceptional Talent in the field of Artificial Intelligence/Data Science in 2022. She has received many research awards for Excellence in Research from various National and International organizations. Her name has been included in the *"Top 2% highly-cited scientists of the world"* list by Stanford University, United States in 2024, 2023, 2022, and 2021. She has published more than 100 peer-reviewed journal papers, 3 written evidences on AI literacy, news integrity and cyber resilience in the UK Parliament (House of Lords and House of Commons), 70+ conference papers with 5 best paper awards. She has successfully guided numerous doctoral Master's thesis candidates. She has been serving as a guest editor in various high-impact journals with reputed publishers. Her research interests are in Natural Language Processing, Social Network and Media analytics, and AI for pervasive healthcare.

Preface

Welcome to *Language Intelligence: Expanding Frontiers in Natural Language Processing*, a comprehensive exploration of the dynamic and evolving field of Natural Language Processing (NLP). This book aims to provide a thorough understanding of both the foundational concepts and advanced techniques in NLP, illustrating its significant impact across various sectors.

Chapter 1 establishes the basics, tracing the historical development of NLP and outlining the different approaches that have shaped its progress. Through examples and case studies, we explore the mechanisms of Natural Language Understanding (NLU) and Natural Language Generation (NLG), setting the foundation for understanding the complexities of the NLP pipeline and its transformative influence on business and societal landscapes.

In Chapter 2, we examine the data landscape essential for NLP, discussing the types of data, methods of acquisition, and the challenges faced in data management. Ethical considerations in data handling are also emphasized, highlighting the need for responsible NLP practices.

Continuing to Chapter 3, the focus shifts to fundamental text processing techniques. From initial text cleaning to detailed parsing and syntactic analysis, this section equips readers with essential skills for preprocessing text data, preparing it for various NLP tasks.

Chapter 4 discusses the linguistic features central to NLP, examining different levels of linguistic analysis and introducing vector space representation, a key concept for many NLP applications today.

In Chapter 5, we explore computational and cognitive approaches that enrich NLP. This includes discussions on how machine learning, memory models, attention mechanisms, and reasoning contribute to the field's advancement, alongside insights into transfer learning and the cutting-edge neuro-symbolic approaches.

Chapters 6–9 provide an in-depth look at practical applications and advanced processing techniques, ranging from affective, psychological, and content analysis to multilingual processing and domain-specific applications in sectors like healthcare, legal, finance, and education. These chapters showcase the versatile and extensive impact of NLP technologies.

Finally, Chapter 10 critically examines the metrics and methods for evaluating the success of NLP, underscoring the importance of accurate and meaningful assessment in developing robust NLP systems.

The Three appendices A, B & C offer detailed explorations of text representation methods, advanced applications of NLP techniques and Python's NLP capabilities, respectively, bridging theoretical knowledge with actionable NLP skills, particularly with Python's rich ecosystem of libraries.

Language Intelligence: Expanding Frontiers in Natural Language Processing is more than just a technical reference; it's a journey through the landscape of linguistic computation, designed to inform, inspire, and ignite a passion for this fascinating field. Whether you are a student, researcher, practitioner, or simply an enthusiast of language and technology, this book aims to enrich your understanding and inspire innovative applications of NLP in the ever-expanding digital universe.

Akshi Kumar

Acknowledgements

As I reflect on the journey that led to the creation of this book, I am filled with immense gratitude towards a group of exceptional individuals who have been my pillars of support, inspiration, and encouragement.

First and foremost, I extend my heartfelt thanks to my parents, Sh. Prem Parkash Kumar and Smt. Krishna Kumar. Their unwavering belief in my capabilities and their endless love and support have been the bedrock of my strength and perseverance. It is to them that I owe my resilience and dedication.

To my brother and his family whose wisdom, guidance, and invaluable advice have been a guiding light throughout this process. His constant encouragement and belief in my work have been instrumental in overcoming the challenges that accompanied this journey.

I am deeply grateful to Professor Jennifer George, former Head of Computing at Goldsmiths, University of London, for her guidance and encouragement. I also extend my thanks to Professor Frances Corner OBE, Warden of Goldsmiths, University of London, for her inspirational leadership and dedication to fostering an environment that champions innovation and excellence. I would also like to express my deepest appreciation to Dr. Saurabh Raj Sangwan, my research collaborator. His insights, expertise, and constructive criticisms have significantly enriched the content and quality of this book. His contribution has been a key factor in shaping and refining the final manuscript.

Last but certainly not least, I thank my son, Kiaan Kumar, whose irresistible enthusiasm and boundless curiosity about the world around us have been a constant source of inspiration. Watching him explore and learn has reminded me of the fundamental wonder that lies at the heart of all knowledge and discovery.

To all of you, I offer my sincere thanks. This book is not just a product of my efforts but a testament to the love, support, and guidance that each of you has generously provided.

In the preparation of this book, I used tools such as ChatGPT and Grammarly to support clarity, sentence restructuring, grammar enhancement, and word count reduction.

Acknowledgements

1

Foundations of Natural Language Processing

Imagine engaging in a conversation where you express enjoyment over a song, and a virtual assistant, like Alexa, responds by acknowledging your preference and adjusting its algorithms accordingly. This is NLP in action—bridging the gap between human communication and computer understanding, allowing for a seamless interaction between the two. Welcome to the fascinating world of Natural Language Processing (NLP)!

NLP is a branch of artificial intelligence that equips computers with the capability to understand, interpret, and respond to human language in a way that is both meaningful and valuable. It encompasses a broad range of tasks and techniques aimed at processing and analyzing both text and speech, serving as a pivotal connection between human natural language and computer data processing. The field of NLP is notably interdisciplinary, drawing from areas such as artificial intelligence, machine learning, linguistics, and social sciences. This amalgamation of fields has led to the development of sophisticated methods that allow machines to process human language in complex ways, ranging from structural and contextual analysis to emotional tone assessment. Every sentence we utter or write carries with it structural, contextual, and emotional cues. While humans can instinctively navigate these cues, for machines, each sentence is a piece of unstructured data that must be meticulously converted into a structured format. Through NLP, what seems like a straightforward sentence like "Alexa, I like this song," is transformed into structured data that machines can comprehend and respond to, leading to actions like playlist modifications and preference learning.

NLP represents a significant stride in the domain of artificial intelligence, where the primary aim is to bridge the gap between human communication and machine understanding. This field involves a series of intricate processes that enable machines to comprehend, interpret, and produce human language in a meaningful way. The core operations of NLP—recognition, understanding, and generation—constitute the backbone of this fascinating AI subdomain.

Language Intelligence: Expanding Frontiers in Natural Language Processing, First Edition. Akshi Kumar.
© 2025 The Institute of Electrical and Electronics Engineers, Inc. Published 2025 by John Wiley & Sons, Inc.

- **Recognition** is the initial phase where machines detect and decipher human language into structured, machine-readable data. This process is crucial for transforming the inherent ambiguity of natural language into a clear-cut format that computers can process. Recognition involves various sub-tasks like tokenization, where text is broken down into words, phrases, or other meaningful elements, and parsing, which involves analyzing the grammatical structure of a sentence. Speech recognition, another facet of this phase, converts spoken language into a digital format. Recognition is heavily dependent on machine learning algorithms that are trained to identify the language's structure and semantics. These algorithms are adept at handling the complexities of language, including syntax, grammar, and even the idiosyncrasies of regional dialects and accents.
- In the **understanding** phase, NLP systems analyze the structured data obtained from recognition to deduce meanings and relationships. This stage involves more advanced NLP tasks such as semantic analysis, which interprets the meaning of words in context, while pragmatics focuses on understanding language. For instance, sentiment analysis discerns the emotional tone behind text data, whether it's positive, negative, or neutral, providing insights into the writer's or speaker's feelings and attitudes. Named entity recognition identifies and classifies key elements in text into predefined categories like names of people, organizations, locations, dates, and more. At this stage, the complexity of human language becomes apparent as the system must understand nuances, humor, sarcasm, and cultural references, which are often challenging for machines.
- The **generation** phase is where NLP systems produce human-like responses from the analyzed data. In this stage, NLP uses Natural Language Generation (NLG) techniques to create coherent, contextually relevant sentences that can be understood by humans. Generation involves converting the structured data back into natural language. This process can be seen in applications like chatbots, virtual assistants, and automated report generators, where the machine communicates with users in a seemingly intuitive and understanding manner. The ability to generate language also encompasses creative aspects of language use, such as composing poetry, writing articles, or generating dialogue in conversational agents.

Despite the technical prowess of NLP, the field still faces significant challenges. One of the primary limitations is the system's ability to fully grasp the intricacies and subtleties of human language. While NLP systems can recognize patterns and analyze text or speech to a certain extent, they often lack the depth of understanding inherent in human communication. The complexity of language, including cultural, contextual, and idiomatic layers, presents a substantial hurdle for AI. Moreover, NLP relies heavily on data-driven, predictive mathematical models that, while being powerful, can sometimes miss the mark in interpreting the ambiguity and fluidity of natural language. Furthermore, most NLP models are trained on vast amounts of text data, which may contain biases and inaccuracies, reflecting the model's language understanding and generation capabilities. These biases can lead to skewed or unfair outcomes, especially in sensitive applications like sentiment analysis, hiring, and law enforcement. Addressing these limitations requires continuous refinement of NLP models, incorporating a broader, more diverse range of data, and developing more sophisticated algorithms that can navigate the nuanced landscape of human language.

1.1 History of NLP

The historical trajectory of NLP is a testament to the evolving interplay between technology and linguistics, an odyssey that commences in the mid-twentieth century and extends into the present era of advanced computing. The foundational stone of NLP was laid in the 1950s, marked by Alan Turing's introduction of the Turing Test, a seminal concept that questioned a machine's ability to exhibit intelligent behavior akin to a human. This period also saw the inception of computational linguistics, where the groundwork for machine understanding of language was established.

As we moved into the 1960s, NLP began to manifest in more concrete forms with systems like ELIZA, created by Joseph Weizenbaum, which demonstrated the superficiality yet potential of human-machine communication. The subsequent development of SHRDLU in 1969 further showcased the ability of computers to comprehend simple English sentences, providing a glimpse into the practical applications of NLP. The 1970s brought a more structured approach to NLP with a focus on rule-based methods, exemplified by the development of conceptual dependency theory. This theory laid the foundation for natural language understanding (NLU) by presenting a model for representing language's conceptual structure. The evolution continued into the 1980s as the field began to pivot from rule-based to statistical methods, signalling a significant paradigm shift. This era also witnessed the creation of Racter, the first chatbot, marking a notable milestone in NLP's history.

The 1990s saw an infusion of machine learning into NLP, catalyzing a transformative phase where algorithms began to learn language patterns, thereby increasing the scope and accuracy of linguistic processing. The culmination of this period was epitomized by IBM's Deep Blue, whose victory in chess underscored AI's potential. The 2000s heralded an age of advanced algorithms and large-scale data, with Google Translate emerging as a quintessential tool, democratizing machine translation for global users. The subsequent decade, the 2010s, was defined by the ascendancy of deep learning and neural networks in NLP. Innovations like sequence-to-sequence models and attention mechanisms significantly improved machine translation, while the introduction of Google's BERT model revolutionized context understanding in NLP.

The present era, the 2020s, continues to witness NLP innovation, with advancements in language generation models like GPT-3 and a heightened focus on addressing bias and ethical considerations in NLP models. The integration of NLP into various industries exemplifies its pervasive impact and the growing recognition of its value in extracting and generating meaningful information from language data. The recent prominence of Large Language Models (LLMs) in NLP has led to a perception that they might render traditional methods obsolete. However, this view overlooks the nuanced and multifaceted nature of NLP. While LLMs have indeed revolutionized the field, offering unparalleled capabilities in generating coherent and contextually relevant text, foundational NLP techniques remain essential for a comprehensive understanding of language processing. Basic foundational NLP remains crucial even in the era of LLMs for several reasons:

- *Understanding Fundamentals:* Foundational NLP provides the groundwork for understanding how language operates at a mechanical level. It encompasses essential processes such as tokenization, parsing, part-of-speech tagging, and syntax analysis. Grasping these basics is vital for interpreting the outputs of more advanced systems like LLMs and for fine-tuning them to specific tasks or languages.
- *Building Blocks for Advanced Models:* The techniques and knowledge derived from foundational NLP serve as building blocks for more sophisticated models, including LLMs. These advanced models often rely on the principles and data processing methods established in basic NLP to function effectively.
- *Customization and Optimization:* Understanding foundational NLP enables researchers and practitioners to customize and optimize LLMs for specific applications. By knowing how language is processed at a fundamental level, one can better tailor these models to meet unique linguistic and contextual requirements.
- *Efficiency and Resource Management:* Foundational NLP methods are often more efficient and require fewer computational resources than LLMs, making them suitable for applications where rapid processing or low resource consumption is essential.
- *Interpretability and Debugging:* A strong grasp of foundational NLP can aid in interpreting the behavior of LLMs and in debugging them when unexpected

results occur. It helps in tracing issues back to their roots in the underlying linguistic processes.

- *Complementarity:* In many cases, foundational NLP methods are used in conjunction with LLMs to enhance performance. For instance, basic NLP techniques can preprocess data to improve the efficiency and accuracy of LLMs or post-process their outputs to refine the results.
- *Educational Value:* For newcomers to NLP, starting with the basics is essential for building a comprehensive understanding of the field. Foundational knowledge equips individuals with the insights needed to effectively engage with, contribute to, and innovate in the domain of NLP.
- *Handling Low-Resource Languages:* Foundational NLP techniques are particularly important for working with low-resource languages, where LLMs may not perform well due to a lack of training data. Basic NLP can provide the necessary tools to process these languages and develop customized solutions.

Throughout its history, NLP has been shaped by the tension and interplay between linguistic theory and computational power, reflecting a journey from simplistic rule-based approaches to sophisticated deep learning models. Each phase of NLP's history not only reflects technological advancements but also a deeper understanding of language's complexity, with ongoing innovations ensuring that the field remains at the cutting edge of artificial intelligence research and application. While LLMs represent a significant leap forward, they do not make foundational NLP techniques obsolete. Instead, these two facets of NLP complement each other, with traditional methods providing the groundwork upon which LLMs build to achieve their impressive feats. Understanding and applying both foundational NLP and LLMs is key to harnessing the full potential of language technology.

1.2 Approaches to NLP

NLP encapsulates a spectrum of methodologies each tailored to parse, interpret, and manifest human language in a form comprehensible to machines. These methodologies span from traditional rule-based systems to advanced machine learning and deep learning paradigms, each contributing uniquely to the evolution of NLP.

- **Rule-Based NLP**, a foundational approach, operates on predefined linguistic rules and grammatical structures. This method, reliant on expert knowledge in linguistics, crafts a deterministic pathway for machines to understand and process language. This methodology, deeply rooted in the traditional study of linguistics, employs a deterministic strategy, where the understanding and processing of language are driven by explicit, handcrafted rules. These rules encompass the gamut of grammatical and syntactic norms that define a language, offering a structured framework for NLP systems to operate within.

At the core of rule-based NLP are comprehensive linguistic resources such as dictionaries, thesauruses, and specialized lexical databases. One notable example is WordNet, a rich lexical database that categorizes English words into sets of cognitive synonyms, known as synsets. Each synset represents a distinct semantic concept, linking words through various relational types, including synonyms (words with similar meanings), hyponyms (words denoting a subclass of a concept), and meronyms (words denoting parts of a whole). This structured semantic network allows rule-based NLP systems to navigate the complex interrelationships of language, enhancing their ability to discern meaning and context.

The application of rule-based NLP is particularly advantageous in tasks where linguistic precision and clear-cut rules are paramount. Information retrieval systems benefit from this approach, as it enables precise querying and filtering of data based on syntactic and semantic criteria. Text summarization, another key application, leverages rule-based methods to distill essential content from larger texts, guided by syntactic structures and meaning encapsulated in the linguistic rules. Basic language understanding, such as parsing sentences and identifying grammatical elements, is also well-suited to rule-based NLP, given its structured and rule-governed nature. Despite its strengths in handling well-defined linguistic tasks, rule-based NLP has limitations. Its deterministic nature means it can be rigid, struggling to adapt to the variability and idiosyncrasies of natural language use in real-world contexts. The creation and maintenance of rule sets require extensive expert knowledge and can be labor-intensive, particularly for languages with complex grammar or those lacking comprehensive linguistic resources. Moreover, rule-based systems might falter in the face of slang, idiomatic expressions, or emerging language use not encapsulated in existing rule sets, highlighting a gap between the structured world of rule-based NLP and the dynamic, evolving nature of human language.

Hence, rule-based NLP offers a deterministic and transparent method for language processing, excelling in specific domains or tasks where the linguistic environment is well-understood and consistent. However, its limitations in handling the dynamic and varied nature of natural language necessitate complementary approaches, especially in broad or informal linguistic contexts.

- Transitioning from heuristics to statistical inference, **Machine Learning-Based NLP** signifies a leap in how machines understand language. Instead of rigid rules, this approach leverages algorithms to learn from data, discovering patterns and relationships in text. Machine learning in NLP can be supervised where models learn from labeled data, or unsupervised, deducing inherent structures within the text. Techniques like support vector machines, decision trees, and neural networks have been instrumental in propelling NLP tasks, including text classification, sentiment analysis, machine translation, and speech recognition. The advent of these statistical models marked a significant advancement in NLP, enhancing both the scalability and accuracy of language processing tasks.

Machine learning in NLP encompasses both supervised and unsupervised learning approaches. Supervised learning methods rely on annotated datasets where the input data is labeled with the correct output, enabling models to learn and make predictions based on this labelled data. Unsupervised learning, on the other hand, digs into raw, unlabelled data to uncover inherent structures and meanings, thus deducing the underlying patterns without explicit guidance. Techniques such as support vector machines, decision trees, and increasingly, neural networks, have become the workhorses of machine learning in NLP, each contributing to various aspects of language processing. These machine learning techniques have been instrumental in advancing core NLP tasks. For instance, text classification has been revolutionized by machine learning algorithms, which can sift through massive volumes of text to categorize content into predefined classes. Sentiment analysis, too, has benefitted from this shift, with algorithms now capable of discerning nuanced emotional tones from text data. Machine translation has seen leaps in quality and efficiency, moving from literal, often stilted translations to more fluid and context-aware renditions of text across languages. Speech recognition, once constrained by the limitations of rule-based systems, has achieved remarkable accuracy under the machine learning regime, enabling real-time, naturalistic voice interactions.

The adoption of machine learning in NLP has not only enhanced the accuracy and effectiveness of language processing tasks but has also significantly expanded the scope and scalability of these tasks. Unlike rule-based systems, which are limited by the confines of their predefined rules, machine learning-based NLP systems thrive on large datasets, continually improving and adapting their performance as they consume more data. This transformative approach to language processing, emphasizing statistical patterns and machine learning, is discussed in depth in Chapter 5 of the book, where we explore the computational and cognitive mechanisms that underpin machine learning in NLP, illustrating how this technology underlies the modern advancements in the field.

- **Deep Learning-Based Methods in NLP** represent the pinnacle of methodological advancement in the field, harnessing sophisticated neural network architectures to capture and interpret the complexities of human language. Technologies such as Recurrent Neural Networks (RNNs), Long Short-Term Memory networks (LSTMs), and more recently, transformers like BERT

(Bidirectional Encoder Representations from Transformers) and GPT (Generative Pre-training Transformer), embody this cutting-edge approach. Deep learning shines in its capacity to learn layered representations of text, adeptly grasping both the immediate and broader contextual cues within language.

The transformative impact of deep learning in NLP is profound, especially in areas like NLU, text generation, and machine translation. These neural network models excel in deciphering the intricate patterns and nuances embedded in language, offering a rich, contextual understanding that enables machines to process and generate text with a level of sophistication akin to human-like comprehension. Unlike earlier methods, deep learning models can inherently capture and utilize the contextual relevance of words and phrases, thus facilitating a nuanced interpretation of language's subtleties. Furthermore, the advent of transformer models has significantly advanced NLP's capabilities. These models, particularly known for their self-attention mechanisms, allow for a more dynamic representation of textual data, enabling the processing of sequences with an efficient understanding of dependencies and relationships. LLMs like GPT have further extended these capabilities, generating text that is not only coherent but also contextually relevant and often indistinguishable from human-written content.

In summary, deep learning-based methods have revolutionized the way machines understand and interact with human language. By learning complex, hierarchical representations of text, these methods have enabled NLP systems to perform a wide array of tasks with unprecedented accuracy and fluency, offering deeper insights into the fabric of language itself. This significant stride in NLP is further elaborated in Chapter 5, focusing on the deep learning paradigms that underpin these advancements.

The journey through the approaches to NLP—from rule-based to deep learning—encapsulates the evolving landscape of language processing. Each approach brings a unique set of strengths and applications, collectively enriching the field of NLP. Rule-based methods, with their reliance on explicit linguistic knowledge, provide a clear, albeit limited, understanding of language structures. Machine learning broadens this horizon, offering scalable and adaptable solutions, while deep learning pushes the boundaries, introducing a level of analytical depth and fluidity that closely mimics human linguistic capabilities. Together, these methodologies define the current state of NLP, a dynamic and rapidly advancing field at the intersection of linguistics, computer science, and artificial intelligence.

1.3 Understanding NLP through NLU and NLG: Examples and Case Studies

NLP encompasses two critical components: Natural Language Understanding (NLU) and Natural Language Generation (NLG). These elements are essential for enabling machines to interpret and produce human language in a context that is meaningful and useful.

- *Natural Language Understanding (NLU):* Involves the machine's ability to understand and interpret human language. NLU is about extracting meaning from text or speech, encompassing tasks like sentiment analysis, entity recognition, and language translation. For example, in sentiment analysis, NLU algorithms examine customer reviews to determine whether the sentiment is positive, negative, or neutral. In the case of entity recognition, NLU is used to identify and categorize key information in text, such as person names, organizations, locations, and dates. A practical case study of NLU is its use in virtual assistants like Siri or Alexa, which understand user commands and queries to perform actions like setting reminders, playing music, or providing weather information.
- *Natural Language Generation (NLG):* On the other hand, is the process where machines generate text or speech from data. This involves converting structured information into human-readable text, ensuring the output is coherent, contextually relevant, and semantically rich. NLG is commonly seen in report generation, where systems convert data into narrative summaries or detailed reports. For example, automated journalism where NLG tools generate news articles based on data inputs like sports statistics or financial reports. Another case study of NLG is in the healthcare sector, where patient data can be transformed into readable clinical reports or personalized patient care instructions.

1.3.1 Practical Case Studies

NLP, through the dual processes of NLU and NLG, offers profound capabilities in interpreting and producing human language. This technology not only enhances interaction between humans and machines but also paves the way for innovative applications across various domains, streamlining processes, and facilitating efficient communication.

- *Customer Service Chatbots*: Incorporating both NLU and NLG, chatbots can understand customer queries (NLU) and generate appropriate responses (NLG). For instance, a chatbot for a bank might understand a customer's request about account balance (NLU) and generate a response detailing the account balance, recent transactions, and other related information (NLG).

- *Automated Content Creation:* News organizations use NLP to automatically generate news articles. For example, The Washington Post's Heliograf has been creating short reports and alerts on topics like the Olympics and elections, where it understands the key facts (NLU) and constructs narrative content (NLG).
- *Language Translation Services:* Translation tools like Google Translate apply NLU to understand the text's meaning in the source language and then use NLG to produce an accurate translation in the target language. This involves a deep understanding of grammatical, syntactic, and semantic nuances across languages.
- *Personal Assistants and Smart Devices:* Virtual assistants like Google Assistant use NLU to comprehend user requests, such as setting up meetings or searching for information online, and NLG to provide responses that are natural and contextually appropriate.

We aim to unpack the intricacies of NLU within this book, highlighting its indispensable role in crafting intuitive and intelligent language processing systems.

1.4 NLP Pipeline

The NLP pipeline, a cornerstone of modern NLP practices, is a systematic journey of transforming raw text into structured, actionable data. This intricate process, fundamental to extracting insights from unstructured text, involves several distinct yet interconnected stages, each contributing uniquely to the overall understanding and generation of natural language. (Fig.1.1) illustrates the NLP pipeline.

- *Data Acquisition and Cleaning:* The journey begins with Data Acquisition, where diverse textual data are sourced from various digital footprints. This

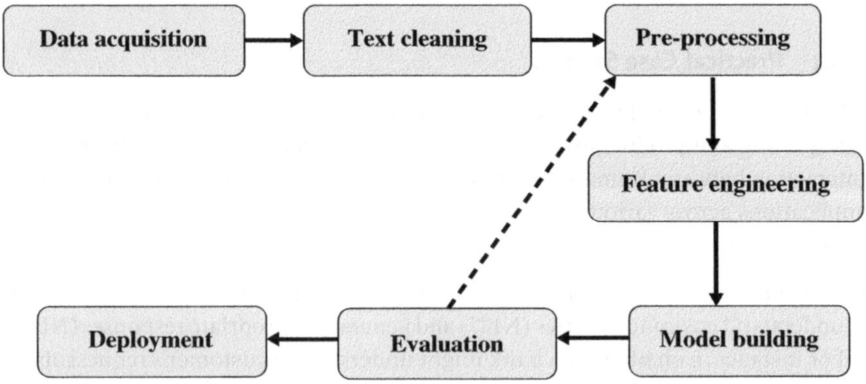

Figure 1.1 NLP Pipeline.

stage addresses the challenge of harnessing a vast array of text data from web pages, social media, official documents, and more, ensuring a rich dataset for analysis. Sophisticated tools like web scrapers and APIs are employed to aggregate this data, necessitating a keen understanding of data relevance and context to align with the end objectives of the NLP tasks at hand.

Following acquisition, Text Cleaning is paramount to refine this raw data. The focus here is on eliminating noise and inconsistencies: removing extraneous HTML tags, correcting spelling errors, and addressing syntactical anomalies. Techniques such as Unicode normalization and regular expression (RegEx) matching are crucial for stripping unwanted characters and formatting the text into a cleaner, more uniform structure. This process is not merely cosmetic but essential, as clean data significantly influences the performance and accuracy of subsequent NLP stages.

- *Preprocessing and Linguistic Analysis:* Text Preprocessing takes the cleaned data through vital steps like sentence segmentation and tokenization, breaking down large text blocks into manageable units of sentences and words, respectively. This breakdown is critical for machines to analyze text at a granular level, facilitating a more detailed and nuanced linguistic understanding.

  In the realm of Linguistic Analysis, the pipeline searches deeper into the grammatical and semantic layers of the text. Here, the focus is on morphological processing (like stemming and lemmatization), syntactic parsing, and semantic analysis, which lay the groundwork for machines to grasp the underlying meaning and context. These processes are intricate, involving complex algorithms to decipher the structure and meaning of language beyond mere word recognition.
- *Advanced Processing and Model Building:* Feature Engineering is the stage where significant attributes or features of the text are extracted and prepared for analytical modelling. This process involves selecting the most relevant aspects of the text, like word frequencies, sentence length, part-of-speech tags, and semantic features, which will be instrumental in training machine learning models.

  Model Building is a pivotal phase where the actual machine learning takes place. Here, various models, from rule-based systems to advanced deep learning networks, are trained on the pre-processed and feature-engineered text. These models learn to perform specific NLP tasks, such as sentiment analysis, entity recognition, or language translation, adapting and improving their accuracy and efficiency over time through iterative training and testing.
- *Evaluation and Deployment:* The Evaluation phase rigorously assesses the model's performance, using metrics like accuracy, precision, recall, and F1 score to ensure that they meet the desired standards of linguistic understanding and generation. This step is crucial for refining the models, tweaking parameters, and validating the effectiveness of the NLP pipeline in real-world scenarios.

Finally, in the Deployment stage, these well-trained and validated models are integrated into applications and systems, ready to interact with end-users and other digital platforms. This stage marks the culmination of the NLP pipeline, where the models are put to the test in live environments, handling real-time language processing tasks, from powering chatbots and virtual assistants to analyzing customer feedback and generating automated content.

Throughout these stages, the NLP pipeline represents a dynamic and iterative process of continuous improvement and adaptation, reflecting the complexity and evolving nature of human language. Each stage, meticulously crafted and executed, contributes to the overarching goal of bridging the gap between human linguistic capabilities and machine understanding, enabling more intuitive and effective human-machine interactions.

1.5 NLP's Transformative Impact on Business and Society

The integration of NLP into various sectors has not only revolutionized business operations but also significantly influenced societal interactions, illustrating the profound impact of this technology. In the realm of business, NLP has become a cornerstone for enhancing customer engagement and support using chatbots and virtual assistants. These intelligent systems, powered by sophisticated NLP algorithms, can understand, and respond to customer queries in real time, improving the overall customer service experience. Similarly, NLP plays a crucial role in market intelligence by analyzing social media and news trends, offering businesses invaluable insights into consumer behavior and market dynamics.

E-commerce platforms leverage NLP to create personalized shopping experiences, recommending products based on customer preferences and search history. This capability not only increases customer satisfaction but also drives sales by presenting users with items that are more likely to appeal to them. Additionally, sentiment analysis on customer reviews using NLP techniques helps e-commerce businesses gauge product performance and customer satisfaction, enabling them to make informed decisions about product improvements and targeted marketing strategies. In the financial sector, NLP contributes to risk management by analyzing news and reports to predict market trends and assess potential risks. Fraud detection is another critical application, where linguistic analysis of financial transactions helps identify suspicious activities, safeguarding against financial fraud. The healthcare industry benefits from NLP in enhancing patient care and monitoring through voice-assisted technologies. Clinical documentation, a time-consuming task for healthcare professionals, is made more efficient and accurate with the automation capabilities offered by NLP, thereby improving the quality of care and reducing administrative burdens.

Furthermore, NLP's influence extends to the education sector, where it facilitates personalized learning experiences. Language learning tools powered by NLP assist users in acquiring new languages, making language learning more accessible and effective. In the public sector, NLP aids policy analysis by analyzing public opinion and feedback on social issues and policies, ensuring that policymaking is informed by the voices of the people.

In summary, NLP's applications across various industries demonstrate its versatility and transformative potential. From improving customer interactions and driving personalized experiences in e-commerce to enhancing patient care in healthcare and supporting data-driven policymaking in the public sector, NLP stands as a pivotal technology shaping the future of business and society.

As we traverse the NLP landscape, we encounter its practical applications in everyday life. From powering search engines and virtual assistants to facilitating real-time translation services, NLP is integral to modern digital experiences. It streamlines email filtering, personalizes social media feeds, enhances customer service interactions through chatbots, and even aids in healthcare by analyzing patient records for improved diagnostic accuracy. In essence, NLP is not just about enabling machines to understand language; it's about fostering an environment where technology comprehensively interacts with human nuances, continually advancing to meet the complexities of human communication.

Knowledge Checkpoint 1

Crossword Puzzle: "Exploring Language and NLP"

Complete the crossword using your knowledge of English grammar and NLP. Each clue corresponds to a term or concept from these fields.

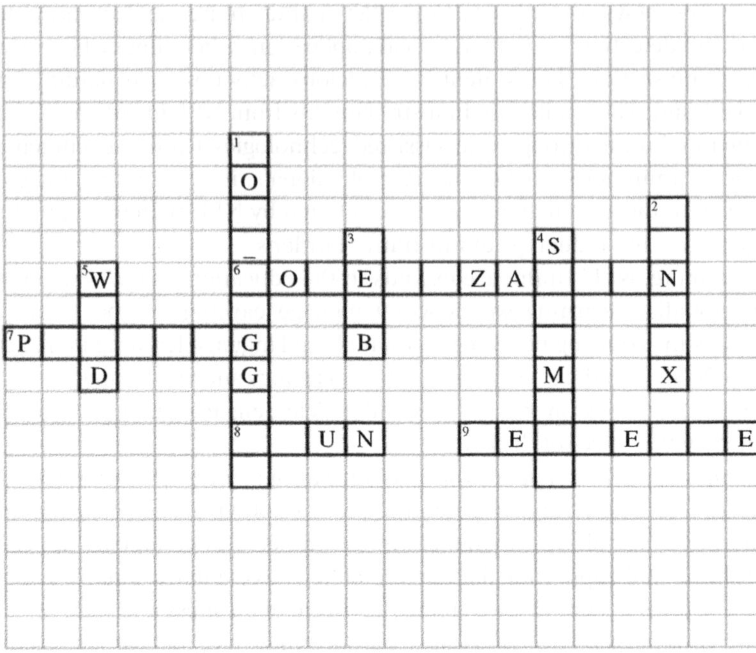

Clues:

Across	Down
6 NLP technique for breaking down text into sentences, words, etc. (13 letters)	**1** NLP task of assigning parts of speech to each word in a sentence. (11 letters)
7 NLP task of determining the structure of a sentence. (7 letters)	**2** The study of sentence structure and the rules that govern the formation of sentences, essential in syntactic analysis in NLP. (6 letters)
8 A linguistic term for the name of a person, place, thing, or idea, crucial in named entity recognition in NLP. (4 letters)	**3** The part of speech that describes an action or occurrence, essential in POS tagging in NLP. (4 letters)
9 In grammar, a group of words that contains a subject and predicate; in NLP, often a unit of analysis.	**4** NLP technique for reducing inflected words to their base or root form.
	5 Basic linguistic unit of meaning, crucial in both grammar and NLP. (4 letters)

2

Navigating the Data Landscape for NLP

In the realm of Natural Language Processing (NLP), data is the lifeblood that powers the algorithms and models essential for interpreting and generating human language. The quest for optimal NLP performance traverses the multifaceted landscape of data characterized by volume, variety, and veracity. Volume refers to the sheer quantity of data required to train robust NLP models. These models, especially in the age of deep learning, thrive on large datasets that provide the breadth of examples needed to understand the complexities and nuances of natural language. However, more data alone does not guarantee success; the variety of data plays a critical role. This encompasses not only the diversity of languages and dialects but also the range of domains and contexts—be it casual conversation, technical reports, literary texts, or social media content—each bringing its own linguistic peculiarities.

The variety in NLP data ensures that models are not just proficient in a narrow context but are adaptable and nuanced enough to handle the unpredictable nature of human language. For instance, training a sentiment analysis model requires data from varied sources to grasp the subtleties of emotional expression across different contexts and cultures. Furthermore, veracity, or the trustworthiness of data, underpins the integrity of NLP models. Data must be accurate, relevant, and representative to avoid biases and misinterpretations that could lead to flawed conclusions or predictions.

Collecting and curating data for NLP is not just about amassing text corpora; it's about building a dataset that mirrors the complex, varied, and rich tapestry of human language. This involves careful annotation, rigorous quality checks, and a strategic approach to data diversity to ensure the models trained on this data can perform effectively and ethically in the real world. For example, an NLP model used in healthcare for analyzing patient records must be trained on accurate, comprehensive, and privacy-compliant data to be both effective and ethical.

Undoubtedly, navigating the data landscape for NLP is a nuanced journey that requires a keen understanding of the volume, variety, and veracity of data.

Language Intelligence: Expanding Frontiers in Natural Language Processing, First Edition. Akshi Kumar.
© 2025 The Institute of Electrical and Electronics Engineers, Inc. Published 2025 by John Wiley & Sons, Inc.

By meticulously addressing these three dimensions, we can develop NLP systems that are not only powerful and intelligent but also fair, unbiased, and adaptable to the ever-changing ways in which we communicate and express ourselves through language.

2.1 Types of Data in NLP

In NLP, data can be categorized into several types based on its nature, structure, and purpose. Here's an elaboration on the main types of data used in NLP:

- *Textual Data:* This is the most common form of data in NLP, encompassing a wide range of written content such as books, articles, blogs, tweets, and more. Textual data can be further classified based on its source and style, including:
  a) **Formal Text:** Found in academic papers, legal documents, and other professional communications, characterized by structured language and complex vocabulary.
  b) **Informal Text:** Includes social media posts, text messages, and casual conversations, often featuring colloquial language, slang, and emojis.
  c) **Web Data:** Encompasses content from websites, including both static pages and dynamic content like user-generated comments and forums.
- *Speech and Audio Data:* Speech data is crucial for tasks like speech recognition, speaker identification, and sentiment analysis through vocal cues. This category includes:
  a) **Recorded Speech:** Audio recordings of spoken language, used in training models for speech-to-text applications.
  b) **Synthetic Speech:** Computer-generated speech used to train and test speech synthesis systems.
- *Multilingual and Cross-Linguistic Data:* With the global nature of communication, multilingual data is vital for developing systems capable of handling multiple languages. This includes parallel corpora for machine translation, where text is aligned across languages, and multilingual datasets that can train models to understand and generate text in various languages.
- *Annotated and Labeled Data:* In supervised learning, annotated data, where text or speech is tagged with labels or categories, is essential. Examples include:
  a) **Sentiment-Annotated Corpora:** Texts labeled with sentiments (positive, negative, neutral) for sentiment analysis tasks.
  b) **Named Entity-Annotated Corpora:** Texts tagged with names of people, organizations, locations, etc., for named entity recognition.
- *Domain-Specific Data:* Certain NLP applications require specialized data reflecting specific fields of knowledge or industry sectors, such as:

   a) **Medical Records:** Used for clinical NLP tasks, these include patient notes, medical journals, and research articles.
   b) **Financial Reports:** Texts like market reports, earnings calls, and financial news, used in economic forecasting and stock market analysis.
- *Unstructured Data:* While not neatly categorized or organized, unstructured data forms a significant portion of the data landscape in NLP. It requires preprocessing to extract meaningful information, including converting raw text and audio files into analyzable formats.
- *Machine-Generated Data:* This includes data produced by AI systems, such as chatbot conversation logs or text generated by language models. It's used for refining AI training processes and enhancing natural language understanding and generation capabilities.

Each type of data in NLP serves different purposes and presents unique challenges, from collection and preprocessing to modelling and analysis. The diversity of data types underscores the multidimensional nature of NLP and the need for comprehensive strategies to handle and leverage this data effectively. In this book, we concentrate on textual data, exploring its intricacies and applications within NLP, while speech and audio data are outside our main scope.

2.2 Data Acquisition

Data acquisition for NLP is the critical first step in building any language model, setting the foundation upon which all linguistic analysis will rest. It involves gathering textual or spoken language material from various sources that reflect the diversity and complexity of human language. The integrity and representativeness of this collected data are vital, as they directly influence the model's subsequent ability to understand, interpret, and generate language. Effective data acquisition ensures that NLP models are not only accurate in their immediate tasks but also versatile and adaptable to different domains and applications. Fig.2.1 outlines various data acquisition techniques and strategies for enhancing datasets, which are fundamental processes in the field of NLP.

The goal is to amass a corpus that is not only vast but also suitable to the problem at hand. For instance, constructing a sentiment analysis model for financial news will require a very different dataset than one intended for medical diagnosis. Sourcing from public datasets can be a starting point, offering a springboard into NLP tasks. These datasets are often curated and well-structured, making them suitable for training models with less preprocessing. For example, the UCI Machine Learning Repository offers datasets that have been used to train models for detecting email spam, while the Hugging Face dataset library serves as

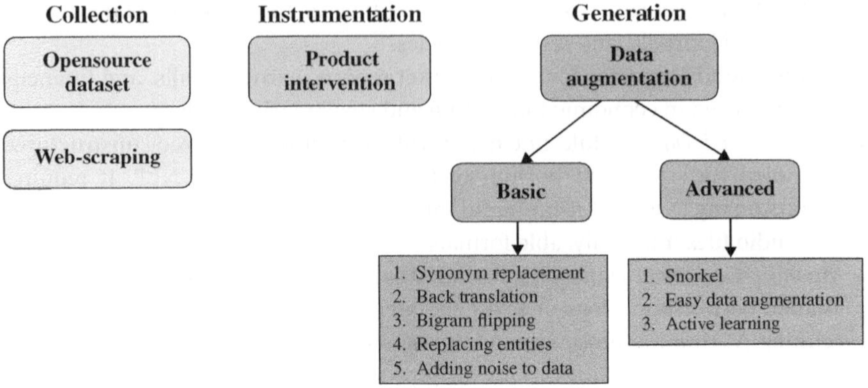

Figure 2.1 Data Acquisition.

a repository for datasets used in more advanced tasks such as question answering and text summarization.

However, the challenge with public datasets lies in their general nature. They may not always provide the niche, domain-specific data required for certain tasks. This is where web scraping, the automated process of extracting data from websites, becomes essential. Tools like Beautiful Soup allow for the parsing of HTML and XML documents, enabling the collection of text from web pages. Selenium extends this capability by interacting with web pages just like a human user, which is particularly useful for extracting data from pages that load content dynamically with JavaScript. The use of these tools presents issues such as handling website layout changes, respecting terms of service and access rates, and dealing with the variability of data formats across different sources.

Beyond textual data found directly on web pages, valuable information is often locked within non-textual formats such as images and PDFs. OCR technology comes into play here, with libraries like Tesseract being used to recognize and extract text from images. This can be especially useful for digitizing printed documents, scanning receipts, or processing handwritten notes. PyPDF2 is another such utility that allows for the extraction of text from PDF files. While OCR technology has made great strides, challenges still persist, such as handling poor image quality, deciphering handwriting with high variability, and interpreting complex layouts like tables or multicolumn formats in documents.

In terms of product intervention, companies like Netflix and Amazon collect vast amounts of data based on user interactions with their services. These interactions, which could include search terms, viewing history, and ratings, are mined to personalize content recommendations. This kind of data is proprietary and specific to the service, offering a rich, contextual dataset that can be used to enhance user experience and refine content delivery algorithms. However, ethical considerations arise concerning user privacy, consent, and data security.

In Python, data acquisition can be conducted through various methods such as utilizing APIs (like the Twitter API for social media data), web scraping with libraries like Beautiful Soup or Scrapy, and accessing databases or reading files directly using Pandas for structured data handling.

2.2.1 Data Requirements and Considerations for NLP Tasks

In the field of NLP, understanding the specific data requirements for various tasks is essential for effective model training. For typical tasks such as text classification, smaller-scale applications might only require a few thousand labeled examples, whereas deep learning models could necessitate tens to hundreds of thousands of samples to capture complex language features. Named Entity Recognition generally needs about 10,000–20,000 annotated sentences for moderate-sized projects, but this number can significantly increase for models intended to perform across diverse contexts. Machine translation for low-resource languages requires several hundred thousand sentence pairs, and this requirement grows to millions for high-resource languages to ensure comprehensive linguistic coverage. Language modelling and text generation tasks vary in their data needs; smaller models can function with data ranging from megabytes to gigabytes, whereas large-scale models like GPT require extensive, Internet-scale datasets. Speech recognition also shows a broad range, with basic models needing hundreds of hours of transcribed speech and more advanced systems requiring thousands.

General considerations also play a crucial role in determining these data requirements. Quality often trumps quantity; high-quality, well-annotated data can sometimes compensate for the sheer volume, making the training process more efficient. Utilizing pre-trained models or engaging in transfer learning can significantly reduce the amount of data required since these models have already been trained on vast datasets and have learned extensive language patterns. Furthermore, domain-specific tasks often require less data if they are focused on a narrower field with limited vocabulary and stylistic variations. Ultimately, the "right" amount of data depends on specific task requirements, the resources available, and the performance benchmarks set for the project. These factors collectively guide the strategic planning of data acquisition and utilization in NLP, ensuring that the models developed are both powerful and efficient.

2.2.2 Data Augmentation

When existing data is insufficient for building robust models, data augmentation can artificially expand the dataset. Data augmentation in NLP is a crucial strategy, particularly when the available corpus is too small to build robust and reliable models. This process involves artificially increasing the size and diversity of the dataset without collecting new data from scratch, thereby enhancing the model's ability to learn and generalize from existing information.

One common method of data augmentation is **synonym replacement**, where words in the text are replaced with their synonyms. For instance, in a sentence like *"The quick brown fox jumps over the lazy dog,"* the word *"quick"* could be replaced with *"fast,"* and *"lazy"* with *"idle,"* creating a new sentence: *"The fast brown fox jumps over the idle dog."* This method relies on thesauri or lexical databases such as WordNet to find synonyms that fit the context, thus expanding the dataset while preserving the original meaning.

Another technique is **back translation**, which involves translating a text into another language and then translating it back to the original language. This process often introduces slight variations in phrasing and word choice, providing a natural form of data diversity. For example, translating the English phrase *"It's raining cats and dogs"* into French and then back into English might result in *"It's pouring very hard,"* which retains the semantic meaning while varying the linguistic structure.

Tools like **Snorkel and NLPAug** offer sophisticated frameworks for automating and scaling these augmentation processes. Snorkel uses weak supervision to generate large datasets by combining and weighting different heuristic rules and external knowledge sources. NLPAug, on the other hand, provides a wide array of augmentation techniques, including not only synonym replacement and back translation but also character-level edits such as inserting, deleting, or swapping characters, and even more sophisticated morphological changes.

However, data augmentation comes with its set of challenges. Ensuring **semantic consistency** is paramount; augmented sentences must maintain the original context and meaning to avoid confusing the model during training. For example, replacing words without considering context can lead to nonsensical sentences or altered meanings, detracting from the model's learning process. Another significant concern is the **potential introduction of bias**. If the augmentation process disproportionately amplifies certain features, linguistic styles, or sentiments, it can skew the model's understanding and performance. For instance, if data augmentation inadvertently emphasizes negative sentiments in customer reviews due to the way sentences are altered, the resulting model may become biased toward perceiving comments as more negative than they are. Last, maintaining the **naturalness of language** is a critical aspect. Augmented data should ideally be indistinguishable from original human-generated text to ensure that the model learns from realistic examples. Over-augmented text or poorly chosen synonyms can lead to awkward phrasings or unidiomatic expressions, which can hinder the model's ability to process natural language effectively.

While data augmentation is a powerful tool for enhancing NLP datasets, it requires careful implementation and consideration of semantic integrity, bias introduction, and linguistic naturalness to ensure the creation of a valuable and effective corpus for model training.

Each stage of data acquisition comes with its own set of considerations and hurdles. The quality of the collected data must be maintained, which requires diligent cleaning and preprocessing to remove noise and standardize formats. Ethical and legal constraints must be navigated carefully, particularly with regard to data privacy and copyright laws. The diversity of the data must be representative to avoid biases in the NLP model. These challenges make data acquisition a complex yet undeniably crucial phase in the NLP pipeline.

2.3 Challenges in NLP Data Acquisition and Management

Acquiring and managing data for NLP tasks present several challenges and issues, stemming from both the inherent characteristics of language and the logistics of data handling. These challenges are multifaceted, affecting the way data is collected, processed, and utilized in NLP models.

- *Volume and Quality of Data:* The first major challenge is obtaining a sufficient volume of high-quality data. NLP models, particularly those based on deep learning, require large amounts of annotated data to learn effectively. However, collecting and labelling such data can be time-consuming and costly. Moreover, the data must be relevant and of high quality; noisy, inconsistent, or biased data can lead to poor model performance and unreliable outcomes.
- *Language Diversity and Complexity:* Language is inherently diverse and complex. It varies greatly across different cultures, regions, and groups, with nuances in dialect, slang, and usage. Capturing this diversity in a dataset is challenging but essential to build robust and inclusive NLP systems. Furthermore, the structural and syntactic complexity of languages, with their rules and exceptions, poses additional challenges in accurately modelling and understanding language phenomena.
- *Annotator Bias and Variability:* In the data annotation process, human annotators introduce their own biases and interpretations, leading to variability in the data. This subjectivity can affect the consistency and reliability of the training data, impacting the subsequent performance of NLP models. Ensuring inter-annotator reliability and minimizing bias is a significant challenge in dataset creation.

- *Domain-Specific Data Requirements:* Many NLP applications require domain-specific knowledge, which can be difficult to encapsulate in general language models. Acquiring specialized datasets in fields like medicine, law, or finance often requires expert knowledge and access to restricted or sensitive information, complicating the data acquisition process.
- *Ethical and Legal Considerations:* Ethical and legal issues are paramount in NLP data acquisition. Ensuring privacy, securing informed consent, and adhering to data protection regulations like GDPR are critical. The use of personal data, especially in sensitive areas, must be handled with utmost care to avoid violations of privacy and confidentiality.
- *Data Drift and Model Relevance:* Language evolves over time, leading to changes in usage, vocabulary, and semantics. This phenomenon, known as data drift, can render existing datasets outdated, necessitating continuous data acquisition and model updating to maintain relevance and accuracy.
- *Access and Resource Limitations:* Accessing comprehensive and diverse datasets can be a barrier, especially for languages or dialects with limited digital presence. Furthermore, the resources required for data storage, processing, and annotation can be substantial, posing challenges for organizations and researchers with limited budgets.
- *Technological and Methodological Challenges:* Finally, the methods and technologies used in data acquisition and processing must be sophisticated enough to handle the volume, variety, and velocity of language data. This includes challenges in web scraping, text extraction from various formats, and the integration of different data sources into a coherent and usable dataset.

Addressing these challenges requires a multifaceted approach, including advancements in machine learning methodologies, improvements in data annotation practices, ethical considerations in data usage, and the development of more sophisticated tools for data acquisition and processing.

2.4 Data Quality Check in NLP

Data quality check in NLP refers to the systematic examination and improvement of datasets used for training and evaluating NLP models. This process is critical because the quality of the data directly influences the accuracy, reliability, and fairness of the models. High-quality data leads to more effective NLP applications, capable of understanding and processing language accurately across various contexts and demographics.

In NLP, data quality is paramount and is defined by several key dimensions: accuracy, consistency, completeness, and fairness. **Accuracy** is crucial as it ensures the data accurately represents the real-world phenomena or information it's meant to depict. This is vital for the model to make correct interpretations and decisions based on the data. For example, in sentiment analysis, the sentiment labels must correctly reflect the emotions conveyed in the text samples. **Consistency** in data is necessary for the reliability of NLP systems. It requires that the data across the dataset maintain uniform formats and conventions. This uniformity is essential for algorithms to process the data correctly, ensuring that, for instance, date formats or terminologies are standardized throughout the dataset. **Completeness** of data is about having a full set of information required for the NLP task at hand, without any missing values or gaps. Incomplete data can lead to biased analyses and skewed outcomes, as the model might not be trained on a representative sample of the real-world scenario. **Fairness** in data aims to prevent biases that could lead to discriminatory or unjust outcomes in model predictions. Ensuring fairness involves scrutinizing the data for any inherent biases and making necessary corrections to avoid perpetuating or amplifying these biases in the NLP models.

Addressing these dimensions of data quality in NLP involves meticulous processes such as **Annotation and Labelling**, which ensures that data is accurately marked with the correct labels or tags, reflecting the true nature or characteristics needed for specific NLP tasks. **Bias Detection and Correction** is another critical aspect, involving the identification and mitigation of any biases present in the data to avoid skewed or unfair outcomes in the model's performance. Lastly, **Data Cleaning and Preprocessing** are fundamental to enhancing data quality, involving the removal of inaccuracies, standardization of formats, and filling in of missing information to ensure the integrity and utility of the data for NLP applications.

The importance of data quality in NLP cannot be overstated, as poor data quality can lead to biased predictions, misinterpretations, and ultimately, the failure of NLP systems to meet their intended purposes. Quality data is the backbone of successful NLP projects, enabling models to learn and generalize well from examples. Thus, here are key aspects to consider during a Data Quality Check.

2.4.1 Checking for Biases

- *Content Bias:* Analyze the data to ensure it does not favor certain topics, ideas, or sentiments unfairly, which could lead the model to make biased predictions. For instance, if a sentiment analysis model is trained on movie reviews predominantly praising action films while criticizing romantic movies, it may unfairly bias its predictions in favor of action movies.
- *Representation Bias:* Ensure that the dataset represents the diversity of the population or phenomena being studied. For example, if you are building a model to

analyze global customer feedback, the data should include multiple languages and cultural contexts. For example, in building a model for global customer feedback, it's crucial to include data from all regions and languages where products are used. Failing to represent any one group, like only using feedback from English-speaking users, can skew the model's understanding and performance.

- *Annotation Bias:* Sometimes, the bias comes from the individuals who annotate the data. Having multiple annotators and cross-verifying their work can mitigate this risk. For example, if the annotators of medical diagnosis data have varying levels of expertise, their annotations might be inconsistent. Using multiple expert reviewers and reconciling differences can mitigate this bias.

2.4.2 Addressing Data Imbalances

- *Class Imbalance:* In classification tasks, make sure that each class is adequately represented. Disproportionate representation can lead the model to favor the majority class. For example, in a text classification task, such as detecting spam emails, if 95% of the data is non-spam and only 5% is spam, models might lean toward classifying all emails as non-spam. Techniques like resampling or synthetic data generation can help balance the classes.
- *Sampling Bias:* Be cautious about how the data is collected. Ensure that the sampling method does not overlook certain segments of the data population. For instance, when collecting data for a political sentiment analysis, if the dataset comprises primarily of one political leaning due to the source of collection, it may not accurately represent the general population's sentiments.

2.4.3 Identifying and Correcting Inconsistencies

- *Annotation Inconsistency:* Check for uniformity in how different annotators label the data. Inconsistencies can confuse the model during training. For example, different annotators may label the emotions in texts differently, leading to mixed signals for training emotion analysis models. Establishing clear annotation guidelines and training for annotators is essential.
- *Data Format Inconsistency:* Standardize the format across the dataset to ensure that the model processes all data uniformly, which is particularly important when merging datasets from different sources. For instance, merging datasets from different sources for a unified NLP model, like combining social media posts with news articles, requires standardizing metadata, text formatting, and encoding to ensure seamless processing.

2.4.4 Ensuring Data Accuracy and Reliability

- *Verify Sources*: Confirm that the data comes from reliable sources and is up-to-date, especially for tasks sensitive to temporal changes like sentiment analysis on current events. For example, for timely tasks like sentiment analysis on current events, it's important to use recent and verified sources to ensure the data reflects the current sentiment accurately.
- *Error Checking:* Regularly review and correct errors in the data, whether they are in the content, labelling, or format.

2.4.5 Evaluating Data Quality Regularly

- Perform regular audits of your dataset, especially after incorporating new data, to maintain its quality over time. For instance, regular audits of an NLP dataset, such as a legal document corpus, might involve re-assessing its relevance, legal compliance, and representativeness after adding new case laws or regulations.

By thoroughly checking for biases, imbalances, and inconsistencies, and ensuring accuracy and reliability, you can significantly improve the quality of your dataset. This, in turn, enhances the performance, fairness, and trustworthiness of your NLP models. Various tools facilitate these aspects of data quality check in NLP:

- *Annotation tools* like Prodigy and Label Studio help in manual data annotation and review, ensuring accuracy and consistency.
- *Data profiling tools* such as Pandas Profiling provide insights into the data's structure and quality, identifying issues like missing values or inconsistent formatting.
- *Bias detection tools* like AI Fairness 360 and Fairlearn are crucial for identifying and addressing biases, thus ensuring fairness in the data and the models trained on it.
- *Statistical and exploratory analysis tools* like R, Python, and data visualization libraries (e.g., Matplotlib, Seaborn) are used to examine data distributions, identify anomalies, and check for data balance and representativeness.

2.5 Ethical Considerations in NLP Data Management

Ethical issues with the data used in NLP stem from various facets of data acquisition, processing, and application. These issues not only concern the technical aspects of NLP systems but also the broader implications of their use on privacy, fairness, and societal norms.

- *Data Bias and Representation:* Data bias is a significant ethical issue where the training data used in NLP systems may not accurately represent the diversity of real-world demographics. This can lead to biased algorithms that systematically discriminate against certain groups. For instance, if an NLP model is trained primarily on text data from a specific demographic, it may perform poorly on text from other demographics or, worse, reinforce stereotypes and prejudices.
- *Consent and Privacy:* The collection and use of text data in NLP often raise questions about consent and privacy. Many datasets are sourced from public or semi-public platforms like social media, forums, and review sites, where users' text contributions are used without explicit consent for their data to be utilized in AI training. This leads to concerns about whether individuals are aware of and agree to their data being used for these purposes, and whether such use complies with data protection laws.
- *Anonymization and De-identification:* Anonymization of text data is crucial for protecting individuals' privacy but is challenging in NLP due to the richness of language, which can inadvertently reveal personal information. Properly de-identifying text data to remove or mask personal identifiers is essential to prevent privacy breaches. However, achieving this without compromising the utility of the data for NLP tasks can be difficult.
- *Transparency and Accountability:* There's often a lack of transparency about the origins, composition, and processing of datasets used in NLP. This opacity can make it hard to assess the ethical considerations of the data used and to hold entities accountable for the outcomes of NLP systems. For example, if an NLP model used in judicial decision-making is trained on historical court records, it's important to understand and critique the data's context, including any potential biases that could affect the model's decisions.
- *Ethical Sourcing and Use:* The ethical sourcing of data for NLP involves ensuring that the data collection processes respect individuals' rights and societal norms. Moreover, the purpose for which NLP systems are employed should align with ethical and legal standards. For instance, using NLP for surveillance or manipulating public opinion can be highly contentious and ethically problematic.

Addressing the ethical issues related to the data in NLP requires a comprehensive approach that includes ethical guidelines, technical solutions, legal compliance, and broad stakeholder engagement. It is about creating NLP systems that are not only technically proficient but also socially responsible, ensuring that the benefits of NLP technologies are realized without compromising individual rights or societal values.

Knowledge Checkpoint 2

Quiz: Understanding Data and Acquisition in NLP

1 Which of the following is a common source of textual data for NLP tasks?
 A Financial models
 B Sensor data
 C Social media posts
 D Weather forecasts

2 What is the significance of multilingual data in NLP?
 A It is used to create more engaging content.
 B It helps in building models that can understand and process multiple languages.
 C It reduces the need for data cleaning.
 D It simplifies the model training process.

3 In NLP, what does annotated or labeled data refer to?
 A Data that is sorted by date
 B Data that is encrypted for security
 C Data that is tagged with specific information like sentiment or entities
 D Data that is synthesized by machine learning models

4 Which technique is used for artificially expanding the dataset when the existing data is insufficient?
 A Data minimization
 B Data augmentation
 C Data compression
 D Data extrapolation

5 Why is domain-specific data important in NLP?
 A It makes data processing easier and faster.
 B It contains specialized vocabulary and knowledge pertinent to a specific field.
 C It is always readily available and easy to use.
 D It is less complex than general data.

6 Data augmentation can lead to biases if not handled properly. What does this imply?
A Augmented data should replace the original data set completely.
B Only new and synthetic data should be used for training NLP models.
C Care must be taken to ensure that augmentation does not skew the distribution or meaning of the data.
D Data augmentation is unnecessary and should be avoided in NLP.

7 What is a parallel corpus in multilingual NLP data acquisition?
A A dataset containing sentences in one language.
B A dataset where each sentence is translated into multiple languages.
C A dataset containing only parallel programming code.
D A dataset used exclusively for speech recognition.

8 In the context of NLP, what is the primary challenge when working with informal text data from social media?
A Lack of sufficient data.
B Standardized and formal language use.
C Presence of slang, abbreviations, and non-standard language.
D High cost of data acquisition.

9 Which dimension of data quality ensures that the data across the dataset maintains uniform formats and conventions?
A Accuracy
B Consistency
C Completeness
D Fairness

10 When addressing data imbalances in NLP, what technique can help balance classes in a dataset that has a disproportionate representation of classes?
A Synonym replacement
B Resampling or synthetic data generation
C Cross-verifying annotations
D Standardizing metadata

11 Which of the following is NOT a common method of data augmentation in NLP?
A Synonym replacement.
B Back translation.
C Decreasing the size of the dataset randomly.
D Adding noise in the form of typos or grammatical errors.

12 How does the concept of data drift affect NLP models over time?

A It increases the model's accuracy as language evolves.

B It makes the model outdated due to changes in language use and semantics.

C It reduces the amount of data needed for training models.

D It enhances the model's ability to process multilingual data.

3

Fundamental Text Processing

Text processing occupies a unique space in the vast landscape of technology, striking a balance between the intricacies of human language and the binary precision of machines. It serves as the bridge that ensures the rich tapestry of human language finds resonance in the structured world of machines. Imagine the sprawling web of information available to us, from centuries-old manuscripts to the endless scroll of social media feeds. The potential knowledge within this data is boundless. However, without the tools to access, decipher, and contextualize this information, its intrinsic value remains locked away. This is where text processing emerges, not merely as a tool but as a critical discipline, acting as the key that unlocks the latent wealth of knowledge in unstructured textual data.

At a cursory glance, language may appear as a simple tool for communication, a linear sequence of symbols and sounds. However, when examined closely from a technical viewpoint, it unravels itself as a masterpiece of intricate design, much like a piece of art. The artistry of language can be understood and appreciated through several technical lenses: its structure, its evolution, and its capability to convey complex information as follows:

- *Structural Complexity:* Technically, language operates on multiple levels of organization, much like the layers of paint on a canvas or the notes in a symphony. Phonemes, the smallest units of sound, combine to form morphemes, the smallest units of meaning. Morphemes further combine to create words, and words are strung together, adhering to syntactic rules, to form sentences. This hierarchical structure is a testament to the intricate design behind every spoken or written statement.
- *Evolutionary Adaptability:* Language is not static; it's dynamic and ever-evolving. Technically speaking, languages undergo both diachronic and synchronic changes. Diachronic changes refer to the historical evolution and transformation of a language over time, while synchronic changes pertain to the structural variations within a language at a given point in time. This ability to morph and

Language Intelligence: Expanding Frontiers in Natural Language Processing, First Edition. Akshi Kumar.
© 2025 The Institute of Electrical and Electronics Engineers, Inc. Published 2025 by John Wiley & Sons, Inc.

adapt makes language akin to an artwork that's perennially in progress, always refining, always improving.

- *Semiotic Depth:* Semiotics, the study of signs and symbols, offers a technical understanding of how language conveys meaning. Every word or phrase is a signifier, pointing toward a signified concept or object. However, the relationship between the two isn't always direct. Metaphors, allegories, and idioms introduce a level of abstraction, where words don't just denote literal meanings but allude to deeper, often cultural, or shared, understandings. This depth of signification and the layers of meaning are what make poetry, prose, and even everyday conversation so rich and textured.

Yet, the science of processing this art is equally compelling. Computers, in their binary world of zeros and ones, need structured, predictable inputs. They don't naturally comprehend the myriad of human expressions and linguistic nuances. Therefore, the challenge and essence of text processing lie in creating methods, algorithms, and systems that can navigate the labyrinth of human expression and bring forth its structure, patterns, and meanings in a way machines can understand. From a technical standpoint, the endeavors to make machines understand human language, through fields like computational linguistics and NLP, underscore the intricate artistry of language. Tokenization, parsing, and semantic understanding are just a few processes that aim to decode the vast and nuanced terrain of human communication.

3.1 Text Cleaning

Text cleaning in NLP is a critical step that involves preparing the raw data for further analysis and processing. This stage is essential for enhancing the quality of the data and ensuring the reliability of the outcomes of NLP tasks.

3.1.1 Techniques and Examples of Text Cleaning

- *Standardizing Case:* The preprocessing pipeline often begins with case normalization, wherein all letters are converted to lower or upper case. This is not merely for aesthetic uniformity but serves a functional purpose. Words at the beginning of sentences or those that are part of proper nouns often start with capital letters, yet they should typically be treated the same as their lowercase counterparts for general processing tasks. Case normalization ensures that "*Apple*," "*apple*," and "*APPLE*" are recognized as the same entity, preventing the fragmentation of word frequencies. In Python, this is commonly done using the **.lower()** or **.upper()** string methods.

- *Unicode Normalization:* Text data often includes diverse characters like emojis, symbols, or special characters from various languages. Unicode normalization standardizes these characters into a consistent form, making the text easier to process. For example, converting accented characters (é, ñ, ü) to their closest ASCII counterparts (e, n, u) simplifies the dataset for algorithms that may not support extended character sets. Python's **unicodedata** module can normalize characters, converting accented characters to their ASCII counterparts, which is especially useful for languages with diacritical marks.
- *Regular Expressions (Regex):* Regex is a powerful tool for searching and manipulating strings based on patterns. In text cleaning, it's used to identify and remove unwanted elements like URLs, email addresses, phone numbers, or any specific patterns that don't contribute to the analytical goals. For instance, removing HTML tags from web-scraped content using a Regex pattern like <[^>]*> ensures that only the textual content is retained for analysis. We can use Python's **re** module to employ regular expressions for identifying and removing or replacing unwanted elements like URLs, email addresses, or HTML tags from the text. For example, to remove HTML tags, one could use a regex pattern like **re.sub(r'<[^>]*>', ", text)**.
- *Spelling Corrections:* Textual data, especially from informal sources like social media, often contains spelling errors. Spelling correction algorithms, or using libraries like TextBlob or PySpellChecker in Python, help rectify these mistakes. For instance, correcting "teh" to "the" or "recieve" to "receive" enhances the coherence of the text data.
- *Handling Numbers and Abbreviations:* Numerals and abbreviations can be informative but may also disrupt textual consistency. For instance, "*3*" and "*three*" should be considered equivalent in a text corpus. A normalization step might involve translating numerals into their written forms or standardizing abbreviated words to their full forms, thus reducing the sparsity of the feature space. In some applications, numerals carry critical meaning and should be preserved or processed differently, such as dates in a historical text analysis or measurements in clinical reports. Similarly, abbreviations can be domain-specific: "*mg*" might be universally normalized to "*milligrams*" in medical documents but left as is in general text.

3.1.2 Challenges in Text Cleaning

The text cleaning process in NLP encounters several challenges, as follows:

- *Contextual Relevance:* Ensuring that cleaning processes do not strip away contextually important information. For example, in sentiment analysis, negations like "not" are crucial and should not be removed.

- *Data Loss:* Aggressive cleaning strategies might lead to the removal of significant parts of the text, potentially losing valuable information or altering the meaning of the data.
- *Standardization:* Finding a balance between over-cleaning (which may lead to a loss of meaningful content) and under-cleaning (which may leave too much noise in the data).
- *Language Diversity:* Text cleaning must adapt to the peculiarities of different languages, considering factors like idioms, compound words, and language-specific punctuation.
- *Automation versus Manual Intervention:* While automated cleaning can process large datasets efficiently, manual intervention might be needed to fine-tune the cleaning process, especially in dealing with nuanced text or domain-specific content.

In essence, text cleaning in NLP entails a delicate balance of techniques aimed at refining the data, ensuring its preparedness for subsequent NLP tasks. The methods selected must be contextually apt to uphold the integrity and usefulness of the data, thereby enabling precise and enlightening language analysis.

3.2 Sentence Splitting

Sentence Splitting, also known as Sentence Boundary Disambiguation or Sentence Segmentation, is a crucial step in many NLP tasks. Its primary goal is to determine where sentences begin and end in a longer text. Simple as it might sound, this task is not always straightforward, given the nuances and intricacies of natural languages. The significance of sentence splitting is manifold. It sets the foundation for subsequent analysis as many NLP tasks, from part-of-speech tagging to parsing to named entity recognition, operate at the sentence level. Properly segmenting a text into individual sentences is crucial for these tasks to function effectively. Furthermore, beyond the analytical perspective, there's a very human aspect to this process. When processing and presenting text to users, knowing where sentences start, and end helps in formatting and improves readability.

However, demarcating sentences is riddled with challenges. One primary obstacle is the ambiguity introduced by punctuation. Periods (or full stops) are commonly used to denote the end of a sentence, but they can also be used in abbreviations, decimal numbers, web URLs, and more. Additionally, the structure of sentences themselves can be a source of confusion. Sentences can contain quoted speech, parentheses, and other punctuations which might confuse a simplistic sentence-splitting algorithm. Compounding these challenges are the varied markers that can conclude a sentence. While periods are common, sentences can also end with exclamation points, question marks, and in some cases, ellipses. Furthermore, sentence boundary rules may differ across languages. An algorithm effective for English might not work well for German or Japanese.

In addressing these challenges, various techniques have emerged. The rule-based approach, for instance, leans on pre-set guidelines. A common heuristic might be to mark a sentence boundary if a capitalized word succeeds a period. However, the rigidity of such methods can be their Achilles' heel, making them prone to overlooking linguistic nuances. Enter machine learning, which offers a more adaptive solution. By training models on data where sentence endings are explicitly labelled, the system learns to predict these boundaries in unfamiliar texts. With the technological march, deep learning has made its foray

Text:
"Ms. Green, who holds an M.Sc. degree, will join the team soon. Meanwhile, I'll check www.example.com. *Can we meet at 2:30 p.m.? Hope to see you there!"*

Sentence Splitting:
A naive approach might split the text every time it encounters a period, resulting in:
1. "Ms."
2. "Green, who holds an M.Sc."
3. "degree, will join the team soon."
4. "Meanwhile, I'll check www.example.com."
5. "Can we meet at 2:30 p.m.?"
6. "Hope to see you there!"

This naive approach, however, introduces errors due to the ambiguity of periods. A more sophisticated sentence splitting algorithm would correctly identify the sentences as:
1. "Ms. Green, who holds an M.Sc. degree, will join the team soon."
2. "Meanwhile, I'll check www.example.com."
3. "Can we meet at 2:30 p.m.?"
4. "Hope to see you there!"

Analysis:
- "Ms." is an abbreviation for a title and should not signal the end of a sentence.
- "M.Sc." is an academic degree abbreviation, and its period doesn't indicate a sentence boundary.
- Web addresses like "www.example.com." can be particularly tricky. A simplistic algorithm might view the last period as a sentence terminator, but in this context, it's part of the web address.
- Time notations like "2:30 p.m." can also confuse basic splitters due to the period after "p.m."

Figure 3.1 Sentence-Splitting Example.

into sentence splitting. Harnessing the power of neural networks, particularly recurrent neural networks (RNNs) and transformative transformers, the task is now approached with increased sophistication. Yet, recognizing the strengths and limitations of each approach, hybrid methods have also emerged. By intertwining rule-based strategies with machine learning models, they aim to capture the best of both worlds.

Let's illustrate the process of sentence splitting with a concrete example (Fig. 3.1).

In Python, sentence splitting, or Sentence Boundary Disambiguation, is a key step in text pre-processing, effectively handled by libraries like NLTK and spaCy. NLTK, a comprehensive NLP library, offers **sent_tokenize** for accurately segmenting text into individual sentences. It uses pre-trained models to recognize punctuation and capitalization patterns that typically mark sentence boundaries. On the other hand, spaCy, known for its performance and ease of integration, processes text through its NLP pipeline, where sentence segmentation is automatically performed as part of its tokenization process.

3.3 Tokenization

Tokenization, at its core, is the process of converting input text into a series of tokens or meaningful pieces. Imagine breaking up a sentence into individual words and punctuation marks; that's a simple form of tokenization. In the field of NLP, this foundational step allows computers to better understand, manipulate, and derive meaning from human language. This section examines the intricacies of tokenization, exploring its significance, methods, challenges, and real-world applications.

When we communicate, our messages are filled with multi-faceted structures: words, phrases, punctuation, and even spaces. To derive meaning or to process these messages, computers must first unpack these structures. This is where tokenization steps in, serving as the first preprocessing step in many NLP tasks, such as text classification, sentiment analysis, machine translation, information retrieval (IR), and speech recognition. Tokenization turns a stream of text into individual pieces, with each piece holding a distinct meaning, making it easier for algorithms to perform subsequent analyses. Tokenization has far-reaching implications in various real-world scenarios:

- *Search Engines:* When you type a query into a search engine, tokenization helps break it down, facilitating accurate and quick results.

- *Machine Translation:* For translating a sentence from one language to another, tools like Google Translate first tokenize the input to work on each segment of text.
- *Speech-to-Text Systems:* Systems that transcribe spoken language, such as Siri or Alexa, utilize tokenization to convert the continuous stream of speech into discrete, processable units.
- *Text Analytics:* Businesses often employ NLP to gain insights from customer feedback, reviews, or surveys. Tokenization helps in segmenting this feedback into analysable chunks.
- *Chatbots and Virtual Assistants*: For chatbots to understand and respond to user inputs, they tokenize sentences to extract meaning and context.

3.3.1 Types of Tokenization

Depending on the granularity of tokens required and the nature of the text, different tokenization strategies are employed. Fig. 3.2 is a hierarchical diagram illustrating the concept of "Tokenization" in NLP. The diagram splits tokenization into three main categories, namely word level, character level, and sub-word level tokenization. Each tokenization strategy has its own use cases and is selected based on the requirements of the specific NLP application.

- *Word-level Tokenization:*
  At this level, the text is broken down into individual words or entities that typically convey a particular meaning in the context. For instance, "*I love NLP.*" becomes ["*I*", "*love*", "*NLP*", "."]. Methods employed include:
  a) **Space and Punctuation Tokenization:** This method utilizes basic string operations to separate words wherever there are spaces, and also treats punctuation like commas, periods, exclamation points, and question marks as

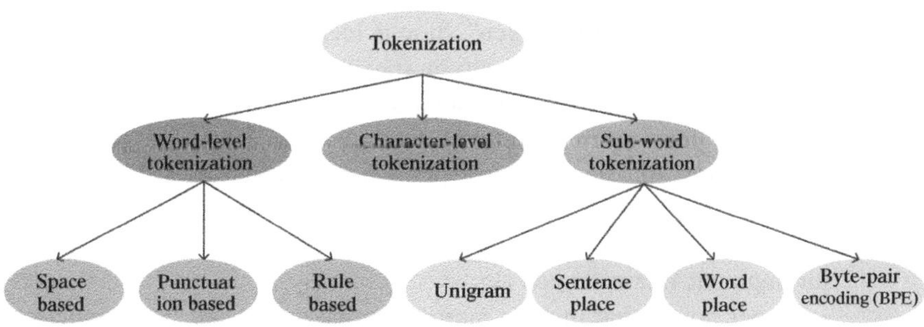

Figure 3.2 Exploring Tokenization Techniques in NLP.

delimiters. This means that the text is segmented each time any of these characters is encountered.

Text Input: "Hello, world! Welcome to San Francisco. Enjoy your ice cream."

Process:

i) **Split at Spaces:** Each space in the string triggers a split, initially dividing the text into segments like ["Hello,", "world!", "Welcome", "to", "San", "Francisco.", "Enjoy", "your", "ice cream."]

ii) **Split at Punctuation:** The algorithm further breaks down any segment containing punctuation, treating the punctuation as separate tokens. The commas, periods, and dashes are all used as points to split the text.

```
Tokenization Result:
          "Hello"
          ","
          "world"
          "!"
          "Welcome"
          "to"
          "San"
          "Francisco"
          "."
          "Enjoy"
          "your"
          "ice"
          "-"
          "cream"
          "."
```

In this case, **"San Francisco"** should ideally be recognized as a single entity because it represents a specific place. However, the space tokenization splits it into two separate words, "San" and "Francisco." Similarly, **"ice-cream"** should be one token because it's a single compound noun. But due to the hyphen being treated as a delimiter, it's incorrectly split into "ice" and "cream." The main limitation of space and punctuation tokenization lies in its simplicity. It does not account for linguistic nuances such as:

- Proper nouns that include more than one word (like "San Francisco" or "New York").
- Compound words joined by hyphens (like "ice cream" or "long-term").
- Situations where punctuation does not signify a break in terms (like email addresses, e.g., "example@example.com").

This method's mechanical nature makes it prone to errors in texts containing specialized language, names, technical terms, or compound words. While effective for very basic tokenization tasks or preprocessing steps, space and punctuation tokenization often requires supplementary processing to correct its misinterpretations or an entirely different method for more accurate text parsing.

b) **Rule-Based Tokenization:** To counter the limitations of simple space-based tokenization, rules are defined to handle common patterns in language. For example, contractions like "*Don't*" can be split into "*Do*" and "*n't*."

```
Text Input: "Don't stop believing."
Rule: Split contractions formed with an apostrophe where part
      of the contraction represents a complete word.
Tokenization Result:
"Don't" → "Do" and "n't"
```

By applying this rule, the tokenizer understands to separate "Do" from "n't" as they represent separate semantic units, with "n't" being a contraction of "not." The challenge here is maintaining consistency across different texts and defining exhaustive rules to handle various linguistic structures.

c) **Regular Expression Tokenization:** Instead of simple rules, regular expressions can be used to tokenize text. This provides more flexibility but requires expertise in crafting suitable patterns.

   i) *Regular Expression Tokenization Example: Capturing Various Data Types*
   Text Input: "Contact me at Akshi.Kumar@gold.ac.uk, check out the website www.gold.ac.uk or my profile at https://www.linkedin.com/in/akshi-kumar-4688b37/. Let's meet at 2pm!"
   Objective: To tokenize this text using regex, we aim to separately identify and extract email addresses, URLs, time expressions, and standard word tokens.
   Regex Patterns Used:

- **Email Addresses: \b[A-Za-z0-9._%+-]+@[A-Za-z0-9.-]+\.[A-Z|a-z]{2,}\b**
  a) Captures typical email formats.
- **Websites (URLs):**
  a) Simple websites: **www\.[a-z0-9\.-]+\.[a-z]{2,}**
  b) Full URLs: **http[s]?://[a-z0-9\.-]+\.[a-z]{2,}(\.[a-z]{2,})?**
  c) These patterns match both simple website addresses starting with "www." and full URLs that include "http://" or "https://."
- **Time Expressions: \b\d{1,2}(am|pm)\b**
  a) Matches times formatted with one or two digits followed by "am" or "pm."
- **Words: \b[A-Za-z']+\b**
  a) Matches sequences of alphabetical characters, accommodating contractions and possessives.

```
Process:
The regex tokenizer will scan through the input text and apply
     each regex pattern in turn, extracting matches as tokens
     and identifying where each type of data appears.
Tokenization Result:
"Contact"
"me"
"at"
"Akshi.Kumar@gold.ac.uk" – identified by the email address
     regex.
","
"check"
"out"
"the"
"website"
"www.gold.ac.uk" – identified by the simple website regex.
"or"
"my"
"profile"
"at"
"https://www.linkedin.com/in/akshi-kumar-4688b37/" –
     identified by the full URL regex.
"."
"Let's"
"meet"
"at"
"2pm" – identified by the time expression regex.
"!"
```

The regex tokenizer effectively distinguishes between different types of tokens based on the patterns defined. Emails, URLs, and time expressions are captured as single tokens despite containing characters that might typically separate tokens, such as dots, slashes, or colons. This method allows for accurate, context-sensitive tokenization that respects the semantic integrity of data types within the text. This example illustrates the versatility and precision of regex tokenization in handling complex text segmentation challenges, where different data types and formats are interleaved within natural language sentences. It shows how regex can be tailored to the specific needs of text processing tasks, ensuring that each type of data is correctly identified and extracted as a single token.

i) *Regular Expression Enhancements in Tokenization:*

- **Disjunction (|):** This operator allows the expression to match one of several possible sub-expressions. For example, the regex **cat|dog** captures either "cat" or "dog" in the text, useful for identifying specific keywords within a corpus.
- **Precedence and Capture Groups:** Parentheses **( )** not only establish precedence in regex operations but also create capture groups that can extract specific parts of the matched text. For instance, the pattern

(\d+)/(\\d+) identifies date formats, capturing both month and day as separate groups.

- **Greediness:** Regular expressions are inherently greedy; they attempt to capture as much text as possible. A pattern like **<.*>** would match the entirety of **<tag>sample text</tag>** as a single string. Using non-greedy qualifiers like **?<**, e.g., **<.*?>**, ensures the match stops at the first closing > making it suitable for parsing nested or repeated HTML tags.

- *Character-level Tokenization:* In character-level tokenization, the text is divided into individual characters. This level is highly granular. The methods employed include:
  a) **Simple Character Split:** Just split the text into individual characters. This approach does not consider any contextual information.
  b) **Regular Expression-Based Split:** Based on specific character patterns, split the text. For instance, you might want to handle certain character combinations differently.

  Character-level tokenization reduces the vocabulary size considerably (as it's limited to the unique characters in the language) but can increase the sequence length, making it harder for models to capture longer dependencies.
- *Sub-word Tokenization:* Sub-word tokenization strikes a balance between word-level and character-level granularity. It's especially beneficial for handling out-of-vocabulary words and morphologically rich languages. The methods employed include:
  a) **Byte-Pair Encoding (BPE):** BPE starts by representing a word as a sequence of characters. For each iteration, it merges the most frequent pair of characters or character sequences. This process continues until a specified number of merges have been completed, resulting in a vocabulary of sub-words.
  b) **WordPiece:** This method is similar to BPE, but merges based on likelihood maximization. The primary difference is in the criterion for merging sequences.
  c) **Unigram Language Model Tokenization:** This approach starts with a large vocabulary and iteratively removes tokens to minimize the likelihood of loss of the training data.
  d) **SentencePiece:** This is a data-driven, unsupervised text tokenizer and detokenizer mainly for Neural Network-based text generation tasks. It provides both BPE and unigram language model methods and doesn't rely on pre-tokenization.
- *Sentence Tokenization:* Sentence tokenization, also known as sentence segmentation or sentence splitting, is the process of dividing a text into individual sentences. Unlike word tokenization, where the goal is to split a text into

individual words, sentence tokenization aims to identify the boundaries of sentences.

The primary challenge with sentence tokenization arises from the fact that punctuation marks, especially periods (.), are not exclusive indicators of sentence boundaries. For instance, abbreviations, decimals, and certain types of domain-specific notations (e.g., "*Mr. Smith*" *or* "*2.5 litres*") contain periods but don't indicate the end of a sentence. The methods employed for sentence tokenization include:

a) **Rule-Based:** Using punctuation marks and capitalization patterns. However, care needs to be taken for cases like "*Dr.,*" "*Mrs.,*" "*U.S.,*" etc., where a period doesn't denote the end of a sentence.
b) **Regular Expressions:** More intricate patterns can be used to recognize sentence boundaries better than simple rule-based methods.
c) **Machine Learning Models:** Trained models on labelled data where the task is to identify sentence boundaries. Decision trees, CRF (Conditional Random Field), and other sequence labelling models have been used for this purpose.
d) **Pre-trained NLP Libraries:** Libraries like NLTK (Natural Language Toolkit), SpaCy, and others offer pre-trained sentence tokenizers. For instance, NLTK provides the Punkt Sentence Tokenizer, a pre-trained unsupervised machine learning-based tokenizer that works for many European languages.

   Tokenization methods are chosen based on the specific requirements of the task at hand. While word-level tokenization is ideal for tasks where word semantics are crucial, character-level tokenization is beneficial for languages with vast vocabularies or when handling out-of-vocabulary words. Sub-word-level tokenization often provides a balance, capturing the semantics while also managing vocabulary size effectively. As NLP continues to evolve, so do tokenization techniques, with the aim of bridging human language intricacies with machine understanding.

3.3.2 Challenges in Tokenization

On the surface, tokenization appears to be a straightforward task—simply breaking down sentences into individual words or units. However, the intrinsic complexity of languages presents numerous challenges that make tokenization far from trivial.

The first major challenge is ambiguity. Consider the phrase "*New York.*" A naive tokenization approach might divide it into "*New*" and "*York,*" treating them as separate entities. However, in the real world, "*New York*" is a singular entity, a city, and should be tokenized as one unit. Similarly, the phrase "*hot dog*" presents another dilemma. While it might be logical to treat "*hot*" and "*dog*" as separate tokens, considering their individual meanings, in many contexts, "*hot dog*" functions more accurately as a single entity or concept.

Next, there's the issue of morphological richness, which is particularly prominent in certain languages. For instance, in Turkish or Finnish, a single word can manifest in various forms due to affixes that indicate tense, mood, possession, and more. This morphological diversity complicates the task of determining what constitutes a meaningful token. Is the root word the token, or are its varied forms to be considered separate tokens? This question becomes pivotal in tokenization for such languages. Another significant challenge arises from the inherent structure of certain languages, particularly those that do not demarcate words using spaces. Languages such as Chinese and Thai present sequences of characters without clear space-separated boundaries. This absence complicates the process of determining where one word ends and another begins. In such scenarios, simple space-based tokenization approaches fall short, necessitating more sophisticated methodologies to identify token boundaries accurately.

Last, the digital age has introduced a slew of new challenges to tokenization. With the ubiquitous use of online communication platforms, we've seen an explosion in the usage of emojis, URLs, and special symbols. These characters and sequences don't fit traditional linguistic structures. An emoji, for instance, can convey a wide range of emotions or meanings in a single symbol, making it essential yet challenging to handle in tokenization. Similarly, URLs or mentions (like @username) in social media platforms are unique constructs that must be tokenized as single units despite their internal structures, demanding special treatment during the tokenization process.

3.3.3 Evolution of Tokenization

Tokenization has come a long way, evolving with the changing dynamics of language, especially in the digital age.

- *Handling Modern Language Trends:* The rise of digital platforms has seen a surge in non-traditional forms of text, like hashtags, mentions (@username), and URLs. Tokenizers now need to account for these, ensuring they don't split them arbitrarily.
- *Multilingual Tokenization:* Global platforms often deal with data in multiple languages. Modern tokenizers are designed to handle multilingual text without requiring separate tokenization logic for each language.
- *Deep Learning and Tokenization:* With the ascent of deep learning in NLP, there's a shift toward models that can tokenize and process text in end-to-end fashions, reducing reliance on standalone tokenization processes.

The implementation of tokenization directly affects the performance of subsequent NLP tasks. Proper tokenization is akin to carefully laying the foundation for a building—it is unseen, yet the integrity of the entire structure depends on it.

3.4 Lemmatization and Stemming

In the realm of NLP, it's crucial to recognize that words have various morphological forms while still expressing similar or related meanings. For instance, "*run,*" "*runs,*" "*running,*" and "*ran*" are all different forms of the same verb. However, treating each form as an independent word can significantly increase the complexity of language data. This is where stemming and lemmatization come into play, two techniques designed to reduce words to a common base or root form.

3.4.1 Stemming

Stemming is the process of reducing a word to its base or root form. The main goal is to map related words to the same stem, even if the stem itself isn't a valid word in the language. For example, the stem of the word "*running*" might be "*runn.*" Stemmers work by algorithmically chopping off prefixes and suffixes from a word. They use a heuristic process with rules, but they don't utilize any knowledge of the word's meaning. As a result, stemmed words might not be actual words. For instance, "*flies*" might be stemmed to "*fli.*"

3.4.2 Advantages and Disadvantages of Stemming

Stemming, a linguistic normalization process, significantly shapes the field of NLP. The simplicity of stemming—its ability to abbreviate words by shearing away prefixes and suffixes—offers several noteworthy advantages and disadvantages.

- *Advantages:*
  a) **Computational Efficiency:** Stemming processes are generally less computationally demanding compared to other word normalization methods like lemmatization. They employ straightforward, rule-based algorithms, which can quickly and efficiently reduce words to their stem forms without involving detailed linguistic knowledge or extensive computational resources.
  b) **Ease of Implementation:** Owing to its rule-based nature, stemming is often easy to implement. Algorithms like the Porter Stemmer are widely recognized and utilized due to their simplicity and ease of incorporation into diverse NLP projects.

c) **Enhanced Recall in Search:** In the context of IR, stemming can augment recall by grouping different inflections and derivations of a word together, making it easier to find related documents even if the exact term isn't used in the search query.

- *Disadvantages:*

a) **Crude Reductions:** The heuristic methods used by stemmers can sometimes be overly simplistic or overly aggressive, potentially stripping words of meaningful linguistic nuances. This is often manifested as over-stemming, where words are truncated excessively, often altering the intended semantic representation.

b) **Under-Stemming:** Conversely, stemming may also lead to under-stemming, where words that should theoretically be reduced to the same stem are not. This happens because stemmers do not possess comprehensive linguistic knowledge and thus might fail to recognize that different word forms share the same root.

c) **Lack of Semantic Precision:** Stemming algorithms typically do not take word meanings into account, and as a result, the produced stems may not always maintain the original semantic meaning, which can be critical in certain applications like semantic analysis or machine translation.

3.4.3 Lemmatization

Lemmatization is a more sophisticated process that involves reducing a word to its base or dictionary form. For example, "*went*" would be lemmatized to "*go*." Lemmatizers achieve this reduction using vocabulary and morphological analysis. They look up a word in a lexicon, consider its part of speech, and then return its lemma or base form. If the word isn't found in the lexicon, the lemmatizer might resort to rules or heuristics, like stemming.

3.4.4 Advantages and Disadvantages of Lemmatization

Unlike the heuristic rules of stemming, lemmatization examines the linguistic properties of a word to derive its base or dictionary form. This profound distinction between the two techniques gives rise to specific advantages and challenges inherent to lemmatization.

- *Advantages:*

a) **Accuracy:** One of the most salient merits of lemmatization is its accuracy. By relying on morphological analysis, it can more precisely reduce words to their dictionary forms. This means "*running*" becomes "*run*" and "*better*" becomes "*good*," preserving the core of the word.

   b) **Lexical Validity:** Lemmatization ensures that the produced root word is lexically valid and belongs to the language in question. Such words are not just truncated versions but are linguistically accurate and can be found in dictionaries, resulting in outputs that are both readable and semantically intact.
   c) **Contextual Sensitivity:** Unlike stemming, which might reduce different words with distinct meanings to the same stem, lemmatization considers word meanings and their context, ensuring that words are treated distinctly based on their semantic value.
- *Disadvantages*
   a) **Computational Intensity:** The sophisticated nature of lemmatization comes at a cost. It tends to be computationally more demanding than the more rudimentary stemming processes. This might impact the speed of processing, especially in tasks involving vast corpora.
   b) **Resource Dependency:** Lemmatization often leans on external resources to function optimally. This includes lexicons, morphological analyzers, and part-of-speech taggers. Their dependency on these tools can make them less agile and harder to implement across diverse languages or in resource-scarce environments.

3.4.5 Stemming versus Lemmatization: When to Use Which?

The debate between stemming and lemmatization isn't about one being universally superior to the other; it's about contextual appropriateness. In scenarios where breadth of retrieval matters most, stemming could be the technique of choice. However, for applications demanding depth, precision, and a fine-tuned understanding of language nuances, lemmatization often emerges as the winner. As with many choices in NLP, understanding the application's needs and the trade-off of each technique is essential to making an informed decision. Consider the following application scenarios:

- *Information Retrieval Systems:* IR systems, including search engines, prioritize retrieving all pertinent documents based on a query. The main metric of concern here is "recall," which measures the proportion of all relevant documents that were retrieved. Stemming is often preferred in IR systems because it groups words more aggressively, increasing recall. Precision might be compromised, but for search systems, recall (finding all relevant documents) is usually more crucial.
- *Text Analysis and NLP Applications:* Lemmatization is preferred when the meaning of words is important. That is when probing into intricate text analysis tasks like sentiment analysis, topic modelling, or semantic relationships mapping, the nuanced understanding of language becomes paramount. In such applications,

distinguishing between words' subtle differences in meaning or sentiment can significantly impact the outcome. Let's consider the words "*book*" (as a noun, referring to a physical or electronic publication) and "*booking*" (the act of reserving something, like a hotel room or a flight). If we apply stemming, both words might be reduced to a root like "*book*." However, with lemmatization, "*book*" would stay as "*book*," while "*booking*" would be identified as a derivative of the verb "*book*" (to reserve or make an appointment) and would likely remain "*booking*." Now let's envision this within the context of analyzing reviews for a travel website:

a) **Sentiment Analysis:** Reviews that mention "*book*" might be discussing the content, usability, or features of guidebooks or e-books available on the site: "*The travel book for Italy was incredibly helpful!*" On the other hand, comments mentioning "*booking*" would likely refer to users' experiences with reserving flights, hotels, or tours: "*The booking process for flights was quick and seamless.*"
b) **Topic Modelling:** Feedback containing the word "*book*" could group around topics related to travel literature, recommendations, or the quality of travel guides provided by the website. In contrast, "*booking*" would generate clusters around reservation processes, payment gateways, or even post-booking services like customer support.

This example highlights how stemming, and lemmatization can lead to varied interpretations, especially when words with shared roots carry different implications in context. By solely relying on stemming, the travel website's team might mistakenly think there's a lot of feedback about their "*book*" offerings when, in reality, customers might be more vocal about the "*booking*" experience. Such an oversight could lead to misplaced priorities and strategies.

To sum up, both stemming, and lemmatization play pivotal roles in NLP by reducing dimensionality and improving the efficiency of various tasks. While stemming is a heuristic approach that's faster and more suitable for tasks like search, lemmatization is a more meticulous process that considers the morphology and meaning of words, making it ideal for deeper language analyses. Choosing the right method is essential for achieving optimal results in NLP tasks. By understanding the nuances of both techniques, developers and researchers can make informed decisions tailored to their specific objectives.

NLTK offers both lemmatization and stemming capabilities; its **WordNetLemmatizer** reduces words to lemmas based on the WordNet's lexical database, while its stemming tools like **PorterStemmer** and **LancasterStemmer** apply algorithmic approaches to trim words down to their stems, often resulting in forms that may not be lexically correct but are consistent for analytical purposes.

3.5 Stop Word Removal

The practice of stop word removal is an essential step in the preprocessing phase of text analysis in NLP, aimed at enhancing the efficiency and effectiveness of subsequent analyses. Stop words are generally high-frequency words in a language that are considered of little value in understanding the content's meaning, such as "*and*," "*but*," "*if*," and "*or*." These words are often filtered out because they can skew the results of text analysis processes, like keyword extraction or frequency distribution analysis, by overshadowing more significant terms that are crucial for understanding text content.

In the context of various NLP tasks, stop word removal can significantly streamline the dataset, reducing its dimensionality and thereby speeding up the processing time. The rationale behind standard stop word removal assumes that these words occur frequently in the language but do not carry significant meaning on their own. This is particularly important in large-scale text analytics applications, where computational resources and efficiency are of concern. For example, in the construction of term frequency-inverse document frequency (TF-IDF) matrices, which are commonly used in text classification and clustering, removing stop words can prevent the over-representation of less informative terms and help the algorithm to focus on more meaningful words that better differentiate the documents.

Despite these advantages, the removal of stop words should be approached with caution. In some NLP applications, such as language modelling and machine translation, stop words can carry crucial syntactic information that helps to maintain the grammatical structure and coherence of sentences. In these cases, eliminating them might degrade the performance of the NLP model. Therefore, the decision to remove stop words must be carefully considered based on the specific goals and requirements of the NLP task at hand.

Moreover, the list of stop words is not universal and can vary depending on the language, context, and application. Custom stop word lists can be created to fit the specific needs of a text analysis project, ensuring that the stop word removal process is both effective and sensitive to the textual content's nuances. Thus, while stop word removal is a common and often beneficial practice in NLP, it requires thoughtful implementation to ensure that it contributes positively to the analytical objectives.

In practice, most NLP libraries and frameworks come with a built-in list of stop words that can be used out of the box. For example, the Natural Language Toolkit (NLTK) in Python provides a list of stop words for several languages, and similar functionalities are available in other tools like Apache Lucene, spaCy, and Gensim. These standard lists have been compiled through extensive analysis of language corpora and are generally sufficient for many text-processing tasks.

3.6 Part-of-Speech Tagging

Part-of-Speech (PoS) tagging is a fundamental task in the field of natural language processing (NLP). It involves assigning a particular tag (or label) to each word in a given text based on its grammatical role, such as whether it's a noun, verb, adjective, etc. For example, in the sentence "*John runs fast,*" "*John*" would be tagged as a noun, "*runs*" as a verb, and "*fast*" as an adverb.

Determining the grammatical roles of words has evolved considerably over time. In the early days, the approach was based on set guidelines, often termed as "*Old School Rules.*" Experts formulated these rules considering the structure and endings of words. For instance, a word finishing with "*-ing*" was typically recognized as a verb, suggesting action. However, as the field matured, researchers began employing statistical methods, harnessing patterns observed in extensive texts. An example of this is if the word "*runs*" frequently appears after the name "John," then there's a high probability that "*runs*" is acting as a verb. As technology advanced, the introduction of machine learning allowed computers to predict tags based on extensive training on labelled examples. By feeding computers numerous sentences along with their corresponding grammatical tags, they started becoming adept at making educated guesses about word roles. In the most recent phase, the NLP community has embraced deep learning. This approach makes computers explore deeper into texts, processing them in intricate layers. This not only allows the identification of word roles but also aids in grasping the underlying meaning of the sentences.

PoS tagging serves as an indispensable tool in the world of NLP, bringing clarity and precision to linguistic structures. One of its fundamental benefits lies in its ability to elucidate meanings. Many words in the English language, depending on their usage in a sentence, can assume different meanings. Take the word "*record*" for instance: when used as a noun, it refers to an object storing information, but as a verb, it denotes the act of capturing or documenting information. Without appropriate tagging, such ambiguities can easily lead to misunderstandings or misinterpretations.

Beyond mere disambiguation, PoS tagging also provides foundational support to advanced linguistic endeavors. As we navigate the intricate path of teaching computers to comprehend and reproduce human language, understanding fundamental grammar becomes pivotal. PoS tags serve as these foundational pillars, especially when we venture into intricate tasks like language translation. The tags offer a blueprint of a sentence's structure, enabling algorithms to discern nuances that are otherwise easily overlooked. Moreover, the importance of PoS tagging is further underscored when we consider the domain of IR. Search engines, which are the gateways to the vast realm of digital information, rely heavily on understanding queries to deliver accurate results. Recognizing the grammatical roles of

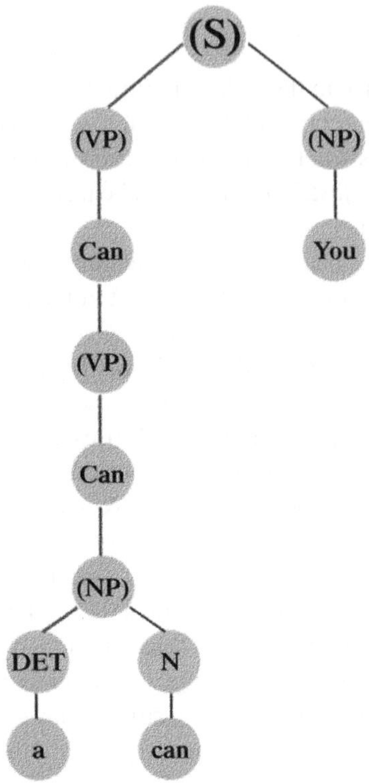

Figure 3.3 Syntactic Tree Diagram.

words within these queries allows these engines to fetch more pertinent results, enhancing user experience.

To visualize the impact of PoS tagging, consider the sentence: "*Can you can a can?*" At first glance, the repetitive use of "*can*" might seem confusing. However, with PoS tagging, each instance is distinctly identified: the first "can" indicates the ability (a verb), followed by the pronoun "*you*," then "*can*" indicating the act of preserving (another verb), the determiner "*a*," and finally, "*can*" as a container (a noun). This intricate differentiation underscores the power and necessity of PoS tagging in language processing. (Fig. 3.3)

3.7 Parsing and Syntactic Analysis

Language, in its raw form, is a cascade of symbols, words, and structures. To truly harness the power of this vast reservoir of information, one must navigate through the intricate layers of language. At the forefront of this navigation is text processing. Among its foundational techniques, parsing and syntactic analysis stand out as primary pillars. These techniques offer a structured pathway into the complexities of language, and in this exploration, we'll explore their methods, nuances, and applications.

3.7.1 Parsing: An Overview

In its essence, parsing refers to the process of analyzing a sequence of symbols (typically words in a sentence) to determine their grammatical structure with respect to a given formal grammar. Think of parsing as a detective trying to determine the roles played by different words in a sentence. Is "*apple*" the subject or the object in the sentence "*I ate an apple*"*?* Parsing provides the answer. The methods in parsing include:

- *Top-Down Parsing:* This approach starts with the highest-level syntax rule (usually the start symbol) and attempts to replace its RHS (right-hand side) components with input symbols. One popular method under this is the Recursive Descent Parsing, which employs recursive procedures to reflect each rule of the grammar.
- *Bottom-Up Parsing:* Here, the input is processed from its beginning to its end, and the parsing constructs a parse tree from leaves to the root. Shift-reduce parsing is a common technique in this category.

Human beings can understand linguistic structures and their meanings easily. But machines are not successful enough for natural language comprehension yet. So, when a machine must parse through one word at a time, it may not be able to fully understand the semantics of a sentence. And these words when given one at a time are known as unigrams. Like in Fig. 3.4, the sentence "*What is Natural Language Processing?*" is parsed one word at a time. Then in a bigram, the sentence "What is Natural Language Processing?" is parsed two words at a time. Finally, in a trigram, the sentence "What is Natural Language Processing?" is parsed three words at a time.

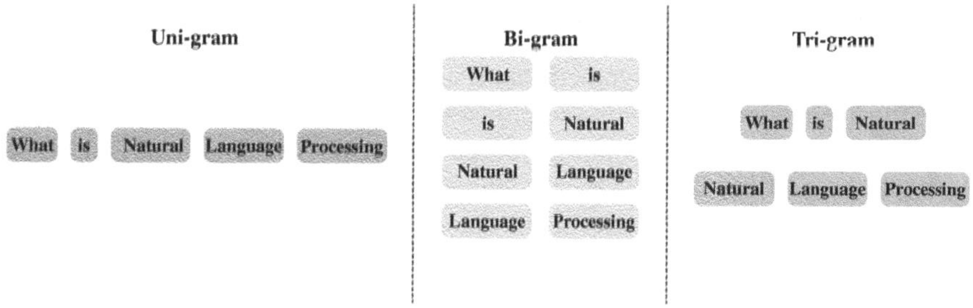

Figure 3.4 N-gram Models in Text Analysis.

3.7.2 Contemporary Relevance of Parsing

In the context of modern NLP, parsing is not just about identifying grammatical structures; it's about gleaning semantic meaning, understanding context, and even predicting intent. For instance, voice assistants like Siri, Alexa, or Google Assistant rely heavily on advanced parsing techniques to comprehend user commands and respond appropriately. When a user says, "Play some calming music," the underlying NLP engine parses this input to deduce not just the structure but also the intent and sentiment behind the request.

- *Top-Down Parsing in Modern NLP:* Traditionally, top-down parsing, with its starting point at the highest level of grammatical structure, offered a theoretical approach to understanding sentence construction. Today, with the advent of neural networks and deep learning, this method has been enriched with probabilistic models. These models, often trained on vast datasets, can predict which grammatical rule is most likely to be applicable next, making the parsing process more efficient and accurate.
- *Predictive Parsing in the Age of Neural Networks:* While Recursive Descent Parsing remains a classic example, contemporary NLP leverages predictive parsing backed by neural architectures. These models can anticipate upcoming words or structures based on context, enhancing the top-down approach's efficiency.
- *Bottom-Up Parsing and Contemporary Techniques:* The bottom-up approach, which builds from individual words or symbols, has found substantial application in modern machine translation systems. As these systems strive to convert a sentence from one language to another, they often start by understanding smaller chunks of input and then piecing together the broader context.
- *Neural Shift-Reduce Parsing:* Traditional shift-reduce parsing has been supercharged in the NLP of today with neural networks. These networks can predict the best time to shift (or read) and when to reduce (or consolidate), optimizing the parsing process for complex and diverse sentences.

3.7.3 Syntactic Analysis: Delving Deeper

Beyond the basic structure, syntactic analysis (or syntax analysis) seeks to understand the arrangement of words and phrases to create well-formed sentences in a language. It's akin to understanding the architecture of a building—not just where the bricks are laid, but how the rooms connect, how the doors lead from one space to another, and how the entire structure stands unified. The techniques in syntactic analysis include:

- *Constituency-based Approaches: The Substructural View:* This technique divides sentences into nested constituents (or sub-phrases), usually represented by a

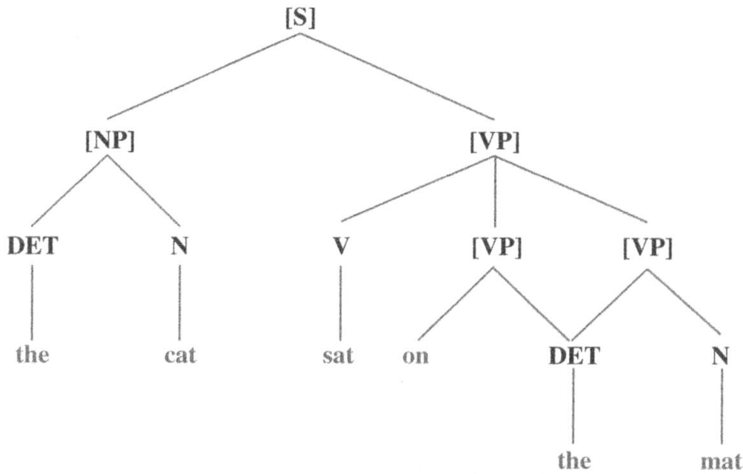

Figure 3.5 Syntactic Structure: "*The Cat Sat on the Mat*".

tree structure. For example, in the sentence "*The cat sat on the mat,*" one can visualize its breakdown: at the top hierarchy, the entire sentence; delving deeper, the division into "*The cat*" (a noun phrase) and "*sat on the mat*" (a verb phrase); and further down, each phrase can be dissected into its atomic components. This tree structure offers insights into how different parts of a sentence relate and group together, forming an integral whole. Fig. 3.5. depicts a visual hierarchy that helps in understanding the sentence structure and relationships between words and phrases.

In this visualization:

- [S] stands for Sentence, which encompasses the whole sentence.
- [NP] stands for Noun Phrase. The subject "*The cat*" is one noun phrase, and the object "*the mat*" in the prepositional phrase is another noun phrase.
- [VP] stands for Verb Phrase. "*sat on the mat*" is a verb phrase that contains a verb and a prepositional phrase.
- [PP] stands for Prepositional Phrase. "*on the mat*" is the prepositional phrase in the sentence.
- DET stands for Determiner. In this sentence, "*The*" and "*the*" are determiners.
- N stands for Noun. "*cat*" and "*mat*" are nouns.
- V stands for Verb. "*sat*" is the verb.

- *Dependency-based Approaches: The Relational View*

  While constituency sheds light on the hierarchical arrangement of words and phrases, dependency-based approaches bring forth the relational dynamics between words. Here, sentences aren't dissected into nested sub-phrases but are instead viewed as networks of interdependent words. For example, in the

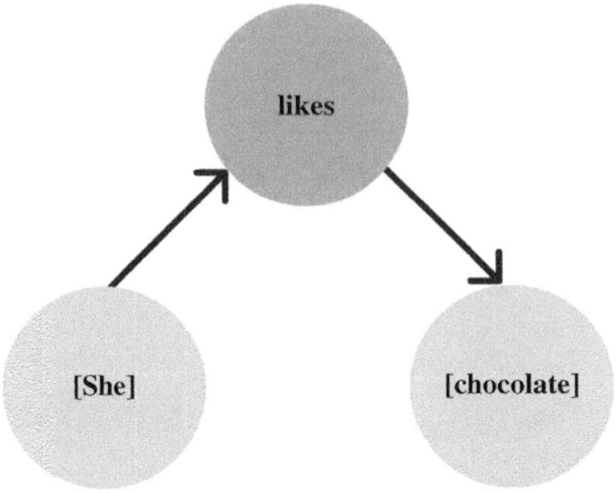

Figure 3.6 Semantic Relationship Mapping: "*She Likes Chocolate*".

sentence "*She likes chocolate,*" the word "*likes*" depends on both "*She*" (the one doing the liking) and "*chocolate*" (the object of affection). Visualizing this sentence using a dependency-based approach paints a clear picture: each word is a node, and arrows (or edges) depict relationships. The word "*likes*" emerges as the central node, with arrows pointing to "*She*" (indicating the subject) and "*chocolate*" (indicating the object). This graph representation captures the inherent dependencies between words, signifying roles, and relationships that each word plays in the context of the sentence. Let's visualize the given sentence using a holistic and inclusive visualization, "*nested bubbles*" as shown in Fig. 3.6.

This approach encapsulates the central idea ("*likes*") and shows how the other components of the sentence relate to and depend on it. In this visualization:

- The outermost rectangle represents the largest bubble, which is labelled with the word "*likes.*"
- Inside this bubble, we have two smaller bubbles represented by square brackets. One is labelled "*She*" and the other "*chocolate.*"
- The arrows (depicted by "↗" and "↘") from the word "*likes*" point to these smaller bubbles, indicating dependency relationships.

3.7.4 Implications of Syntactic Analysis for Modern NLP

The significance of syntactic analysis in today's NLP landscape is profound. From chatbots that need to comprehend user queries to machine translation systems striving for accurate translations, understanding sentence structure is paramount. For instance, while translating between languages with differing word orders, dependency analysis can be invaluable, ensuring that relationships between words remain consistent.

- *The Dawn of Conversational AI:* The rise of conversational AI, epitomized by chatbots and voice assistants, has transformed user-machine interaction. Users now expect more human-like responses, emphasizing the machine's capability to understand not just words, but also the context and intricacies of sentences. Herein lies the quintessential role of syntactic analysis. For instance, when a user inquires, "*What's the weather like today and tomorrow in Paris?*", a chatbot must decipher that the query relates to two distinct timeframes and is centered around weather conditions in Paris. Syntactic analysis helps break down such queries, ensuring chatbots respond accurately.
- *Machine Translation:* Bridging Linguistic Gaps: Machine translation systems, such as Google Translate or DeepL, hinge on their ability to convert text from one language to another seamlessly. But this is not a mere word-to-word substitution. Languages come with their unique syntactic structures. A sentence structure that is perfectly valid in English might be unnatural or even incomprehensible in, say, Japanese. Syntactic analysis, especially dependency-based approaches, provides these systems with the tools to maintain the relational integrity of words in translations. For example, if a subject in an English sentence becomes an object in its Japanese counterpart due to syntactic differences, dependency analysis ensures this transformation is handled coherently.
- *Semantic Search and Information Retrieval:* Search engines have evolved from keyword-based systems to semantic search platforms. Users no longer want results based merely on the presence of specific words; they seek results relevant to their query's intent. Syntactic analysis aids in discerning this intent. Consider the search "*Apple company history versus apple fruit origin.*" Without syntactic analysis, a search engine might struggle to distinguish between "*Apple*" the tech giant and "*apple*" the fruit. But by understanding the structure and relationships of words in the query, search engines can more effectively differentiate and provide pertinent results.
- *Content Generation and Summarization:* Modern NLP is not just about comprehension; it's also about creation. Platforms that generate content, whether articles or summaries, rely heavily on syntactic analysis. When summarizing a lengthy article, for instance, these platforms must determine which sentences or phrases are crucial and how they interrelate. Syntactic analysis ensures the generated summary is coherent and retains the original content's essence.
- *Personal Assistants and Task Automation:* Virtual personal assistants, such as Siri or Alexa, are tasked with multi-step operations based on user commands. A user might say, "*Send an email to John about the meeting tomorrow and set a reminder for 9 AM.*" Here, syntactic analysis plays a dual role: First, by breaking down the user's instruction into distinct tasks (sending an email and setting a reminder), and second, by understanding the specifics of each task (the recipient is John, the topic is a meeting, and the reminder time is 9 AM).

Thus, in the rapidly evolving world of NLP, parsing stands out not just as a theoretical cornerstone but as a hands-on, foundational tool driving a multitude of applications. Every interaction we have with voice assistants, real-time translations, or sentiment analysis tools invariably taps into sophisticated parsing techniques. As AI systems weave more seamlessly into our daily routines, the precision of syntactic analysis becomes indispensable, ensuring that these machines grasp and respond to human language adeptly. While machine learning and NLP advance at an unprecedented pace, the significance of parsing and syntactic analysis persists, anchoring our ongoing quest to enhance machine understanding of human speech and text.

3.8 Tools and Libraries for Text Processing

In the ever-evolving domain of NLP, choosing the right tools often hinges on the preferred programming language. Here, we categorize some popular tools based on their primary or most user-friendly programming language.

3.8.1 Python

Python has established itself as a premier language for NLP, attributed to its user-friendly nature and a plethora of dedicated libraries.

- *Text Cleaning:* Python's NLTK library includes functions to remove HTML tags, non-alphabetic characters, and other extraneous elements from text. SpaCy, known for its efficient text processing pipelines, offers robust methods for text normalization, including lowercasing, lemmatization, and removing punctuation or numbers.
- *Sentence Splitting:* Both NLTK and spaCy are adept, with spaCy's hybrid approach of rule-based and ML methods standing out.
- *Tokenization:* NLTK is a foundational tool, with spaCy prized for its efficiency in large datasets. The Transformers library from HuggingFace, tailored for transformer models, and Gensim, primarily known for topic modelling, also offer tokenization functionalities.
- *Lemmatization and Stemming:* NLTK offers a WordNet lemmatizer, while spaCy features a rule-based alternative.
- *Stop Word Removal:* Both NLTK and spaCy come with predefined lists of stop words.
- *Part-of-Speech Tagging:* TextBlob offers a beginner-oriented interface, complemented by the robust capabilities of NLTK and spaCy.
- *Parsing and Syntactic Analysis:* spaCy provides dependency parsing, while the BLLIP Parser emerges from rigorous academic research.

- *Miscellaneous:* FastText, by Facebook's AI Research, specializes in embeddings and classification. Scikit-learn, though broader in scope, also furnishes text-processing utilities.

3.8.2 Java

Java's performance-oriented design makes it apt for enterprise-level NLP applications.

- *Text Cleaning:* While Java-based NLP tools often focus more on analysis, text cleaning can be implemented using regular expressions or custom Java methods to strip unwanted text elements.
- *Sentence Splitting:* Both Stanford NLP and OpenNLP offer competent tools.
- *Tokenization*: OpenNLP stands out with its diverse NLP toolkit.
- *Stop Word Removal:* Stanford NLP and OpenNLP both provide mechanisms for filtering out stop words, facilitating the refinement of text data to focus on content-rich tokens for further NLP tasks.
- *Part-of-Speech Tagging:* Stanford's POS Tagger emanates from deep NLP research, while OpenNLP offers a dependable counterpart.
- *Parsing and Syntactic Analysis:* The Stanford Parser is renowned in parsing circles for its precision.

3.8.3 C++ (with Python Bindings)

Blending C++'s speed with Python's accessibility results in tools that are both performant and intuitive.

- *Parsing and Syntactic Analysis:* Google's Parsey McParseface (under SyntaxNet) offers top-tier performance, while UDPipe, aligned with the Universal Dependencies framework, ensures versatility and linguistic consistency.

Each platform and library brings its own strengths to the table. Selecting the right tool often depends on the project's specific needs, the data's scale, and the team's expertise with the chosen platform.

Knowledge Checkpoint 3

Fundamental Text Processing Scenarios

1) **Scenario 1:** You are tasked with cleaning a dataset containing social media posts for sentiment analysis. How would you handle common text cleaning challenges such as slang, misspellings, and emoticons to ensure the analysis is accurate?
2) **Scenario 2:** Imagine developing a chatbot that needs to understand and respond to customer queries. How would sentence splitting and tokenization play a crucial role in this project, and what tools would you use to implement these processes?

3) **Scenario 3:** As a data analyst working on a machine translation tool, why would you prefer lemmatization over stemming for processing text data? Provide examples where lemmatization proves to be more effective.
4) **Scenario 4:** You're analyzing a large corpus of ancient texts with many outdated words and phrases. Discuss the importance of context in stop word removal and how aggressive filtering might affect the meaning of historical documents.
5) **Scenario 5:** A software company is developing a document summarization tool. How would parsing and syntactic analysis contribute to creating accurate and coherent summaries of long articles?
6) **Scenario 6:** Consider a multinational corporation that wants to analyze customer feedback in multiple languages. How would you approach tokenization in this multilingual context, and which tools would be most effective?
7) **Scenario 7:** You are part of a team working on a search engine optimization (SEO) project. How would text cleaning and stop word removal impact the performance of the search engine, and what factors would you consider in customizing the stop word list?
8) **Scenario 8:** In a project focused on voice recognition software, how does sentence splitting affect the system's ability to accurately transcribe spoken language into text? Discuss the role of machine learning in improving sentence boundary disambiguation.
9) **Scenario 9:** For a sentiment analysis task, how would you decide between using stemming or lemmatization? Provide a scenario where the choice significantly impacts the analysis outcome.
10) **Scenario 10:** Your company is developing an AI-driven news aggregation platform. How would tokenization, particularly sub-word tokenization, help in dealing with the diverse and dynamic nature of news language?
11) **Scenario 11:** In legal document analysis, precision is critical. How would you ensure that the parsing and syntactic analysis processes maintain the legal text's integrity and meaning?
12) **Scenario 12:** You're tasked with improving a language-learning app that helps users understand complex sentences. Which syntactic analysis methods would be most beneficial for teaching sentence structure and why?

Knowledge Checkpoint 4

Fundamental Text Processing Quiz

1 What is the purpose of Unicode normalization in text cleaning?
A To remove all non-ASCII characters
B To standardize characters into a consistent form

C To increase the size of the text
D To identify and correct spelling errors

2 Why is sentence splitting challenging in text processing?
A Because sentences are too long
B Because punctuation marks like periods can serve multiple functions
C Because it is difficult to read
D Because it requires understanding the meaning of each word

3 What is the main goal of tokenization in NLP?
A To create a large database of words
B To convert text into a series of tokens or meaningful pieces
C To find and correct grammatical errors
D To translate text from one language to another

4 How does lemmatization differ from stemming?
A Lemmatization only works on verbs, while stemming works on all parts of speech
B Lemmatization reduces words to their root form based on actual language usage, whereas stemming cuts off the ends of words heuristically
C Lemmatization is faster than stemming
D There is no difference; they are the same

5 In what scenario might removing stop words be detrimental to text analysis?
A When performing keyword extraction
B When doing sentiment analysis and context is important
C When counting the number of words in a text
D Stop words are always removed; there are no detrimental scenarios

6 What is the significance of Part-of-Speech (PoS) tagging in NLP?
A It helps in sorting words alphabetically
B It assigns grammatical labels to words, aiding in understanding sentence structure
C It changes the font size of the text
D It reduces the text to its stem form

7 What is the main function of parsing in NLP?
A To translate the text from one language to another
B To check the spelling of the text
C To analyze the grammatical structure of the text
D To count the number of paragraphs in the text

8 Which Python library is known for its efficient text processing pipelines and robust methods for text normalization?
A NumPy
B spaCy
C Pandas
D TensorFlow

9 Which of the following best describes Unicode normalization?
A Converting all text to uppercase
B Removing numeric characters from text
C Standardizing text to a uniform encoding standard
D Translating text into Unicode language

10 What is the use of regular expressions (Regex) in text cleaning?
A To calculate the frequency of word occurrence
B To search and manipulate strings based on patterns
C To automatically correct grammatical errors
D To convert text from one language to another

11 Which technique is NOT typically used for sentence boundary disambiguation?
A Rule-based methods
B Machine learning models
C Dictionary lookups
D Neural networks

12 What is the main advantage of sub-word tokenization?
A It can handle large documents faster.
B It helps in handling out-of-vocabulary words.
C It simplifies grammatical analysis.
D It replaces stop words efficiently.

13 Part-of-Speech tagging is crucial for which of the following NLP tasks?
A Password encryption
B Sentiment analysis
C Data storage
D Website design

14 What is a significant challenge in text cleaning?
A Increasing the size of the text
B Deciding which text style to use

C Maintaining the meaning and context of the text
D Changing the font of the text

15 Why is stemming particularly useful in information retrieval systems?
A It ensures accurate spelling.
B It groups different forms of a word together.
C It translates text into different languages.
D It increases the length of the text.

16 Why might stop words be retained in language modelling tasks?
A They are necessary for correct spelling checks.
B They contribute to understanding the grammatical structure.
C They increase the database size for machine learning.
D They make the text look longer and more detailed.

17 Dependency parsing primarily focuses on:
A The order of paragraphs in a document
B The hierarchical structure of sentences
C The relationships between words in a sentence
D The alphabetical arrangement of words

18 In machine translation, lemmatization is important because:
A It shortens sentences for easier translation.
B It helps in maintaining the meaning of words across languages.
C It increases the speed of translation.
D It translates proper nouns more accurately.

19 How does tokenization benefit machine translation?
A It enhances the encryption of the text.
B It separates text into tokens, making it easier to translate individual elements.
C It improves the printing quality of the text.
D It increases the number of fonts available for translation.

20 Which Python library is NOT primarily used for text processing in NLP?
A Matplotlib
B NLTK
C spaCy
D Gensim

4

Linguistic Features in NLP

This chapter introduces the concept of linguistic features, which are the fundamental building blocks in the field of NLP. Linguistic features refer to the attributes that can be derived from text and speech to help a computer system understand and generate human language. They are the characteristics of language that can be quantified or categorized to facilitate language processing tasks. These features encompass a wide range of language components, from the basic units of sounds (phonemes) to the complexities of discourse.

Linguistic features serve as pivotal reference points that inform and shape the development of NLP technologies. They are the components that enable machines to parse speech and text, extract meaning, detect sentiment, and even create language that mimics human fluency. In the context of NLP, these features are not merely academic constructs but practical tools that provide a framework for the development of algorithms and systems capable of processing language in myriad forms. The inclusion of linguistic features into NLP models transforms raw language data into structured formats that machines can navigate. For instance, the identification and tagging of parts of speech in a sentence allow algorithms to understand the role each word plays and how words relate to each other, which is essential for tasks like translation or summarization. Similarly, the analysis of syntactic structures helps machines comprehend the grammatical composition of sentences, facilitating tasks such as parsing and text generation.

Linguistic features also extend beyond individual words and sentences, encapsulating the broader context and intent behind language use. This is where semantics and pragmatics play a critical role. By deciphering the intended meaning behind phrases and interpreting the subtleties of context, NLP systems can respond to queries, participate in conversations, and even detect nuances like sarcasm or irony. Linguistic features are the tools that help construct the bridge between human linguistics and machine understanding. This bridge is not

Language Intelligence: Expanding Frontiers in Natural Language Processing, First Edition. Akshi Kumar.
© 2025 The Institute of Electrical and Electronics Engineers, Inc. Published 2025 by John Wiley & Sons, Inc.

static but a dynamic, continually evolving construct. As language itself evolves, so too must the NLP systems that seek to interpret it. The ongoing research into linguistic features is driven by the recognition that language is not a fixed code but a living, changing medium of human expression.

One of the critical aspects of this bridge-building is the development of context-aware systems that can interpret the meaning and intent behind words used in varying contexts. Such systems need to account for the cultural, social, and situational factors that impact language use. It involves not only the semantic analysis of words and sentences but also the pragmatics of language use—how meaning is shaped by context and how language is used to achieve specific communicative goals.

Moreover, the quest for machines to understand human language necessitates a multi-disciplinary approach. Insights from linguistics, psychology, computer science, and cognitive science converge to inform the design of algorithms that can handle the complexity and subtleties of human communication. This interdisciplinary approach is what animates the field of NLP, imbuing it with the capacity to innovate and refine the ways in which machines engage with human language. In the pursuit of this goal, the NLP community continues to push the boundaries of what is possible. Advancements in machine learning (ML) and deep learning have led to models that can not only understand but also predict and respond to human language with increasing accuracy and nuance. These models are fed with rich linguistic data, informed by the wealth of knowledge from the field of linguistics, and honed through the power of computational algorithms. The bridge between human linguistics and machine understanding, though not yet complete, is continually being extended. With each linguistic feature that is understood and incorporated into NLP systems, the gap narrows, leading us closer to a future where machines can understand and interact with human language with the same ease and depth as we do.

4.1 Levels of Linguistic Analysis

Linguistic analysis in NLP is a multi-tiered approach that dissects language into distinct yet interrelated layers. Each stratum examines different components and structures of language, ranging from the elemental to the complex, and collectively, they contribute to the comprehensive understanding and automated processing of human language (Fig. 4.1).

4.1.1 Phonetics and Phonology: Sounds of Language

Linguistic analysis begins with the examination of sounds. Phonetics and Phonology, though often working in tandem, address distinct facets of language sounds.

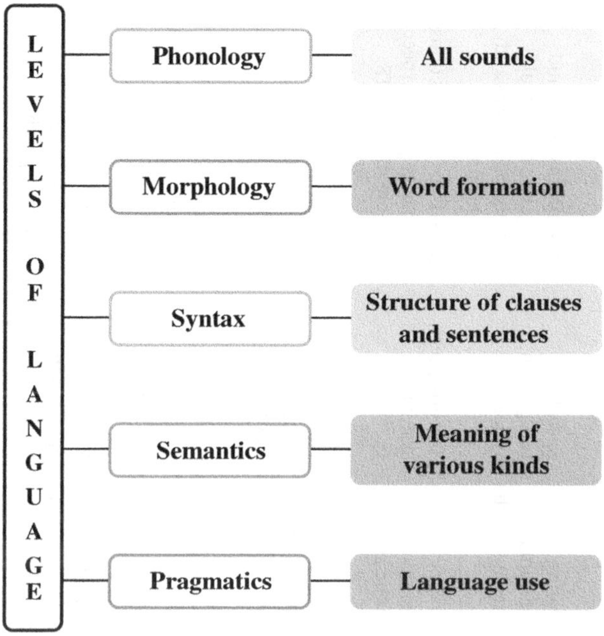

Figure 4.1 Levels of Linguistic Analysis.

Phonetics focuses on the physical production and auditory perception of speech sounds, breaking down the elemental units into vowels and consonants, and further into features like voicing and aspiration. Phonology goes a step further to understand how these sounds are organized and used in languages. In the realm of NLP, this level is fundamental for applications involving speech—whether it's recognizing spoken words in voice-operated software or generating speech from text in text-to-speech systems. Table 4.1 categorizes the information systematically, providing a clear understanding of the methodologies, techniques, and applications in phonetics and phonology within the context of NLP and speech processing technologies.

While the table provides a comprehensive overview of phonetics and phonology methodologies, techniques, and applications, it's important to note that this book primarily focuses on text-based processing. As such, we do not explore these areas in depth, as they are more pertinent to speech processing and analysis.

Morphology: Word Structure and Formation

Morphology dives into the construction of words, analyzing how morphemes—the smallest units of meaning—combine to form words. Understanding morphology is

Table 4.1 Overview of Phonetics and Phonology in Speech Processing: Methodologies, Techniques, Applications, and Examples.

Level	Methodology	Description	Application	Example	Implementation
Acoustic Phonetics	Spectrogram Analysis	Analyzes the physical properties of sound waves in speech.	Visual analysis of sound properties	Speech analysis applications	Used to create visual representations of the speech spectrum.
Articulatory Phonetics	Phonetic Transcription	Studies how speech sounds are produced by the mouth and vocal tract.	Transcribing sounds into written symbols	Language documentation	Phonetic symbols represent sounds to study and document pronunciation.
Phonological Analysis	Phoneme Recognition	Investigates systematic sound patterns in languages.	Differentiating between minimal sound units in speech	Speech recognition systems	Algorithms detect and categorize individual sounds for analysis and recognition.
Prosodic Analysis	Prosody Modelling	Examines elements like intonation, stress, and rhythm in speech.	Understanding speech's emotional and rhythmic aspects	Text-to-speech systems	Models to infer emotions or emphasize parts of speech for more natural TTS.
Auditory Phonetics	Auditory Perception	Studies how humans perceive and interpret speech sounds.	Recognizing and interpreting different speech sounds	Hearing aids, language learning tools	Analyzing how listeners differentiate and understand speech sounds.
	Accent Recognition	Identifies speaker's accent to improve communication systems.	Tailoring speech recognition to accommodate different accents	Customer service interfaces	Training ASR and TTS systems to recognize and adapt to various accents.
Phonetic Alignment	Automatic Speech Recognition (ASR)	Aligning phonetic data with audio for accurate representation.	Converting spoken language into written form	Voice-to-text applications	Aligning transcribed text with spoken words to enhance speech recognition accuracy.

key for NLP systems when it comes to tasks like word segmentation, particularly in languages where words are not clearly separated by spaces, or for parsing complex word formations in agglutinative languages. It also aids in generating different word forms and in grasping the nuances of meaning that different morphemes can contribute to a word. Table 4.2 represents a structured summary of the methodologies, techniques, and applications of morphology in the field of NLP, showcasing how these elements are implemented across different contexts to enhance language processing and understanding.

4.1.2 Syntax: Sentence Structure and Grammatical Rules

The syntactic level takes the spotlight when it comes to structuring language. Syntax is not just about what words are used; it's about where they are placed. Sentence parsing, one of the most fundamental tasks in NLP, relies on syntactic analysis to decompose sentences into their constituent parts and understand their grammatical relations. It's the syntactic scaffolding that supports the interpretation of sentences and ensures that language generation models produce linguistically coherent outputs. Table 4.3 encapsulates the syntax level in NLP, highlighting methodologies, techniques, and their applications in the real world. It shows how syntactic analysis is crucial in grammar checking, machine translation, and understanding natural language, underlining the practical implementations of these syntactic methodologies in various NLP applications.

4.1.3 Semantics: Meaning of Words and Sentences

The semantics level is where meaning takes center stage. It's not enough for NLP systems to recognize words and their structures; they must also comprehend what those words signify. Semantic analysis encompasses the interpretation of individual words, the relationships between words, and how combinations of words convey complex concepts and facts. It is the semantic prowess of an NLP system that enables it to extract facts, answer questions, and engage in dialogue with users by truly understanding what is being communicated. Table 4.4 provides an overview of the semantic aspect of NLP, describing the methodologies involved in understanding word and sentence meanings, the techniques used to disambiguate and label semantic roles, and their applications in real-world scenarios like search engines, chatbots, and text summarization.

4.1.4 Pragmatics: Language in Context and Usage

Pragmatics extends the analysis to the realm of speaker intent and contextual meaning. It acknowledges that what we say is often just the tip of the communicative iceberg, with much of the message lurking below the surface of explicit

Table 4.2 Overview of Morphology in NLP: Methodologies, Techniques, and Applications.

Level	Methodology	Description	Technique	Application	Example
Morphemic Analysis	Identifying morphemes	Identifying and categorizing morphemes to understand word structure.	Stemming	Reducing words to their base form, used in search engines.	Text analysis tools
Inflectional Morphology	Analyzing word forms	Analyzing word forms to express different grammatical categories like tense, case, number.	Lemmatization	Converting words to their lemma, typically involving complex morphology.	Language learning apps
Derivational Morphology	Creating new word forms	Exploring the process of creating new words and word forms, using prefixes and suffixes.	Morphological Parsing	Decomposing words into morphemes and analyzing their structure.	Predictive text input
Computational Morphology	Algorithmic analysis	Employing algorithms to understand and generate the morphological structure of words.	Morphological Generation	Generating grammatically correct word forms in various contexts.	Multilingual platforms
Lexical Morphology	Encoding lexicon entries	Studying the role of morphemes in encoding lexicon entries and their meanings.	Finite State Transducers (FSTs)	Representing morphological rules to generate or analyze word forms.	

Table 4.3 Overview of Syntax in NLP: Methodologies, Techniques, and Real-World Applications.

Level	Methodology	Description	Technique	Application	Example
Constituency Analysis	Analyzing structure	Analyzing sentence structure by breaking down sentences into sub-phrases forming higher-level phrases.	Parse Trees	Visualizing sentence structure	Grammar checking software
Dependency Analysis	Identifying relations	Examining sentence structure by identifying dependency relationships between head words and their dependents.	Context-Free Grammars	Predicting sentence structure independently of language specifics	Machine translation
Grammatical Parsing	Algorithmic analysis	Utilizing algorithms to analyze grammatical structure of sentences to understand each word/phrase's role.	Syntactic Parsing	Determining sentence meaning in context	Natural Language Understanding systems

Table 4.4 Overview of Semantics in NLP: Methodologies, Techniques, and Real-World Applications.

Level	Methodology	Description	Technique	Application	Example	Implementation
Lexical Semantics	Investigating word meaning	Investigating the meaning and relationships of individual words.	Word Sense Disambiguation	Determining the context-specific meaning of words	Search Engines	Enhancing search accuracy by understanding the specific meanings of words in queries.
Compositional Semantics	Integrating word meanings	Exploring how individual word meanings combine and are interpreted in larger expressions.	Semantic Role Labelling	Identifying roles of words in sentences to understand sentence meaning	Chatbots	Interpreting user queries accurately by analyzing the sentence semantics.
Semantic Analysis	Understanding text meaning	Utilizing knowledge of word and sentence level meanings to process language.	Semantic Parsing	Analyzing the logical structure of sentences to derive meaning	Text Summarization	Extracting essential semantic content to produce concise summaries of large texts.

language. NLP systems that can navigate the subtleties of pragmatics can infer user intent, recognize indirect requests, and appreciate the social dynamics of language use. This level is crucial for applications where human interaction is central, such as in conversational agents and social media analysis. Table 4.5 presents an overview of pragmatics in NLP, detailing how methodologies like Speech Act Theory, Conversational Implicature, and Contextual Reasoning play a pivotal role in interpreting and understanding language beyond its literal meaning, through techniques like Pragmatic Enrichment, Discourse Analysis, and Indirect Speech Act Recognition, and their applications in real-world technologies like digital assistants, customer service bots, and sentiment analysis systems.

4.1.5 Discourse: Structure and Coherence in Texts

Discourse analysis in the realm of NLP extends beyond the scrutiny of individual sentences, venturing into the examination of how these sentences interconnect to forge structured and meaningful narratives. This analytical domain is pivotal for it encapsulates the essence of communication, exploring the seamless flow of conversations and the sustained context across interactions. The discipline is instrumental in crafting and refining NLP systems capable of engaging in or dissecting prolonged dialogs, ensuring the coherence of discourse over time and accurately maintaining thematic and referential continuity.

In the nuanced field of pragmatics within NLP, methodologies like **Cohesion and Coherence Analysis** alongside Narrative Structure Analysis stand out as fundamental. Cohesion and Coherence Analysis aim to scrutinize and ascertain the logical sequence and consistency within the text, guaranteeing that the narrative is not only intelligible but also follows a logical trajectory. This examination is thorough, tracing how individual sentences and concepts intricately weave together to form a unified narrative thread, thereby fostering a cohesive and coherent reading experience. **Narrative Structure Analysis**, conversely, immerses itself in the narrative fabric of the text, dissecting the narrative architecture to discern the progression of events and the evolution of characters. This methodology unravels the narrative's scaffold, enlightening the structural and thematic intricacies that underpin the storyline, thereby offering profound insights into the narrative's underlying fabric and significance.

In sophisticated discourse analysis, several techniques are pivotal for maintaining clarity and coherence. **Anaphora Resolution** is one such technique that focuses on identifying the referents of pronouns and other anaphoric elements, which is essential for preserving clarity in the discourse. For instance, in a narrative where *"John put on his jacket because he was cold,"* anaphora resolution helps identify *"he"* as referring to *"John,"* clarifying the narrative's context. Additionally, **Discourse Parsing** plays a crucial role by segmenting

Table 4.5 Overview of Pragmatics in NLP: Methodologies, Techniques, and Real-World Applications.

Level	Methodology	Description	Technique	Application	Example	Implementation
Speech Act Theory	Examining language use	Examining how speakers use language to perform actions and convey intentions beyond literal meanings.	Pragmatic Enrichment	Inferring implied meanings in language	Digital Assistants	Analyzing user commands to understand intentions and perform appropriate actions.
Conversational Implicature	Investigating implied meanings	Investigating the meanings implied in communication not directly expressed, contributing to conversation understanding.	Discourse Analysis	Understanding how meaning is constructed in conversations	Customer Service Bots	Interpreting customer queries and responses to provide contextually relevant reactions.
Contextual Reasoning	Assessing context effect	Assessing how context influences language interpretation in different situations.	Indirect Speech Act Recognition	Identifying communicative intent beyond literal sentence meaning	Sentiment Analysis	Evaluating opinions and emotions by understanding the pragmatic aspects of communication.

text into discernible discourse units like stories, events, or thematic entities. This segmentation facilitates a deeper understanding of the text's structure and relational dynamics, aiding in the comprehensive analysis of the discourse. Complementing this, **Topic Segmentation** methodically divides the text into segments based on thematic transitions, enhancing both comprehension and information retrieval.

Anaphora resolution not only involves syntactic analysis but also investigates semantic understanding, leveraging contextual clues to accurately connect pronouns with their corresponding entities. **Coreference Resolution** expands this scope to include all expressions referring to the same entity, ensuring the text's semantic integrity. For example, "*Dr. Smith spoke to the patient and then he prescribed medication*" illustrates how coreference resolution links *"he"* to *"Dr. Smith,"* thus maintaining narrative consistency.

The challenge in both anaphora and coreference resolution lies in the inherent ambiguity of natural language, where expressions can be vague, and multiple antecedents may exist, necessitating a deep contextual understanding. Variability in linguistic and cultural nuances further complicates this process, demanding a nuanced approach to correctly interpret referential expressions.

In practical settings, these analytical methods are crucial. Legal document analysis, for instance, relies on precise reference resolution to comprehend case specifics and involved parties accurately. Similarly, in literature analysis, understanding character actions and narrative development hinges on effective anaphora and coreference resolution. Interactive AI systems like chatbots also depend on these techniques to ensure conversations remain coherent and contextually relevant.

Moreover, summarization tools and sentiment analysis algorithms exemplify the application of these discourse analysis techniques. Summarization tools leverage discourse understanding to create condensed yet comprehensive versions of texts, while sentiment analysis algorithms employ these insights to accurately gauge emotional undertones, considering the narrative and discursive shifts within the text. These implementations highlight the critical role of discourse analysis in enhancing NLP systems, enabling them to navigate and interpret the intricate landscape of human communication with nuanced precision and insight.

4.2 Features in NLP

Within the field of NLP, the concept of **"features"** is pivotal to transforming raw text into analyzable data. A feature, in this context, refers to an individual measurable property or characteristic of a phenomenon, often extracted from the text, used to construct a numerical or categorical representation that ML models can process and analyze.

The **feature space** in NLP is the multi-dimensional space where each dimension corresponds to a specific feature that represents some aspect of the text. For example, in a simple bag-of-words model, each dimension might represent the occurrence of a distinct word in the text corpus, thereby creating a feature space where each text sample is a vector indicating the presence or frequency of each word. **Feature engineering** is the process of using domain knowledge to extract and select the most relevant features from raw data. In NLP, this might involve choosing which aspects of the text are important and how to quantify them. This process can be quite intricate, involving several sub-processes like feature extraction and feature selection:

- *Feature Extraction:* This is the initial step in transforming text into a form that ML algorithms can understand. It involves converting text data into numerical or categorical values. For example, extracting the length of sentences, the frequency of specific words, or the presence of named entities like people or places.
- *Feature Selection:* This involves selecting the most significant features from the set extracted. Not all features are equally informative; some might be redundant or irrelevant to the task at hand. Feature selection aims to identify and retain those features that contribute most to the predictive power of the model.

Features in NLP serve as the foundational elements that transform the amorphous and unstructured nature of language into structured, analyzable data. Through meticulous processes of feature extraction and selection, enriched by domain knowledge and advanced modelling techniques, NLP professionals can craft powerful models that grasp and interpret the multifaceted essence of human language, enabling a myriad of applications from automated translation to emotion detection and beyond. For instance, in sentiment analysis, the frequency of certain adjectives might be a powerful feature, as adjectives often carry strong sentiment indicators. Feature extraction in this case might involve counting how often words categorized as positive or negative adjectives appear in a text. In spam detection, feature extraction might focus on specific keywords often found in spam emails, while feature selection would determine which of these keywords are truly predictive of spam.

With advancements in NLP, feature engineering has evolved to include sophisticated techniques like word embeddings, where words are converted into vectors of real numbers, capturing semantic relationships based on the context of their occurrence in the corpus. This technique allows for a more nuanced representation of text, facilitating the processing of language's subtle linguistic features.

4.3 Vector Space Representation in NLP

Vector space representation in NLP is a cornerstone technique that effectively bridges the gap between the rich, nuanced domain of human language and the precise, quantitative realm of ML algorithms. This technique entails converting textual data into a structured numerical form, enabling algorithms to perform a wide array of tasks ranging from classification to clustering and beyond. The principle of vector space representation lies in its ability to encapsulate linguistic elements as vectors within a multi-dimensional space. Each dimension within this space represents a distinct characteristic or feature extracted from the text, typically words or phrases. For instance, in a corpus of documents, each unique term can be considered a dimension in the vector space, and the value in each dimension reflects the significance or occurrence of that term in the context of a particular document or a set of documents.

The transformation process starts with tokenization, where text is segmented into its constituent tokens, which could be words, phrases, or even characters. Following tokenization, various methods are employed to quantify these tokens and encode them into numerical vectors. The numerical encoding can be as simple as counting the frequency of each word in a document (as in the Bag of Words model) or as complex as calculating the contextual relevance of words across the entire corpus (as in TF-IDF).

In vector space representation, the position and magnitude of a vector in the space can significantly convey the linguistic features of the text it represents. For example, similar documents are often located close to each other in this space, while dissimilar ones are positioned further apart. This spatial arrangement is pivotal for ML models, as it allows them to discern patterns, detect anomalies, and make predictions based on the geometric properties of the vectors. Moreover, the high-dimensional nature of this vector space often necessitates dimensionality reduction techniques, such as Principal Component Analysis (PCA) or t-distributed Stochastic Neighbor Embedding (t-SNE), to simplify the data and unveil underlying structures. These reduced representations can be more manageable for algorithms, especially when dealing with large datasets, enabling more efficient processing and analysis.

Vector space representation lays the groundwork for extensive NLP tasks, enabling advanced language analysis and processing with remarkable accuracy and depth. The following sections will explore four essential techniques in vector space representation, each playing a pivotal role in translating textual information into a numerical format that can be easily processed by algorithms.

These techniques include:

- *Bag of Words (BoW):* This approach tallies the occurrence of each word within a document, disregarding the order and context, to create a simple yet effective representation of text content.
- *TF-IDF (Term Frequency-Inverse Document Frequency):* Building upon the BoW concept, TF-IDF measures not only the frequency of words in a document but also their relative importance across a corpus, offering a more nuanced text representation.
- *N-gram Model:* This model captures context by considering contiguous sequences of "n" words or characters, providing a richer and more contextually aware representation of the text data.
- *One-hot Encoding:* A method where each word in the vocabulary is represented as a binary vector with one "hot" element, distinguishing each word uniquely in the vector space.

By employing these methods, NLP practitioners can transform the abstract and unstructured nature of language into structured, analyzable data, paving the way for ML models to interpret and act upon the intricacies of human language effectively. In Python, vector space representation of text can be achieved using libraries like Scikit-learn or Gensim, which convert text into numerical vectors using methods like TF-IDF or word embeddings, facilitating the analysis of text data in ML models.

4.3.1 Bag of Words (BoW): Vector Space Models and Frequency Distributions

In the field of NLP, the Bag of Words (BoW) model has been a linchpin for the transformation of textual information into a format that can be handled by algorithms. BoW paves the way for many ML and NLP tasks, providing a baseline against which more sophisticated models are measured. This section probes the intricacies of the Bag of Words model, exploring its conception, functionality, and applications, as well as its limitations and the advancements that have been made to overcome them.

At its core, the Bag of Words model is a representation of text that converts unstructured data into a structured form. It is called a "bag" because it implies that the text is treated as a collection of words without considering the grammar or the word order—much like pulling words out of a bag at random. Each word holds a slot in a vector, and the value in that slot reflects the presence of the word in a given document.

- *Mechanics of BoW: From Text to Vector:* The transformation from raw text to a BoW representation involves several steps:
  a) **Vocabulary Creation:** First, a vocabulary of all unique words in the training corpus is constructed. This vocabulary becomes the feature set.

b) **Document-Term Matrix:** Each document is then represented as a vector within this feature space. The simplest form of BoW encodes this vector with binary values—indicating the presence or absence of a word in the document.

c) **Term Frequency:** More often, BoW employs term frequency, quantifying how many times a word appears in the document. This numeric representation is crucial as it conveys the prominence of certain terms within the text.

The BoW approach is tightly linked with the vector space model, a fundamental framework in information retrieval. Documents are mapped into a multi-dimensional space, where each dimension corresponds to a word in the vocabulary. In this space, the frequency of the word affects the vector's magnitude along that dimension. Collections of such vectors form a document-term matrix, which serves as the bedrock for further analysis, be it for clustering, classification, or similarity searches. While raw frequency counts can be informative, they often give undue prominence to common words that carry little topical information. Techniques like Term Frequency-Inverse Document Frequency (TF-IDF) weigh the word frequencies by how common they are across all documents, helping to highlight terms that are more interesting and distinctive to a document. The Bag of Words model, with its inherent simplicity, has provided a gateway into more sophisticated language modelling techniques. It remains a starting point for feature representation in text-based applications. The NLTK library in Python can be used to create a bag-of-words model with its **FreqDist** or **Counter** functions to tally word occurrences within a corpus.

4.3.2 Term Frequency-Inverse Document Frequency: Weighing Terms in Documents

The TF-IDF metric stands as one of the most influential techniques in the realm of information retrieval and text mining. This statistical measure evaluates how relevant a word is to a document within a collection of documents, known as a corpus. The relevance increases proportionally to the number of times a word appears in the document but is offset by the frequency of the word in the corpus. The TF-IDF value therefore reflects both the term's significance in a particular document and its rarity across all documents. TF-IDF builds upon the BoW model by diminishing the weight (importance) of terms that appear frequently across documents, thus highlighting terms that are unique to a particular document.

- **Term Frequency (TF):** This is a measure of how frequently a term occurs in a document. It's calculated by dividing the number of times a term t appears in a document d by the total number of terms in the document:

$$\text{TF}(\text{t}, \text{d}) = \frac{\text{Number of times term t appears in document d}}{\text{Total number of terms in document d}}$$

- **Inverse Document Frequency (IDF):** This measures the importance of the term across a set of documents. The IDF of a term is calculated by taking the logarithm of the number of documents D divided by the number of documents that contain the term t:

$$\text{IDF}(t, D) = \log\left(\frac{\text{Total number of documents D}}{\text{Number of documents containing term t}}\right)$$

- **TF-IDF Score:** The TF-IDF score is computed as the product of TF and IDF: $\text{TF} - \text{IDF}\ (t, d, D) = \text{TF}\ (t, d) \times \text{IDF}\ (t, D)$

Let us consider a simple example to illustrate how TF-IDF works. Imagine we have a corpus with 3 documents:

- **Document 1:** "The sky is blue."
- **Document 2:** "The ocean is deep and blue."
- **Document 3:** "The sunset is red."

To calculate the TF-IDF for the word "blue" in Document 1, we perform the following steps:

1) **Calculate TF:**
   - "blue" appears 1 time in Document 1.
   - There are 4 words in Document 1.
   - So, TF ("blue", Document 1) =14 = 0.25TF ("blue," Document 1) =41 = 0.25.
2) **Calculate IDF:**
   - We have 3 documents in our corpus.
   - "blue" appears in 2 of these documents.
   - So, IDF ("blue", D) = $\log\left(\frac{3}{2}\right) = 0.1761$ (using the natural logarithm).
3) **Calculate TF-IDF:**
   - TF-IDF ("blue", Document 1, D) = $0.25 \times 0.1761 = 0.044025$.

By repeating this calculation for each word in each document, we would end up with a matrix where each row corresponds to a document and each column corresponds to a TF-IDF score for a term in the vocabulary. Higher TF-IDF scores indicate a term's greater importance to a particular document relative to other documents in the corpus. In Python, the **TfidfVectorizer** function from the **sklearn.feature_extraction.text** module can be used to calculate the TF-IDF. TF-IDF is particularly effective for the following reasons:

- *Discrimination of Common Words:* Words that appear frequently across documents (like "the" or "is") are penalized. This reduces their influence when comparing documents.
- *Highlighting Unique Terms:* Terms that are unique to a document but not common across other documents are given more significance, enhancing the document's unique topical footprint.

- *Scalability and Simplicity:* The computation of TF-IDF does not require complex models and scales well with the size of the corpus.
- *Versatility:* TF-IDF can be used as a feature vector for a plethora of ML models and is effective for tasks ranging from document classification to clustering and information retrieval.

TF-IDF provides a numerical weightage that is instrumental in reflecting how important a word is not only in a document but within the entire corpus. This dual importance—balancing term frequency with document frequency—makes TF-IDF a powerful tool in the arsenal of text analysis and natural language processing. Despite the emergence of more complex algorithms in recent years, TF-IDF remains robust and straightforward. TF-IDF has been applied in systems like search engines, which rank the relevance of documents to a user's query. It's also prevalent in document clustering, aiding in the identification of documents that share common themes. Furthermore, TF-IDF serves as a cornerstone feature in many supervised learning tasks, such as spam detection or sentiment analysis.

However, TF-IDF has several limitations that affect its performance. It treats each word independently and lacks the capability to grasp context or word order, essential for understanding textual semantics. This approach fails to account for polysemy, treating words with multiple meanings the same across different contexts. Furthermore, TF-IDF only relies on statistical word frequency, ignoring semantic relationships between words, such as synonyms. The method also tends to overemphasize rare terms due to its inverse document frequency component, potentially misrepresenting their importance. Additionally, TF-IDF cannot handle new words not present in its training corpus, which limits its effectiveness in dynamic or evolving language contexts. Moreover, in very short texts like tweets or SMS messages, TF-IDF scores may be less meaningful due to limited word occurrence and context. Lastly, it does not differentiate between types or qualities of documents, treating all sources as equally authoritative.

In conclusion, while TF-IDF is a powerful tool for certain applications, these limitations make it less suitable for tasks that require a deep understanding of language, such as semantic search, word sense disambiguation, or processing of very short or dynamically changing texts. This has led to the development and adoption of more advanced techniques like word embeddings and neural network-based models in natural language processing.

4.3.3 N-Gram Language Model

An N-gram language model is a type of probabilistic language model used for predicting the next item in a sequence of words. The "N" in "N-gram" refers to the number of words used to predict the next one. For example, in a bigram (2-gram) model, the next word is predicted based on the previous one. In a trigram

(3-gram) model, the next word is predicted based on the two words that precede it, and so on.

The concept of the N-gram model is not new. It originated from the field of computational linguistics and information theory. Its roots can be traced back to Claude Shannon's work on the mathematical theory of communication in the late 1940s. The foundation of an N-gram model is probability. The model calculates the probability of a word given the previous "N-1" words. This is known as conditional probability. The model is trained on a corpus of text, learning the probabilities of word sequences within that corpus. In Python, the NLTK library's **ngrams** function allows for easy generation of n-grams from text data.

The mathematical representation of an N-gram model for predicting a word sequence $w1, w2, \ldots, wn$ is:

$P\,(wn|wn-1, wn-2, \ldots, wn-N+1)$

The probability of word wn is conditional on the preceding "N-1" words.

- *Building an N-gram Model: Example and Steps*
  a) *Corpus Selection:* Choose a corpus of text relevant to the context where the language model will be used.
  b) *Tokenization:* Break the text into tokens (words).
  c) *Building N-grams:* Construct the N-grams from the corpus. For instance, the sentence "The cat sat on the mat" would yield the following bigrams: "The cat," "cat sat," "sat on," "on the," and "the mat."
  d) *Calculating Probabilities:* Determine the probability distribution of each N-gram.
  e) *Smoothing:* Apply smoothing techniques to deal with zero-probability issues for unseen N-grams.
  f) *Evaluation:* Assess the model using a hold-out dataset or cross-validation to ensure it generalizes well.

Despite their simplicity, N-gram models are a crucial stepping stone in the evolution of language modelling. They provide a fundamental understanding of how probabilistic models can grasp the structure of language and are still used as baseline models in many NLP tasks.

4.3.4 Conversion of Categorical Data to Numerical Data in NLP and One-Hot Encoding

In NLP, handling categorical data—such as labels or categories associated with text—is crucial for processing and analyzing the language effectively. Converting categorical data into numerical format allows ML algorithms to operate on text data, facilitating various NLP tasks, including sentiment analysis, topic classification, and named entity recognition. The techniques for conversion include:

- *Label Encoding:* Transforms each category into a unique integer based on the category's occurrence order, suitable for categories with a natural ordering but may inadvertently introduce a numerical hierarchy where none exists.
- *Frequency Encoding:* Assigns numbers to categories based on their frequencies, emphasizing the prevalence of certain categories within the dataset.

One-hot encoding stands out as a pivotal technique for converting categorical variables into a binary matrix representation. It ensures that the model treats each category equally without implying an unintended ordinal relationship. Consider a dataset comprising movie reviews labeled with sentiments like "positive," "negative," and "neutral." In sentiment analysis, these categorical labels are converted into numerical data to train the model:

a) Text: "I loved the movie!" - > Label: "positive"
b) Text: "It was the worst film I've ever seen." - > Label: "negative"
c) Text: "An average movie, nothing special." - > Label: "neutral"

Using one-hot encoding, the sentiments are numerically represented as follows:

- "positive" [1, 0, 0]
- "negative" [0, 1, 0]
- "neutral" [0, 0, 1]

This conversion creates a distinct binary vector for each sentiment category, allowing a ML algorithm to process and learn from the sentiment labels associated with the textual data effectively.

One-hot encoding's clear demarcation of categories enhances model performance by preventing the algorithm from assuming an unintended order among categories. However, it can lead to increased dimensionality, especially with a large number of categories, resulting in sparse matrices that may be computationally intensive to process.

In practical NLP applications, these vector space representations, especially through one-hot encoding, are instrumental in transforming the nuanced and abstract nature of text into structured, algorithm-friendly data. This process underpins sophisticated NLP tasks, enabling the nuanced interpretation and prediction of textual content in a variety of applications, from automated sentiment assessment to intricate language understanding systems.

4.4 Semantic Features in NLP

The evolution of NL from traditional ML feature extraction to automatic feature learning through deep learning signifies a monumental shift toward semantic-rich feature representation. In traditional ML approaches, feature extraction often requires extensive manual effort to identify and codify linguistic elements as numerical values, focusing mainly on surface-level text attributes like word frequencies, n-grams, or syntactic patterns.

As we transitioned into the era of deep learning, the scope and capability of feature representation expanded dramatically. Deep learning models, particularly in NLP, autonomously learn to identify and encode features from raw text, delving into the semantic essence of language. This shift means that features in modern NLP systems are inherently semantic, capturing the underlying meanings, themes, and contextual nuances of text in a way that traditional methods could not.

Semantic features in NLP, empowered by deep learning, encapsulate the complex and multi-layered nature of language. These features are derived from sophisticated models and techniques that understand and represent the text's semantic content:

- *Lexicons* in NLP have evolved with these advancements, now being used in tandem with ML algorithms to provide nuanced semantic annotations and insights, enhancing the semantic depth of the extracted features.
- *Ontologies* play a crucial role in enriching text processing with domain-specific knowledge and hierarchical relationships, offering a structured semantic framework that deep learning models can exploit to gain a better understanding of context and entity relationships.
- *Knowledge graphs* integrate seamlessly with deep learning, providing a semantic network of entities and relationships that models can query and reason with, enabling a more nuanced and interconnected understanding of text.
- *Word embeddings,* a breakthrough in representing text as dense vectors, capture latent semantic and syntactic properties, allowing models to discern word meanings based on usage contextually.

In the modern NLP landscape, the distinction between feature extraction and feature learning blurs as deep learning models inherently learn to identify and leverage semantic features from large corpora of text. This progression has led to a more intuitive and context-aware approach to NLP, where features are not just indicators of text but rich semantic representations that convey the depth and breadth of human language. As a result, NLP systems today are capable of more advanced and nuanced language understanding and processing, mirroring the complexity and subtlety of human communication more closely than ever before.

4.4.1 Lexicons

Lexicons, in the context of NLP, are comprehensive repositories of words, their definitions, and various linguistic attributes. They are akin to dictionaries but are structured in a way that machines can process and understand. Lexicons serve as a fundamental resource in NLP, providing essential data that fuels both traditional and modern language processing tasks.

A lexicon in NLP is not just a list of words but includes detailed information such as part-of-speech tags, morphological patterns, semantic meanings, synonyms, antonyms, and usage examples. This rich set of data allows NLP systems to perform more accurately in tasks like text analysis, language translation, and sentiment analysis by understanding the nuances of language usage.

- *Examples of Lexicons in NLP:*
  a) **Sentiment Lexicons:** These contain words associated with sentiments or emotions and are often used in sentiment analysis. For example, words like "happy," "joy," and "exciting" might be labeled as positive, while "sad," "depressing," and "terrible" as negative.
  b) **Domain-specific Lexicons:** Tailored to specific fields or industries, such as medical, legal, or technical domains, these lexicons contain specialized vocabulary and terminology. In a medical lexicon, for instance, terms like "bradycardia" or "tachycardia" are defined with their clinical implications.
- *Use Cases of Lexicon in NLP:*
  a) **Semantic Analysis:** Lexicons are crucial in semantic analysis, where the goal is to understand the meaning conveyed in text. They help in disambiguating words with multiple meanings based on context. For example, in a sentence like "He was interested in the Java programming language," a technology-focused lexicon would ensure "Java" is recognized as a programming language rather than an island.
  b) **Language Translation:** Lexicons facilitate the translation process by providing translations of words and phrases, including context-specific meanings, which are essential for accurate and coherent translation between languages.
  c) **Speech Recognition:** In this domain, lexicons help in converting speech to text by providing the system with a database of words, their pronunciations, and possible variations, improving the accuracy of speech-to-text conversion.
  d) **Spell Checking and Correction:** Lexicons serve as the reference for spell-checkers, helping to validate the correctness of words and offering suggestions for misspelled terms based on lexical proximity.
- *Challenges and Considerations:* While lexicons are invaluable in NLP, they also pose challenges. Keeping lexicons up-to-date with evolving language use, slang, and new terminology is a constant endeavor. Additionally, the effectiveness of a lexicon can be limited by its scope and the quality of its entries, necessitating careful curation and maintenance.

While lexicons in NLP are more than just word lists; they are dynamic databases that encapsulate the essence of language. They are instrumental in a myriad of NLP applications, from enhancing machine translation to powering sophisticated semantic analysis. By providing detailed and structured information about words and their uses, lexicons enable NLP systems to process and understand human language more effectively, underpinning the success of numerous language processing and analysis tasks.

4.4.2 Ontologies

Ontologies in NLP represent a structured framework of knowledge that categorizes and defines how entities and concepts are related within a particular domain. Unlike lexicons, which primarily focus on individual words and their meanings, ontologies provide a more comprehensive and hierarchical structure of knowledge, offering insights into the relationships and attributes of concepts.

An ontology in NLP is essentially a formal representation of knowledge as a set of concepts within a domain, along with the relationships between those concepts. It is used to model the data in a way that not only defines entities but also categorizes these entities and specifies the possible relations and rules that govern them. Ontologies are crucial for tasks that require an understanding of domain-specific knowledge and the semantic relationships between different entities.

Examples of Ontologies in NLP:

a) **Medical Ontologies:** These define and organize concepts related to healthcare and medicine, such as diseases, symptoms, treatments, and drug interactions, facilitating tasks like medical records analysis and clinical decision support.
b) **Business Ontologies:** Used in the corporate world to define the entities and relationships relevant to a particular business or industry, aiding in data integration, business intelligence, and semantic search.

Use Cases of Ontologies in NLP:

a) **Semantic Web Services:** Ontologies play a crucial role in the semantic web, enabling machines to process and understand the content of web pages and services for more effective information retrieval, automation, and integration.
b) **Knowledge Representation and Reasoning:** In AI and NLP, ontologies support complex reasoning about entities and their relationships, enhancing the capabilities of systems to perform tasks like automated reasoning, question answering, and intelligent data retrieval.
c) **Information Extraction and Classification:** Ontologies help in extracting and classifying relevant information from large datasets by providing a structured context that machines can interpret.

4.4.3 Knowledge Graphs

While ontologies and knowledge graphs are related and often used interchangeably in discussions, they are distinct concepts:

- *Ontologies* provide a schematic outline, often abstract, defining the types of entities and relationships within a specific domain. They are more about the structure and rules of how entities can be related rather than about the entities themselves.
- *Knowledge Graphs*, on the other hand, are large networks of entities and relationships derived from real-world data. They are practical implementations populated with specific instances of the entities and relationships defined in ontologies. Knowledge graphs are dynamic and can grow as new data and relationships are added, representing the actual interconnected knowledge within or across domains.

Knowledge graphs are essential tools in the advancement of NLP, providing a wealth of structured semantic knowledge that goes beyond the realm of word meanings. These graphs exist as intricate networks, mapping out the myriad relationships between different entities—people, places, concepts, and more—in a way that machines can understand and process. The entities become nodes within the graph, while the edges are the relationships that connect them, constructing a web of interconnected information. Fig. 4.2 depicts an example knowledge graph that represents information in a structured form.

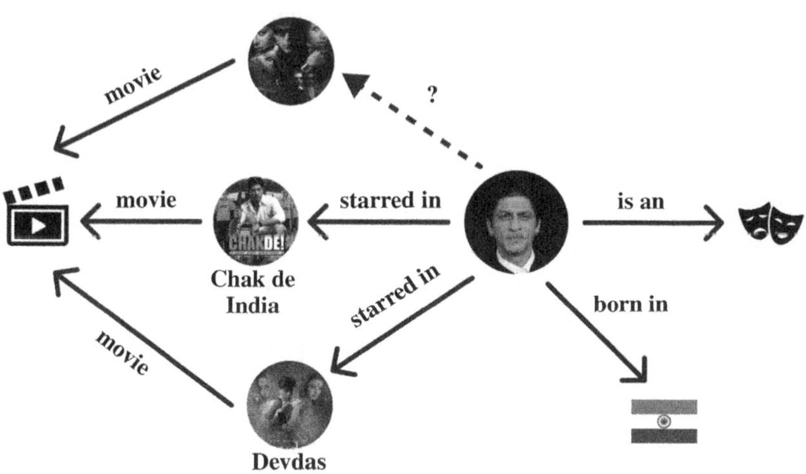

Figure 4.2 Example Knowledge Graph.

The central node in the knowledge graph represents a prominent figure in the Indian film industry, Shah Rukh Khan, linked with three movies through the relationship "*starred in*". This figure is also connected to the Indian flag, signifying "*born in*" India, and to a pair of theater masks, indicating a profession in the performing arts. A camera icon is present, labeled "*movie*", and is connected to three films, with "*Chak de India*" and "*Devdas*" being explicitly named, while the third film remains unidentified. The dotted line with a question mark points to an unknown or additional connection, which might lead one to consider other films or aspects related to the actor's career not shown on the graph.

In the context of NLP applications, knowledge graphs serve as reservoirs of contextual and factual information that can greatly enrich language understanding. They bring clarity to ambiguity and support inference, offering a depth of understanding that cannot be gleaned from raw text alone. For instance, when it comes to question-answering systems, the ability to comprehend how entities relate to each other is paramount. A knowledge graph helps in precisely this aspect, by allowing the system to draw connections and understand the context surrounding the entities involved.

Knowledge graphs' influence extends beyond just comprehension. They are also instrumental in semantic search, information retrieval, and even content recommendations, where understanding the deeper, sometimes non-explicit connections between entities can lead to more accurate and relevant results. Integrating these graphs with NLP systems results in a more robust understanding of language, one that encompasses not only the words and their meanings but also the world knowledge and logical inferences that underpin human communication. This integration allows machines to mimic a more human-like understanding of language, considering not just what is said but also what is meant, which can be especially valuable in nuanced and complex communicative scenarios.

4.4.4 Word Embeddings

Word embeddings have been a transformative concept in the field of NLP, where they serve as dense vector representations of words. These embeddings are more than just an array of numbers; they encapsulate the very essence of words' meanings by placing vectors of semantically similar words in close proximity within a sprawling, high-dimensional space. The theoretical underpinning for this method is the distributional hypothesis, which suggests that words found in similar contexts are likely to have similar meanings as shown in Fig. 4.3 where "*Mathematics*" and "*Statistics*" are similar concepts and thus would be located near each other in a high-dimensional word embedding space. Similarly, "Tiger" and "Lion" are both large wild cats and thus also would be represented by points that are close together

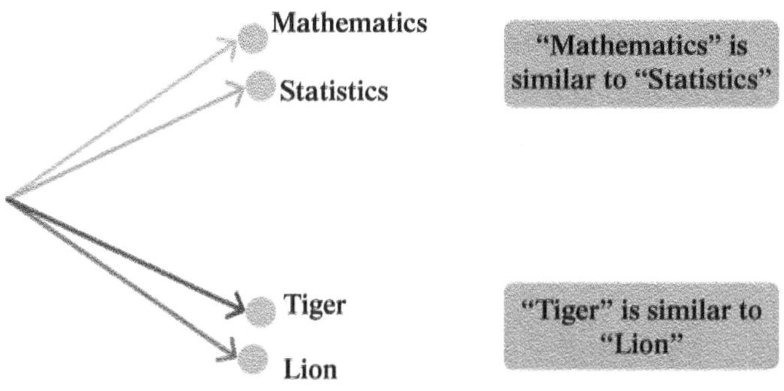

Figure 4.3 Understanding Word Embedding.

in the embedding space... By adopting this hypothesis, word embeddings are able to reflect the nuanced way in which language operates.

In practice, each word is assigned a distinct vector in a continuous vector space during the training process. The specifics of these vectors—their length and the values they contain—are not crafted by human design but are instead derived from patterns within the training data. The model learns these patterns, adjusting the vectors as it goes, to best capture the different contexts in which a word can appear. Consequently, words that often share the same context are naturally modeled as vectors close to one another, forming clusters that reflect their semantic relationships. There are various models that have been crafted to generate these embeddings, each with its unique approach to modelling word meanings. Word2Vec, a groundbreaking method developed by researchers at Google, offers two strategies for creating embeddings: the Continuous Bag-of-Words (CBOW) and the Skip-Gram model. CBOW predicts a word based on its context, while Skip-Gram does the reverse, predicting the surrounding words from a given word.

Then there's GloVe, short for Global Vectors for Word Representation, which takes an unsupervised learning approach. Unlike Word2Vec, which considers local context, GloVe generates word embeddings by leveraging global word-word co-occurrence statistics from a corpus, capturing both local and global linguistic information. FastText, a model brought forth by Facebook, builds upon the Word2Vec paradigm by incorporating sub-word information into its embeddings. This model breaks down words into smaller units—such as prefixes, suffixes, and roots—recognizing that these components often carry significant semantic weight. This is particularly advantageous for understanding the nuances of morphologically complex languages and for addressing words that are not in the model's initial vocabulary.

Undoubtedly, word embeddings mark a leap forward in how machines process and understand human language. Through these advanced models, computers can now grasp semantic relationships and nuances that were once the exclusive

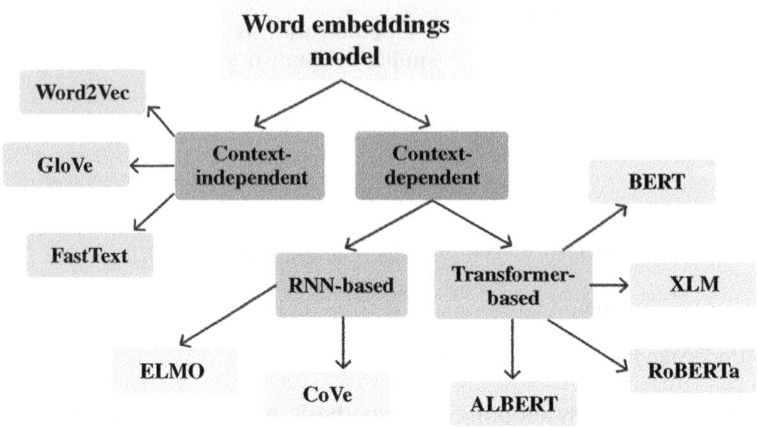

Figure 4.4 Word Embedding Models.

province of human cognition. Word2Vec, GloVe, and FastText each contribute distinct methodologies to the development of embeddings, expanding our ability to capture the complexity and variability of language in ML applications.

Fig. 4.4 shows the classification of word embedding models, distinguishing between context-independent models like Word2Vec, GloVe, and FastText, and context-dependent models including RNN-based like ELMo and CoVe, and transformer-based like BERT, ALBERT, XLM, and RoBERTa.

While traditional word embeddings offer a static representation of word meanings, capturing a word as a singular point in vector space irrespective of its context, contextual embeddings represent a significant leap forward. These dynamic representations shift the way we understand words in computational linguistics, as they generate different vectors for the same word when used in different contexts. This is crucial since many words are polysemous and their meanings change subtly or drastically depending on the sentence in which they appear. For example, the word "*bank*" can be associated with financial institutions or the land alongside a river, and contextual embeddings can differentiate these meanings based on context.

Contextual embeddings consider not only the words themselves but also their sequence, syntactic dependencies, and semantic roles in sentences. This allows for a more nuanced understanding and representation of language, mirroring the fluid nature of human speech and writing. This evolution from static to dynamic word representations is exemplified in models like ELMo, BERT, and the GPT series. ELMo uses a deep bi-directional LSTM network, allowing it to capture context in a way that wasn't possible with previous embedding techniques.

Each word's embedding is a function of the entire sentence, leading to a richer understanding of its usage.

BERT, utilizing the innovative Transformer architecture, takes things further by pre-training on a large corpus with a deep bidirectional understanding. Unlike its predecessors, BERT considers both the left and right context simultaneously in all layers, leading to a profound comprehension of a word's use across different contexts. The GPT models, including the one facilitating this conversation, approach contextual embeddings with a unidirectional focus, pre-training on a diverse range of internet text to grasp a broad spectrum of language applications. They then fine-tune through supervised learning on specific tasks to adapt their understanding to contexts or applications.

The development of contextual embeddings has transformed the way machines interpret language, enabling a dynamic and context-aware approach that aligns more closely with the complexity of human communication. These models—ELMo, BERT, and various iterations of GPT—have set new standards in NLP, enabling applications that can more effectively process, understand, and generate human-like text.

4.5 Feature Generation in NLP: Manual versus Automatic Approaches

In NLP, the creation and utilization of features are critical for building models that accurately understand and interpret language. Features in NLP can be broadly categorized into two types: manual (handcrafted) and automatic (learned). The choice between these two types of features hinges on several considerations, each with its advantages and limitations based on the task at hand, data availability, computational resources, and the overarching objectives of the NLP project.

- *Manual (Handcrafted) Features:* Manual features in NLP are explicitly designed and implemented by human experts. These features often stem from linguistic knowledge and involve extracting specific attributes from the text, such as part-of-speech tags, syntactic parsing trees, named entities, and keyword counts. Handcrafted features in NLP come with distinct advantages and disadvantages that impact their application in various tasks. One of the key advantages is their precision; these features are often meticulously designed to capture specific linguistic phenomena, making them highly relevant and precise for targeted NLP tasks. For example, in sentiment analysis, handcrafted features might include specific sentiment-laden words or phrases identified through linguistic research, providing precise indicators of emotional tone.

Moreover, handcrafted features afford greater control over the model's input, facilitating a more detailed interpretation and explanation of the model's behavior. This control can be particularly beneficial in applications where understanding the basis of the model's decisions is crucial, like in legal document analysis where each decision needs to be thoroughly justified.

However, the disadvantages of handcrafted features lie in their scalability and flexibility. Developing these features can be labor-intensive and may not effectively scale with large datasets or complex linguistic phenomena. This limitation becomes apparent in tasks like language translation or large-scale text mining, where the diversity and volume of language use can overwhelm manually crafted feature sets. Additionally, handcrafted features often lack flexibility and may require significant re-engineering to be applicable in new contexts or domains. For instance, a feature set designed for analyzing formal language in legal documents might perform poorly on informal language used in social media, necessitating a substantial overhaul to adapt to the new context.

- *Automatic (Learned) Features:* Automatic features are derived from the data directly by the model, typically through ML and deep learning methods. Models like neural networks can automatically learn to represent text as dense vectors (embeddings) that encapsulate various linguistic patterns and semantics.

  Learned features in NLP bring significant advantages in terms of adaptability and efficiency but also face challenges with interpretability and data dependency. The adaptability of learned features is one of their strongest points, as these features are generated automatically by the model, allowing them to capture the linguistic nuances of various contexts and domains seamlessly. For instance, deep learning models trained on diverse text corpora can identify and leverage subtle patterns and semantics relevant to different languages or dialects, which handcrafted features might overlook.

  In terms of efficiency, once an ML model is appropriately trained, it can rapidly generate features from new text data, processing vast amounts of information at scale. This efficiency is exemplified in applications like real-time language translation or content recommendation systems, where models continuously adapt and respond to new data inputs without the need for manual feature redesign. However, these learned features come with the drawback of reduced interpretability. The complexity of the algorithms, especially in deep learning models, often makes it difficult to trace how and why specific features influence the model's decisions, leading to the notorious "black box" problem. This lack of transparency can be a significant issue in scenarios requiring clear decision-making rationale, such as in legal or medical applications.

  Additionally, the performance of models generating learned features heavily depends on the quality and quantity of the training data. Insufficient or biased training data can lead to poorly learned features, which in turn can compromise the model's accuracy and reliability. For example, a sentiment analysis model trained on limited or unrepresentative text samples might misinterpret the sentiments in broader or more diverse datasets, illustrating how critical the underlying data is for the effectiveness of learned features in NLP.

4.5.1 Choosing Between Manual and Automatic Features

The decision between manual and automatic feature generation in NLP should consider the following factors:

- *Complexity of the Task:* Simple tasks might benefit from straightforward handcrafted features, while complex tasks involving nuances of language might require the sophisticated pattern recognition capabilities of learned features.
- *Data Availability:* Handcrafted features can be more suitable for projects with limited data, whereas learned features generally require large datasets to capture linguistic patterns effectively.
- *Computational Resources:* Learning features typically demand more computational power and time, especially when using deep learning models, compared to generating manual features.
- *Project Goals:* If the project requires highly interpretable models, manual features might be preferred. Conversely, if the goal is to capture deep semantic patterns or the task is highly domain-specific with ample data, automatic features might be more appropriate.

The selection between manual and automatic features in NLP is a strategic decision that must align with the project's specific needs and constraints. A balanced approach, often combining both manual and automatic features, can sometimes offer the best of both worlds, leveraging the precision of handcrafted features and the learning power of automated systems to achieve optimal performance in language processing tasks.

Knowledge Checkpoint 5

"Exploring Language as Data"
This worksheet guides you through a series of activities exploring how we can analyze language using different methods. The goal is to think creatively about language structure and usage, rather than finding the "right" answers.

Text Sample: Goldsmiths, University of London, is a renowned public research university located in New Cross, London. Established in 1891, it became part of the University of London in 1904. Goldsmiths is celebrated for its creative and innovative approach to education and research, particularly in the fields of arts, design, humanities, and social sciences. The university has a vibrant, diverse community with students and staff from over 130 countries. Its alumni include influential artists, musicians, and filmmakers, who have significantly impacted the cultural landscape. Goldsmiths' campus blends historic architecture with modern facilities, providing an inspiring environment for learning and creativity. The university is also known for its commitment to social justice and sustainability, actively engaging in various community projects and initiatives. Goldsmiths continues to push boundaries in higher education, fostering an environment where critical thinking and artistic expression are highly valued.

Part 1: Word Frequency Analysis

1) **Count the Words:** List down the words in the text sample and count how many times each word appears.
2) **Reflection:**
   - What did you notice about the most frequent words?
   - Were there any surprises in the word frequency?

Part 2: Word Relationships

1) **Identify Word Pairs:** Find pairs of words that often appear together in the sample text. List at least three pairs.
2) **Reflection:**
   - Why do you think these words often appear together?
   - How does identifying word pairs help in understanding the text?

Part 3: Word Prediction Game

1) **Guess the Word:** Try to Guess the Missing Word Based on the Surrounding Words. Write Down Your Guess

"The United Kingdom is known for its diverse landscapes, from the rolling hills of the English countryside to the rugged Scottish Highlands and the picturesque Welsh ________."

Part 4: Categorizing Words

1) **Categorize the Words:** Categorize at least ten words from the text into different types (e.g., nouns, verbs, adjectives).
2) **Reflection:**
   - What patterns did you notice in the way words are used in the sample text?
   - How could categorizing words be helpful in analyzing language?

Part 5: Creating Word Representations

1) **Represent Words Visually:** Choose five words from the sample text and represent them using only symbols or simple drawings.
2) **Reflection:**
   - How did you choose to represent each word?
   - What challenges did you face in visually representing these words?

Knowledge Checkpoint 6

"Linguistic Analysis and NLP Techniques"
Analyze the linguistic differences between two given sentences and suggest NLP approaches to interpret them accurately.

Part 1: Sentence Analysis

Instructions: Read the following sentences carefully:

1) "He heated the soup in the microwave until it was hot."
2) "He heated the soup in the microwave until it was boiling."

Questions:

1) Identify the subject, verb, and object in each sentence.
2) What does the pronoun "it" refer to in each sentence? How does the context influence its interpretation?

Part 2: Linguistic Differences

Instructions: Discuss the linguistic differences between the two sentences.

Questions:

1) How does the change of one word ("hot" to "boiling") alter the meaning of each sentence?
2) What grammatical or syntactic features support the differing interpretations of "it"?

Part 3: NLP Approaches

Instructions: Suggest two different NLP approaches that could be used to correctly interpret the meaning of each sentence.

Questions:

1) How would a dependency parsing technique help resolve the ambiguity in these sentences?
   - Provide a brief outline of what dependency parsing is and how it might apply here.
2) Explain how a coreference resolution algorithm could determine the referents of "it" in both scenarios.
   - Describe what coreference resolution is and discuss a potential algorithm or model that could be used.

Part 4: Practical Application

Instructions: Imagine these sentences are part of a voice-activated smart kitchen appliance that controls a microwave. Discuss how accurate interpretation of these sentences is crucial.

Questions:

1) What could be the consequences of misinterpreting these sentences in a smart kitchen context?

2) Suggest ways the appliance could verify the user's intent to prevent operational errors, such as overheating the soup.

Part 5: Reflective Questions
Instructions: Reflect on the role of context in interpreting sentences in NLP.
Questions:

1) Why is understanding the context important for NLP systems?
2) Discuss how advanced NLP systems might handle such ambiguities more effectively in the future.

5

Computational and Cognitive Approaches in Natural Language Processing

In the modern era of technological advancement, the field of Natural Language Processing (NLP) stands at the forefront of a revolution that is bridging the gap between human cognitive capabilities and AI. The quest to endow machines with the ability to understand, interpret, and generate human language has been ongoing for decades, and it has reached an inflection point with the advent of cognitive and advanced learning techniques. This chapter aims to explore the fascinating world of these techniques that are at the heart of state-of-the-art NLP systems. We will explore the intricacies of how these systems are not merely coded to perform tasks but are designed to learn, adapt, and interact in ways that are remarkably similar to human cognition.

The cognitive revolution in NLP began with a shift from rule-based systems, which were limited by the sheer complexity and variability of human language, to machine learning (ML) models that learn from vast amounts of data. However, early ML models, too, had their limitations; they were often like sponges that could soak up information but lacked the ability to reason or handle complexities that humans navigate with ease. Enter advanced learning techniques—inspired by the inner workings of the human mind, these techniques have provided a new lens through which NLP systems can be designed to mimic cognitive processes such as memory, attention, and learning from a few examples.

One of the fundamental cognitive capabilities is memory—the ability to store and recall information. Early NLP models had short-term memory at best, struggling with long sequences and context-dependent interpretations. Memory and recall models in modern NLP, such as Long Short-Term Memory (LSTM) networks and Gated Recurrent Units (GRUs), have transformed the landscape, allowing machines to remember and utilize past information effectively. These models are akin to the neural pathways in the human brain, where information is retained over time and recalled when relevant. However, having a good

Language Intelligence: Expanding Frontiers in Natural Language Processing, First Edition. Akshi Kumar.
© 2025 The Institute of Electrical and Electronics Engineers, Inc. Published 2025 by John Wiley & Sons, Inc.

memory is only part of the cognitive puzzle. The ability to focus and pay attention to certain stimuli while ignoring others is crucial in processing the vast amount of information we encounter. Attention mechanisms in NLP, particularly the ones used in transformer models like GPT (Generative Pre-trained Transformer) and BERT (Bidirectional Encoder Representations from Transformers), have revolutionized the field by enabling models to selectively weigh the importance of different pieces of information when making decisions. This selective attention is strikingly similar to how humans focus on relevant information while reading or listening. As NLP systems interact more with humans, understanding and estimating cognitive load—how much mental effort is required for a task—becomes increasingly important. Cognitive load estimation in NLP is an emerging field that considers the user's perspective, adapting the interaction to ensure that information is neither overwhelming nor too simplistic. This consideration is essential in educational technology, where the goal is to tailor learning experiences to individual needs.

The pinnacle of cognitive capabilities is arguably human-like reasoning—the ability to draw inferences, understand implications, and make decisions based on incomplete information. Modern NLP systems strive to emulate this by incorporating commonsense knowledge and reasoning abilities. While still in their nascent stages, these efforts are groundbreaking as they move machines from the realm of rote learning to the domain of understanding and reasoning. Moreover, the ability of a system to learn effectively is crucial. Transfer learning has been a game-changer in this domain, allowing NLP models to learn from one task and apply that knowledge to another. This approach is similar to how humans apply knowledge from one area to another—learning concepts in one context and transferring them to solve problems in different contexts.

In addition to learning from large datasets, there is a growing interest in how machines can learn from minimal data—mirroring the human ability to learn quickly from a few examples. Zero-shot, few-shot, and one-shot learning techniques push the boundaries of what machines can learn without the need for extensive data. This capability is vital for the development of NLP systems that can adapt to new languages or specialized domains where data is scarce. Adversarial training, where models are exposed to malicious inputs to improve their robustness, is another advanced technique that has parallels with the human learning process. Just as humans learn from their mistakes and become more resilient when exposed to challenges, adversarial training helps models not only anticipate but also resist attempts to deceive or confuse them. Finally, interactive learning encapsulates the dynamic and reciprocal nature of human learning. By engaging in dialogue and using feedback, NLP systems can refine their understanding and improve their performance. This technique emulates the natural human learning process, where interaction and feedback are fundamental to acquiring knowledge.

5.1 Machine Learning for NLP

The integration of ML into NLP has indicated a paradigm shift in how machines understand and process human language. This fusion has given rise to sophisticated models capable of performing a multitude of tasks that were once the exclusive domain of human cognition. In this section, we explore the transformative role of ML in NLP, the various tasks that NLP can accomplish with ML, and explore case studies that illustrate these advances.

The journey of ML in NLP began with the recognition that rule-based systems, although meticulously crafted, were inherently limited. They lacked the flexibility to adapt to the nuances and variability inherent in human language. The advent of ML introduced a new era where systems could learn from vast amounts of data, discern patterns, and make decisions with minimal human intervention. These data-driven models were able to capture subtleties that rule-based systems could not, from recognizing the sentiment behind a piece of writing to translating languages with near-human accuracy.

At its core, ML for NLP relies on statistical learning models that can infer linguistic structures from annotated corpora. Initial forays into ML utilized algorithms such as Naive Bayes, Decision Trees, and Support Vector Machines to classify texts and understand their content. However, the true potential of ML in NLP was unlocked with the introduction of neural network-based models, particularly with the development of deep learning. Deep neural networks, with their capacity to learn complex representations, have become the backbone of modern NLP systems.

5.1.1 Tasks Accomplished by ML in NLP

ML has dramatically transformed the capabilities of NLP, enabling systems to perform a variety of complex tasks with increasing accuracy and sophistication. Here's a detailed look at some key tasks achieved by ML in NLP:

- *Text Classification:* Text classification involves categorizing pieces of text into predefined groups. It's widely used for spam detection in emails, where ML models are trained to recognize and filter out unwanted messages. Another common application is sentiment analysis, particularly on social media platforms, where ML algorithms analyze text to determine the writer's sentiment, be it positive, negative, or neutral. This task has broad implications, from monitoring brand reputation to gauging public opinion on various topics.
- *Machine Translation:* Machine translation is the process of translating text from one language to another using ML models. Advances in deep learning have notably enhanced the quality of machine translations, bringing them closer to

the accuracy and fluency of human translators. This improvement is pivotal in global communication, allowing for seamless interaction across language barriers and fostering international collaboration.

- *Named Entity Recognition (NER):* NER is a process where ML models identify and classify key elements in text into predefined categories like names of people, organizations, locations, dates, and more. This task is crucial for extracting useful information from large datasets, aiding in tasks ranging from automating customer support to enhancing search engine performance by understanding the context of user queries.
- *Speech Recognition:* Speech recognition technology converts spoken language into text. With ML, systems like Siri, Alexa, and Google Assistant have become more proficient in understanding and processing natural speech, facilitating hands-free operation and enabling efficient voice-driven interactions. This technology has revolutionized user interfaces and accessibility, making technology more intuitive and accessible to a broader audience.
- *Question Answering:* Question-answering systems are designed to understand and respond to questions posed in natural language. This functionality is central to search engines and chatbots, which use ML to parse the query, understand the context, and retrieve the most relevant answers. The sophistication of these systems, from simple fact retrieval to complex problem-solving, showcases the depth of understanding that ML can bring to NLP.
- *Summarization:* Automatic summarization generates a brief, coherent summary of a larger text document. ML models in this area learn to identify key points and condense information without losing the original meaning, making it easier for users to digest large amounts of information quickly. This is especially beneficial in areas like legal document review, academic research, and news aggregation.
- *Language Generation:* Language generation involves creating text that mimics human writing. The advent of models like OpenAI's GPT series has demonstrated the potential of ML in generating coherent, contextually relevant text across various genres and styles. This capability has applications in content creation, interactive storytelling, and even in generating code, expanding the possibilities of automated and assistive writing.

Each of these tasks highlights the versatility and power of ML in enhancing NLP systems. From interpreting and categorizing text to generating human-like dialogue and summaries, ML has opened new frontiers in understanding and leveraging natural language, making it an indispensable tool in the ongoing evolution of NLP technology. These ML-driven NLP tasks are detailed across chapters: Chapter 6 covers Named Entity Recognition (NER) and summarization, while Chapter 7 dives into text classification, including sentiment and emotion recognition, irony, sarcasm, humor detection, psychometric analysis, and digital content moderation. Translation is explored in Chapter 8. However, speech recognition and language generation fall outside this book's scope.

5.1.2 Selecting the Right Machine Learning Model for NLP Tasks

Selecting the right ML model for an NLP task involves considering several factors to ensure the model aligns with the specific requirements and goals of the task. Here's a general guide to help in selecting an appropriate ML model for NLP tasks:

- *Understand the Task Requirements:*
  a) **Complexity:** Assess the complexity of the NLP task. Simpler tasks like text classification may require less complex models, while tasks like machine translation or sentiment analysis in nuanced contexts might need more advanced models like deep neural networks.
  b) **Data Type and Size:** Consider the type (text, speech, etc.) and size of your dataset. Larger datasets can train more complex models without overfitting.
- *Evaluate Model Performance:*
  a) **Accuracy:** Choose models known for high accuracy in similar tasks. Benchmark studies and literature can provide insights into which models perform best for specific NLP tasks.
  b) **Speed and Efficiency:** Consider the model's inference time and resource requirements. Real-time applications require fast, efficient models.
- *Consider Data Availability and Quality:*
  a) **Training Data:** Some models require large amounts of labeled data, while others can work well with less data. For instance, transfer learning with models like BERT can be effective with smaller datasets.
  b) **Data Preprocessing Needs:** Some models may require extensive preprocessing of data (e.g., tokenization, lemmatization) to perform optimally.
- *Model Interpretability and Flexibility:*
  a) **Interpretability:** If understanding how the model makes decisions is important, prefer models that are more interpretable or transparent.
  b) **Adaptability:** Choose models that can easily adapt to changes in the task or data, especially if you anticipate future changes in requirements.
- *Utilize Pre-trained Models and Transfer Learning:*
  a) **Pre-trained Models:** Utilize models pre-trained on large datasets that are similar to your task, as they can significantly reduce development time and improve performance.
  b) **Transfer Learning:** Adapt these pre-trained models to your specific task, which is particularly useful if you have limited data for training.
- *Technical Considerations:*
  a) **Computational Resources:** Assess the computational cost of training and deploying the model, ensuring it aligns with the available resources.

b) **Tools and Infrastructure:** Ensure compatibility with existing tools and infrastructure. Some models may require specific hardware (like GPUs for training deep learning models).

By systematically evaluating these factors, you can make an informed decision on the most suitable ML model for your NLP task, balancing between performance, efficiency, and practicality to meet the specific needs of your application.

5.1.3 Evolution and Impact of ML in NLP

The evolution of ML in NLP has brought significant advancements but also challenges. One of the primary hurdles is the need for large, annotated datasets for training ML models, as these datasets are crucial for the models to learn and understand language nuances but are often labor-intensive and costly to produce. Bias in ML models represents another critical issue, where the prejudices existing in the training data can be learned and perpetuated by the model, leading to biased outcomes in language processing tasks. This problem is particularly evident in applications that involve decision-making based on language analysis, such as hiring processes or loan approvals, where biased models can result in unfair or discriminatory outcomes. Additionally, the often-opaque nature of ML algorithms can pose challenges in terms of interpretability and transparency. Understanding the decision-making process within these models can be complex, making it hard to explain outcomes, diagnose errors, or improve model performance.

Despite these challenges, the integration of ML in NLP has been overwhelmingly positive, revolutionizing the field by enabling automated, efficient processing of language at scale. This integration has led to the creation of new services and products that enhance productivity and offer novel solutions in various sectors. With continued research and development, the future of ML in NLP promises further sophistication in applications, improving existing technologies and potentially unlocking new realms of language processing capabilities.

5.2 Memory and Recall Models

In the realm of human cognition, memory is not a singular monolithic entity but a complex, multifaceted function that involves various processes of encoding, storing, and retrieving information. Similarly, in the field of NLP, memory and recall models are sophisticated systems designed to mimic these intricate processes. These models serve as the cornerstone of understanding sequences and context, enabling NLP systems to perform tasks that require an awareness of previous interactions or information. In this section, we will explore the mechanisms that enable NLP models to retain and utilize past information—akin to human memory and recall.

5.2.1 Working with Long-Term Dependencies

One of the foremost challenges in NLP is managing long-term dependencies—where the relevance of information stretches over long sequences of text. Traditional neural networks struggle with this; as sequences grow longer, they suffer from vanishing or exploding gradients, which lead to loss of information and computational difficulties.

- *Understanding LSTM (Long Short-Term Memory) Networks:*
  To tackle the challenge of long-term dependencies, LSTM networks, introduced by Hochreiter and Schmidhuber in 1997, have been designed with the ability to remember information for prolonged periods. They are an extension of recurrent neural networks (RNNs), specifically engineered to avoid the long-term dependency problem. The architecture of LSTM includes (Fig. 5.1):
  a) **Forget Gate:** It decides what information should be thrown away or kept. It looks at the previous state and the current input and outputs a number between 0 and 1 for each number in the cell state, where 0 means "completely forget this" and 1 means "completely retain this."
  b) **Input Gate:** It updates the cell state with new information. It filters out which values will be updated based on the current input and the past state.
  c) **Cell State:** This acts as the "memory" of the LSTM, carrying relevant information throughout the sequence of data.
  d) **Output Gate:** It determines the next hidden state, which contains information on the previous inputs. The hidden state can be used for predictions.

  LSTM Networks are akin to a writer's careful notes, which preserve essential plot points to weave a coherent story. LSTMs manage long-term dependencies by selectively retaining important information while discarding the irrelevant, akin to a reader focusing on the narrative arc and forgetting trivial details. This selective memory enables them to excel in language translation and text generation, where context from far back in the text can drastically alter meaning. For example, consider an NLP system designed to summarize

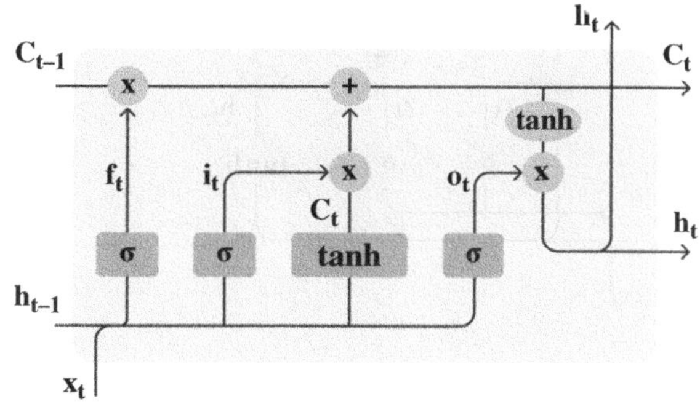

Figure 5.1 Architecture of LSTM.

news articles. When processing a lengthy article about an election, an LSTM can retain critical events mentioned early in the text (like the profiles of the candidates) and use this information to understand and emphasize the importance of the election results at the end of the article.

- *Exploring GRU (Gated Recurrent Unit) Networks:*
  GRUs are a variant of LSTMs designed to be simpler and more efficient. Introduced in 2014, GRUs combine the forget and input gates into a single "update gate" and merge the cell state and hidden state, resulting in a model that is easier to compute and has fewer parameters. The architecture of GRU includes (Fig. 5.2):
  a) **Update Gate:** Determines the degree to which the unit updates its activation, or state.
  b) **Reset Gate:** Decides how much of the past information to forget.
  c) **Hidden State:** Carries information throughout the processing of the sequence, serving a similar purpose to the cell state in LSTMs but is less complex.

GRUs have been shown to perform on par with LSTMs on certain tasks and are particularly effective when working with smaller datasets or when computational efficiency is vital. GRU Networks are the speed readers of ML. With fewer parameters than LSTMs, they rapidly absorb and process information, making them ideal for tasks where speed and efficiency are paramount. Think of GRUs as a person skimming through emails, quickly determining which messages are important and which can be ignored. Imagine you're asking a voice assistant to remind you of your appointments. You might say, "Remind me of my appointment," followed by, "It's with Dr. Smith." A GRU network would efficiently recall that "it" refers to your appointment without needing the extensive context that an LSTM might use.

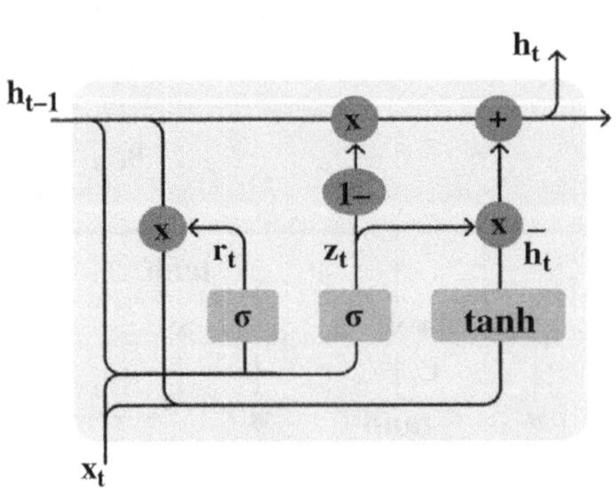

Figure 5.2 Architecture of GRU.

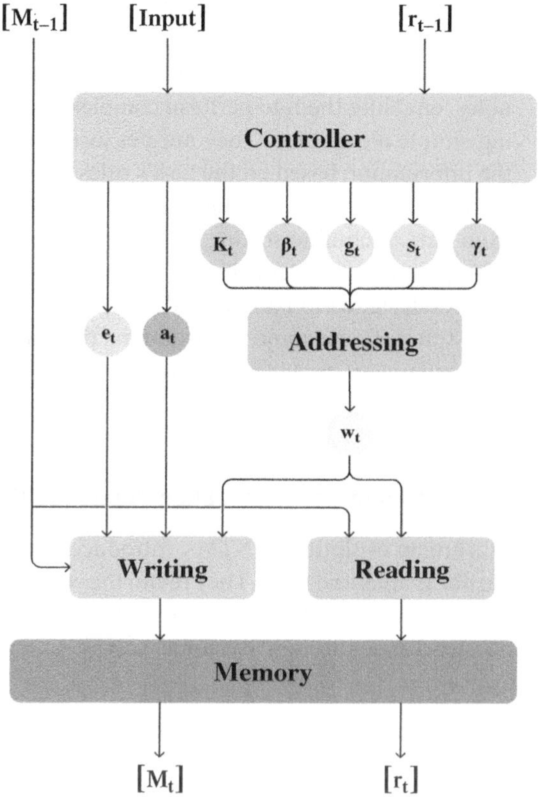

Figure 5.3 Architecture of NTM.

5.2.2 Neural Turing Machines (NTMs)

NTMs, are a breakthrough in NLP, marrying the concepts of neural networks with external memory resources. NTMs are designed to mimic the way humans use scratch paper to extend their memory and computation capabilities. The capabilities of NTMs include (Fig. 5.3):

- **External Memory Bank:** A large, addressable memory that the system reads from and writes to, which helps in tasks requiring data retention over time.
- **Controller Network:** Typically, an LSTM or another form of RNN, which manages the read and write processes.
  a) **Read and Write Heads:** Mechanisms that define how the memory is accessed and modified, using differentiable attention processes that allow the network to be trained via gradient descent.

NTMs offer a more sophisticated approach. They resemble a chess player keeping track of past moves using a notebook. NTMs combine the pattern recognition capabilities of neural networks with an external memory akin to writing notes, enabling them to perform complex tasks such as sorting and even learning simple algorithms. They are not just remembering but also manipulating the information based on the task's rules, just as a chess player might strategize their next move based on the game's history. NTMs can learn simple algorithms from data, including sorting, copying, and associative recall tasks, showcasing their potential for algorithmic reasoning. Take the case of a customer service chatbot designed to handle banking queries. An NTM-equipped chatbot could keep track of a customer's past interactions and current queries, ensuring that the guidance it provides on navigating banking services is both contextually informed and accurate.

5.2.3 Differentiable Neural Computers (DNCs)

DNCs are an evolution of NTMs, introduced to handle more complex data structures like graphs and trees. They retain the concept of a neural network augmented with an external memory bank but enhance the capabilities to navigate intricate data structures through dynamic access patterns. Features of DNCs include (Fig. 5.4):

a) **Dynamic Memory Allocation:** Allows the DNC to efficiently use its memory by freeing and allocating space as needed.

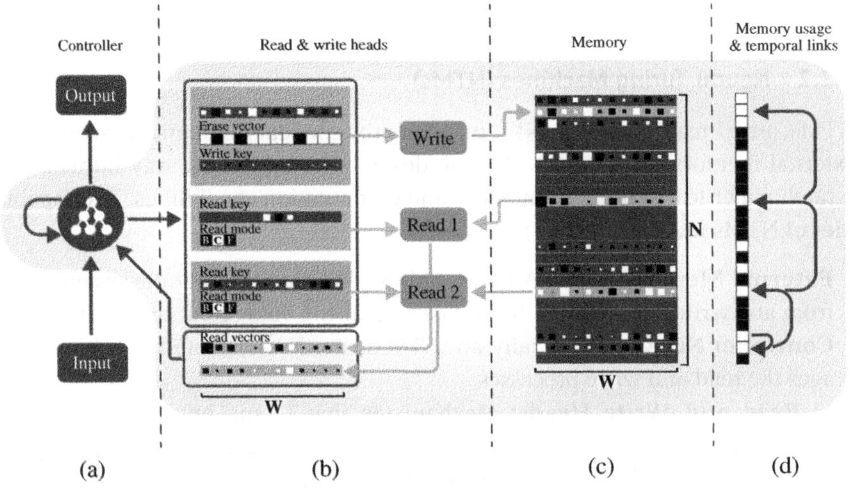

Figure 5.4 Architecture of DNC.

b) **Temporal Linkage Matrix:** Keeps track of the order in which information is written, enabling the DNC to recall sequences of information.
c) **Duality of Interface:** The system has discrete interfaces for reading and writing, akin to read/write heads in NTMs, but with enhanced capabilities for complex data management.

DNCs represent the pinnacle of this memory-recall architecture, integrating the best of NTMs with enhanced capabilities to handle intricate data. They are the equivalent of an expert researcher navigating through complex information with a system of tabs, annotations, and bookmarks to solve problems. DNCs excel at tasks that require understanding relationships and hierarchies, like interpreting a legal document or navigating a complex web of interrelated scientific research. DNCs can be applied to tasks that require relational reasoning, such as answering questions about relationships between entities in a story. Envision using a virtual assistant to manage a project with many moving parts. A DNC-powered assistant could keep track of each component, how they interrelate, and the project's progression over time, thus providing timely suggestions and reminders.

Through the development of memory and recall models in NLP, we move closer to achieving a level of artificial intelligence (AI) that can process and utilize information like a human, over long periods and across complex structures. These advanced models are not just milestones in NLP but stepping stones towards creating systems that can learn, think, and remember with the flexibility and efficiency that characterizes human cognition.

5.3 Attention Mechanisms

The concept of attention in NLP is similar to the human ability to focus intensely on one conversation in a noisy room or on a particular detail of a complex image. In the realm of language processing, attention mechanisms empower models to dynamically prioritize certain parts of the input data over others, thereby enhancing the prediction and understanding of language. For instance, when translating the sentence "The cat sat on the mat" into French, a simple model might translate it word-for-word without considering context, possibly resulting in an awkward or incorrect translation. With attention mechanisms, the model learns to "focus" on the word "cat" and its importance in the sentence, giving it the context needed to find the right translation for "cat" in French ("chat") and placing it correctly in the sentence structure.

5.3.1 Transformer Models

The Transformer model represents a significant shift from traditional sequence-based models that process inputs sequentially, such as RNNs and LSTMs.

By utilizing parallel processing and focusing on the attention mechanism, the Transformer greatly improves speed and efficiency, particularly when handling long sequences of data.

The core idea of the Transformer is to use self-attention mechanisms to weigh the influence of different parts of the input data. The attention mechanism computes a score that signifies how much focus to place on other parts of the input sequence when encoding a particular piece of data. These scores are then used to produce a weighted sum of all the input data, which provides context for any point in the sequence.

Architecture

The architecture of the Transformer model is primarily divided into two components: the encoder and the decoder. Both consist of stacks of identical layers, each containing two main sub-layers: a multi-head self-attention mechanism and a position-wise feed-forward network. As shown in Fig. 5.5.

- **Encoder:** The encoder's role is to process the input data and map it into an abstract representation that encapsulates the information in the entire sequence. This representation contains the context for each word, obtained through the attention mechanism, which is sensitive to the position and significance of each word in the sequence.
- **Decoder:** The decoder takes the encoder's output and generates a sequence output, one piece at a time. It uses the encoder's output and what it has produced so far to predict the next item in the sequence. In addition to the two sub-layers present in the encoder, the decoder has a third sub-layer that performs multi-head attention over the encoder's output.

The key features of transformer models include:

- **Multi-Head Attention:** This type of attention mechanism allows the model to jointly attend to information at different positions from different representational spaces. By having multiple "heads," the Transformer can focus

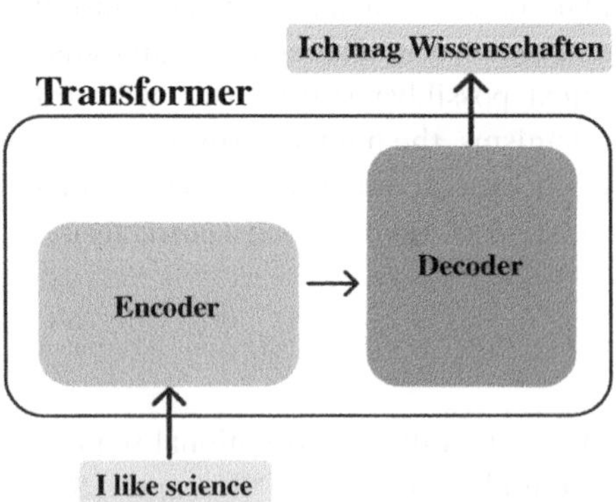

Figure 5.5 Architecture of Transformer Model.

on different words and different parts of each word, for a comprehensive understanding of each term in context.

- **Positional Encoding:** Since the model lacks any recurrent or convolutional layers, it uses positional encodings to make use of the order of the sequence. These encodings are added to the input embeddings at the bottoms of the encoder and decoder stacks, providing a notion of word order that the self-attention mechanism alone would not capture.
- **Layer Normalization and Residual Connections:** Each sub-layer in the encoder and decoder, including attention and feed-forward neural networks, has a residual connection around it followed by layer normalization. This design helps in stabilizing the learning process and allows for deeper models by preventing the vanishing gradient problem.

Table 5.1 reflects the rapid development and diversification of Transformer models to address various challenges and achieve more efficient processing, adaptability, and performance across a range of language tasks.

Large Language Models (LLMs), such as GPT and BERT, are specific implementations of the transformer architecture that have been trained on extensive amounts of text data. They are called "large" due to their massive size in terms of the number of parameters and the breadth of data they are trained on. LLMs leverage the transformer's capabilities to understand and generate human language with remarkable proficiency, performing tasks like translation, summarization, question-answering, and text generation often at or near human-level performance.

- *Relationship and Differences:*
  a) **Foundation:** Both LLMs and transformers are based on the same foundational architecture. LLMs are essentially an application or scaling-up of the transformer architecture to create models that can process and understand language on a vast scale.
  b) **Purpose and Scope:** Transformers are a more general architecture used in various models and applications beyond just language processing, including areas like image and audio processing. LLMs specifically refer to the application of transformer architecture in creating very large models for language processing tasks.
  c) **Training and Functionality:** LLMs are trained on a much larger scale compared to typical transformer models. They are often pre-trained on a diverse range of text data, enabling them to gain a broad understanding of language which can then be fine-tuned for specific tasks.

In summary, while all LLMs like GPT and BERT are based on the transformer architecture, not all transformers are LLMs. The term "transformer" refers to the underlying neural network architecture, whereas a "Large Language Model"

Table 5.1 Overview of Transformer Models.

Model Name	Brief Description	Key Points
Transformer (Original)	The first model to use self-attention to process sequences of data.	• Introduced self-attention mechanism. • No recurrence or convolutions used.
GPT (Generative Pre-trained Transformer)	Aims to generate text by predicting the next word in a sentence.	• Autoregressive model. • Fine-tuned for specific tasks after pre-training.
BERT (Bidirectional Encoder Representations from Transformers)	Uses a bidirectional approach to understand the context of a word based on all its surrounding words.	• Masked language model • Fine-tuning approach differs from GPT.
T5 (Text-to-Text Transfer Transformer)	Converts all NLP problems into a text-to-text format, where the input and output are always text.	• Encourages consistent approach to a variety of tasks. • Pre-trained on a large corpus.
XLNet	Combines the best of GPT and BERT and learns bidirectional contexts by maximizing the expected likelihood over all permutations of the input sequence tokens.	• Permutation-based training. • Captures bidirectional context without masking.
RoBERTa (A Robustly Optimized BERT Pre-training Approach)	An optimized version of BERT designed to improve pre-training using more data and compute resources.	• Longer training with bigger batches and more data. • Removes the Next Sentence Prediction (NSP) task.
GPT-2/GPT-3	An improved version of GPT with more parameters, trained on a larger dataset for better performance.	• Scaled-up versions of GPT. • Zero-shot learning capabilities.
ELECTRA	A model that is trained to distinguish "real" input tokens from "fake" ones generated by another network.	• Efficient pre-training method. • Can be trained on relatively less compute resources.

ALBERT (A Lite BERT)	A version of BERT optimized for memory and speed by sharing parameters across layers.	• Parameter-reduction techniques. • Embedding factorization.
DistilBERT	A smaller version of BERT designed to be faster and lighter, while retaining most of its performance.	• Distillation technique used • Reduced size and complexity.
BART (Bidirectional and Auto-Regressive Transformers)	Combines the benefits of bidirectional and autoregressive Transformers.	• Sequence-to-sequence model. • Pre-trained as a denoising autoencoder.
DeBERTa (Decoding-enhanced BERT with Disentangled Attention)	Enhances BERT and RoBERTa models with a disentangled attention mechanism.	• Disentangled attention mechanism. • Enhanced token representations with position information.
GPT-4	The next iteration of the GPT series with more parameters and improved performance.	• Improved upon GPT-3's performance. • Advanced natural language understanding.

refers to the scale and application of this architecture in creating extensive models capable of a wide range of language understanding and generation tasks.

5.3.2 Multi-Head and Self-Attention

The concept of multi-head attention can be viewed as an extension of the basic attention mechanism, where multiple sets of attention weights (or "heads") are calculated. Each set focuses on different parts of the input sequence, allowing the model to capture a range of perspectives. This can be equated to examining a situation through multiple lenses—each lens offers a unique viewpoint, and a comprehensive understanding is achieved by integrating these viewpoints. For example, in a complex sentence like *"The trophy didn't fit in the suitcase because it was too big,"* a model needs to understand what "it" refers to. Multi-head attention enables one "head" to focus on the word "trophy," another on "suitcase," and another on the phrase "too big," collectively resolving that "it" refers to the "trophy."

Self-attention, specifically, is where a single sequence updates itself in the light of other elements in the same sequence, effectively enabling each part of the sequence to consider the rest of the sequence when encoding its own representation. To understand self-attention, consider a block of text with the pronoun "she." To know who "she" refers to, a model uses self-attention to weigh the relevance of all previous mentions of potential referents and decides which one aligns best contextually. The self-attention mechanism learns these patterns during training and applies them when encountering similar structures in new text.

- *Types of Attention:*
  The advent of attention mechanisms has significantly enriched the toolkit of NLP, equipping models with the ability to discern and prioritize different segments of input data. There are various methods for models to selectively focus on different parts of input data. These methods vary in complexity and applicability, with each offering distinct advantages and challenges. Primarily, there are three main types of attention: Soft, Hard, and Local.
  a) **Soft Attention:** Soft attention is a fully differentiable mechanism that allows for gradient-based learning, which fits neatly into the backpropagation paradigm used to train neural networks. It can be viewed as a weighted average of features, where the weights represent the model's attention to each feature and sum to one, forming a probability distribution. As a result, the model can learn to allocate its focus softly over the entire sequence, adjusting these weights during training to improve performance. In practice, soft attention is calculated using a set of scores, often obtained by a compatibility function between two sets of features. For instance, in the context of machine translation, the model might compute attention

scores that reflect how relevant each word in the source sentence is when translating a particular word in the target language. However, one notable downside is its computational cost, especially with long sequences, as it requires calculating attention weights for every element in the sequence for every single operation. This can lead to significant resource consumption and longer processing times.

b) **Hard Attention:** Hard attention is akin to a sampling method; it randomly selects a subset of inputs to attend to and entirely ignores the rest. This selective focus can be imagined like a spotlight moving across a stage, intensely illuminating specific actors (the inputs being attended to) while leaving others in the shadows (the ignored inputs). The randomness in selection means that each forward pass through the network may consider a different subset of inputs, making the attention mechanism non-differentiable. Due to its non-differentiable nature, training models with hard attention mechanisms typically involves variance reduction techniques and reinforcement learning. These models are trained using methods like the REINFORCE algorithm, which estimates the gradients stochastically. Hard attention can significantly reduce the computational burden, as it processes a smaller subset of the input data. However, the trade-off comes with the challenge of ensuring that the model focuses on the right features, and the increased complexity in training the model due to its stochastic nature.

c) **Local Attention:** Local attention strikes a balance between soft and hard attention. It limits the focus of the model to a subset of input features, constructing a window around each point of interest. Within this window, the attention is soft, allowing gradients to flow and enabling the model to learn which features to focus on during training. However, outside of this window, the attention is effectively zero. By restricting the computational scope, local attention can offer a compromise between the expressiveness of soft attention and the efficiency of hard attention. This type of attention is particularly useful when there's some prior knowledge that input features of interest are likely to be located near each other in the sequence, such as in certain types of language modelling or sequence labelling tasks. Local attention reduces computational load compared to soft attention and can be especially advantageous when dealing with very long sequences where it's impractical to attend to every element. At the same time, it maintains the differentiability that allows for straightforward training with standard optimization techniques.

The choice of attention type depends on the specific requirements of the task at hand, the nature of the input data, and the computational resources available. Each type offers a different way for the model to learn to focus its "attention" and, as a result, to process language data with the nuance and sophistication that is increasingly approaching human-level understanding.

- *Methods and Improvements:*
  Attention mechanisms have been augmented with various methods to improve efficiency and performance. These include:
  a) **Scaled Dot-Product Attention:** This method, used in the Transformer model, scales the dot products by the inverse square root of the dimension of the key vectors, preventing overly large dot product values that can result in gradients that are too small for effective learning.
  b) **Positional Encodings:** Since Transformer models do not inherently consider the sequential nature of data, positional encodings are added to the input embeddings to give the model information about the position of the words in the sequence.
  c) **Attention with Convolutional Features:** Attention mechanisms can be combined with convolutional neural networks (CNNs) to capture local context within larger sequences, providing a hybrid approach that leverages both the local feature extraction capabilities of CNNs and the global context sensitivity of attention.

The attention mechanisms have become an indispensable component in the toolbox of NLP models, helping them to process language with a nuance and sophistication that approaches human-level understanding. Through various types and methods, these mechanisms offer flexibility and adaptability, catering to the diverse range of challenges presented by natural language.

Together, these mechanisms represent a sophisticated tapestry of techniques that transform how machines handle human language, moving from rigid, sequential processing to a fluid, context-aware approach. As we continue to explore these mechanisms, we'll see how they are not merely technical innovations but represent a stride towards endowing machines with a semblance of human-like comprehension.

5.4 Human-Like Reasoning

Human thought processes are complex, involving not only the straightforward retrieval of information but also the ability to draw inferences, understand context, and apply common sense knowledge to interpret nuances and subtleties in language. NLP systems traditionally excel at tasks with clear rules and patterns, but human-like reasoning requires moving beyond pattern recognition to a deeper understanding of meaning and implication.

5.4.1 Analyzing NLP Systems with Human Reasoning Capabilities

To infuse NLP systems with human reasoning capabilities, researchers have been exploring various strategies, which include:

- *Inferential Thinking:* Inferential thinking is foundational to human cognition. When we read a story or engage in a conversation, we do not simply process the words as they are; we read between the lines, make assumptions, and draw conclusions that extend beyond the explicit statements. For instance, take the scenario where someone says, "I left my umbrella at home and got soaked." A human would effortlessly infer that it was raining and that the speaker likely walked through it.
  Transferring this capability to NLP systems involves developing algorithms that can understand the implications and unspoken nuances of language. This is typically approached through sophisticated ML models that have been fed vast amounts of text and have learned to predict not just the next word in a sentence but also the unseen consequences or preconditions of a stated event. This requires not just a literal understanding of language but a predictive capacity that can anticipate unstated facts based on learned patterns.
- *Abductive Reasoning:* Abductive reasoning, or the process of creating plausible explanations for a set of observations, is another dimension of human-like reasoning that is particularly challenging for NLP systems. When a human hears a loud bang followed by silence in a familiar context, such as their own home, they might abduce that a book has fallen off a shelf. For an NLP system, reading a text that describes a sudden loud noise followed by quiet, it would need to draw on a wide array of background knowledge and context to make a similarly plausible inference.
  To endow NLP systems with abductive reasoning abilities, researchers use techniques like narrative chaining—where a system learns to link events in a story in a causally coherent manner—and large-scale language modelling, where the system generates hypotheses based on contextually rich representations of language.
- *Analogical Reasoning:* Analogical reasoning is a powerful cognitive process where an individual draws from known experiences to understand new ones. For example, understanding the workings of an atom by comparing it to a solar system. In NLP, enabling a system to perform analogical reasoning requires it to identify patterns that transcend the literal content of text.
  To achieve this, some NLP systems are designed to recognize and interpret metaphors and similes, which are linguistic expressions of analogical thought.

By training on examples of analogical language, these systems can begin to apply similar patterns when encountering new scenarios or concepts.

- *Common Sense:* Common sense reasoning presents a unique challenge for NLP systems, as it requires an understanding of implicit knowledge that humans acquire through everyday experiences. Phrases like "it's raining cats and dogs" or "he broke the ice" convey meaning that goes beyond the literal combination of words.

  One way to approach this in NLP is to integrate databases of common-sense knowledge that contain facts about the world, logical relations, and cultural idioms. However, the subtlety and context-specific nature of common sense make it difficult to cover all possible scenarios. ML models, particularly those based on neural networks, have the potential to internalize some aspects of common sense through extensive exposure to human language.

5.4.2 Commonsense Knowledge and NLP

Commonsense knowledge encompasses the basic facts about the world that people generally know and agree upon. It allows NLP applications to make sense of the text in a way that aligns with human understanding and expectations. Here's a summary of the methodologies to embed commonsense knowledge into NLP, with use cases in Table 5.2.

In conclusion, integrating human-like reasoning, especially commonsense knowledge, into NLP systems remains a significant and ongoing challenge. However, the integration of structured knowledge bases, advanced ML techniques, and insights from human cognition continues to push the boundaries of what NLP can achieve in terms of mimicking human thought processes.

One of the biggest challenges in mimicking human thought processes is the sheer breadth and flexibility of human reasoning. Rule-based systems can capture explicit knowledge but fail to generalize. ML approaches, especially deep learning, offer more flexible mechanisms to capture patterns of reasoning but require extensive data. Techniques such as transfer learning, where a model trained on one task is adapted to another, and few-shot learning, which involves training models on very few examples, are among the promising solutions for this challenge. These techniques are discussed in the subsequent sections.

5.5 Transfer Learning in NLP

Transfer Learning has emerged as a paradigm-shifting approach in NLP, enabling models to achieve remarkable performance across a range of language tasks. This section unpacks the mechanisms and benefits of Transfer Learning, with

Table 5.2 Summary of Methodologies and Use Cases for Embedding Commonsense Knowledge in NLP Systems.

Methodology	Description	Use Cases in NLP
Knowledge Graphs	Structured representation of real-world entities and their interrelations, often used to enhance reasoning capabilities.	• Enhancing chatbots to understand and process real-world entities. • Semantic search engines to find more relevant results.
Pre-trained Language Models	Language models trained on vast corpuses of text that implicitly learn commonsense knowledge which can be fine-tuned for specific tasks.	• Automated story generation that includes natural plot development. • Advanced sentiment analysis that understands context and idioms.
Hybrid Models	Combining the fluid understanding of pre-trained models with the structured data from knowledge graphs to provide a more comprehensive understanding.	• Multimodal AI systems that can interpret text in the context of images or vice versa. • More accurate machine translation that understands cultural nuances.
Custom Datasets	Datasets designed to explicitly test and train NLP systems on commonsense reasoning, with targeted tasks that require understanding beyond literal text.	• Enhancing academic testing systems to evaluate student responses with deeper understanding. • Refining legal document analysis tools for better context interpretation.
Psycholinguistic Insights	Utilizing cognitive theories and insights into how humans process language to design NLP systems that mimic human mental strategies.	• Developing more natural conversational agents for therapy and counselling. • Improving voice-activated systems to understand commands in a more human-like context.

a focus on its implementation through pre-training and the ability to generalize across tasks.

5.5.1 Power of Pre-Training

Pre-training is a formative step in preparing an NLP model for complex tasks. It involves training a model on a large, general dataset before fine-tuning it on a smaller, task-specific dataset. The foundational training objectives commonly used during pre-training are Masked Language Modelling (MLM) and Next Sentence Prediction (NSP).

- *Masked Language Modelling (MLM):*
  a) **Conceptual Overview:** In MLM, a certain percentage of the input tokens are randomly masked, and the objective of the model is to predict the original identity of these masked tokens. This is akin to filling in the blanks in a sentence, which encourages the model to understand context, grammar, and the relationships between words.
  b) **Implementation Details:**
     - **Token Selection:** Various strategies for selecting which tokens to mask (randomly, by part of speech, etc.) can be explored.
     - **Masking Mechanisms:** Discuss the use of special **[MASK]** tokens and alternative methods like replacing words with random words or other words in the vocabulary.
     - **Context Utilization:** The model must use the surrounding unmasked tokens to infer the correct masked tokens, leveraging both left and right context in a bidirectional manner.
  c) **Learning Dynamics:** It's important to discuss how MLM forces the model to develop an understanding of not just the words but also their use in various contexts, essentially teaching the model about word usage patterns, relationships, and dependencies.
- *Next Sentence Prediction (NSP):*
  a) **Conceptual Overview:** NSP trains a model to predict whether a given sentence logically follows another. During training, the model is presented with pairs of sentences and must learn to predict if the second sentence is the subsequent sentence in the original document.
  b) **Implementation Details:**
     - **Pair Selection:** Explanation of how sentence pairs are chosen, with some pairs being actual consecutive sentences (positive examples) and others being random sentences paired together (negative examples).
     - **Representation Learning:** The model learns to understand narrative flow and coherence, which is essential for tasks involving understanding of document structure, such as summarization and question answering.

c) **Learning Outcomes:** NSP training enhances the model's ability to capture relationships across sentences, an understanding of discourse, and an intuition for what makes a coherent text.

- *Fine-Tuning Process:* Once a model has been pre-trained on large datasets, the next step is to fine-tune it on a specific task. This fine-tuning process involves adjusting the pre-trained model's parameters so that it can apply its general understanding of language to the nuances of a particular task. This section provides a comprehensive guide on how to execute this critical phase effectively.

a) Selecting an Appropriate Learning Rate
  - **Starting Point:** Begin with a learning rate that is smaller than the one used for pre-training, as large updates can disrupt the pre-trained weights.
  - **Learning Rate Scheduler:** Implement a scheduler to decrease the learning rate as the training progresses, which helps the model stabilize its learning on the new task.

b) Deciding on the Number of Fine-Tuning Epochs
  - **Task Complexity:** Simpler tasks may require fewer epochs, while more complex tasks might need more time for the model to adapt.
  - **Dataset Size:** A smaller dataset typically needs fewer epochs to avoid overfitting; conversely, a larger dataset can sustain a higher number of epochs.
  - **Early Stopping:** Monitor validation performance and stop training when performance plateaus or starts to decrease, indicating that the model is no longer learning useful patterns.

c) Preventing Overfitting on Smaller Datasets
  - **Data Augmentation:** Generate synthetic data by altering the training samples in ways that are consistent with the task to increase the effective size of the dataset.
  - **Regularization Techniques:** Employ methods like dropout or weight decay to prevent the model from becoming too fitted to the training data.
  - **Cross-Validation:** Use techniques like k-fold cross-validation to ensure that the model generalizes well across different subsets of the data.

d) Fine-Tuning Methodology
  - **Warm-Up Phase:** Start fine-tuning with a "warm-up" period where the learning rate is gradually increased from zero or a very small value to the target learning rate.
  - **Gradual Unfreezing:** Unfreeze and train one layer at a time, starting from the top layers and progressively going deeper, which prevents catastrophic forgetting of pre-trained knowledge.
  - **Hyperparameter Tuning:** Experiment with different hyperparameters, including learning rates, batch sizes, and optimizer types, to find the best combination for the task.

- **Evaluation Metrics:** Select appropriate metrics to evaluate the model's performance, ensuring they align well with the goals of the specific NLP task.

e) Practical Considerations

- **Compute Resources:** More epochs and larger batch sizes will generally require more computational resources, so adjust based on availability.
- **Task-Specific Architectural Changes:** Sometimes, it's necessary to modify the model's architecture by adding task-specific layers or heads; these changes must be made before fine-tuning begins.

These pre-training objectives teach models to understand and generate language in a way that mirrors some aspects of human language comprehension. It's crucial to understand that pre-training serves as a general education for the model, teaching it about language in a broad sense, without any specific task in mind. This wide-ranging foundation is what makes models versatile when they're later fine-tuned for specific tasks. Table 5.3 summarizes the benefits of pre-training. The table can serve as a concise reference for understanding why pre-training has become a ubiquitous strategy in NLP model development.

Pre-training language models on vast and diverse datasets is a foundational step in the creation of models that can understand and generate human language with a high degree of proficiency. Table 5.4 provides a snapshot of some of the primary datasets employed in the pre-training of NLP models, highlighting their compositions, contributions, and typical use cases in the field of language processing.

This table underscores the diversity and specificity of datasets suitable for pre-training, which are instrumental in developing NLP models with a rich understanding of language nuances.

5.5.2 Models that Generalize

In the realm of NLP, the generalization capability of models is pivotal. It refers to the ability of a model to perform well on new, unseen data that was not present during the training phase. This generalization is not only about maintaining performance across similar types of data but also about adapting to entirely different tasks with minimal adjustments. In this section, we will explore models that are particularly adept at this form of generalization, with a focus on the architecture and training methods that enable this flexibility.

Generalization in NLP models is an attribute that indicates the model's ability to apply learned knowledge from one context to another effectively. A model that generalizes well can understand the underlying patterns and structures of language that are common across various tasks, from text classification to machine translation. This is a critical aspect because it means that once a model

Table 5.3 Key Benefits of Pre-Training in NLP Models.

Benefit	Description	Implications for NLP
Improved Data Efficiency	Pre-trained models require less task-specific data to achieve high performance, reducing the need for large, labelled datasets.	Faster adaptation to new tasks with limited data.
Better Generalization	Models pre-trained on diverse data sources can generalize better to unseen data, reducing overfitting.	Enhanced ability to handle a wide variety of language tasks and domains.
Robust Feature Extraction	Pre-training helps in learning robust and transferable features that are useful across multiple tasks.	Common linguistic features are captured, improving overall language understanding.
Accelerated Convergence	Fine-tuning a pre-trained model often converges faster than training a model from scratch.	Reduced training time and computational resources for downstream tasks.
Improved Performance	Pre-trained models often achieve state-of-the-art performance on various NLP tasks.	Higher accuracy and more nuanced understanding in tasks such as translation.
Handling of Contextual Nuances	Pre-training on large corpora allows models to better understand context and disambiguate word meanings.	More sophisticated handling of context, idioms, and ambiguous language.
Scalability	Pre-trained models can be continuously updated with new data, scaling their understanding and capabilities.	Ability to adapt to emerging linguistic trends and terminologies.
Domain Adaptation	Pre-trained models can be fine-tuned to adapt to specific domains, even if they are substantially different from pre-training data.	Tailored performance in specialized fields like legal or medical NLP applications.
Enhanced Language Coverage	Pre-training on extensive and diverse datasets covers more of the language spectrum, including rare words and phrases.	Reduction in the model's exposure bias, handling edge cases more effectively.
Resource Efficiency	Pre-training, often done once, allows reuse of the same model across many tasks, optimizing resource use.	Lower energy and hardware costs due to shared pre-trained models across projects.

Table 5.4 Prominent Datasets Used for Pre-Training NLP Models.

Dataset	Composition	Contribution to Pre-training	Use Cases
Books Corpus	Over 11,000 books across various genres.	Rich narrative and dialogue structures, diverse vocabulary.	Story generation, dialogue systems.
Wikipedia Dumps	Comprehensive text from Wikipedia articles across all topics.	Encyclopedic world knowledge, formal writing style.	Information retrieval, content summarization.
Web Crawl Data	Text data from the broader internet, including websites and forums.	Informal language use, slang, and contemporary dialogue.	Sentiment analysis, social media monitoring.
Legal Corpora	Text from legal documents, court cases, and law journals.	Technical language and formal legal terminology.	Legal document analysis, compliance software.
Medical Corpora	Text from medical research papers, clinical case reports, etc.	Medical terminology and jargon, patient care language.	Medical informatics, clinical decision support systems.
Multilingual Data	Texts in multiple languages from the OPUS collection and others.	Cross-lingual understanding, translation capabilities.	Machine translation, cross-linguistic NLP applications.

is trained, it can be applied to a variety of tasks with little to no change in its architecture, making it incredibly efficient and versatile. The significance of generalization in NLP cannot be overstated. As models become more generalized, they become more useful across different domains, reduce the need for extensive retraining or model redesign for each new task, and help overcome the limitations posed by dataset-specific quirks or biases.

In the discussion of models that generalize, next, we discuss one of the most illustrative cases of a versatile NLP framework designed for broad applicability, T5, or the Text-to-Text Transfer Transformer. The T5 model stands as a paragon of generalization in the NLP landscape. It encapsulates the ethos of recent developments in transfer learning, where a single model learns to perform a multitude of tasks, often with state-of-the-art performance.

- *Architecture Overview:* The architecture of T5 is a variation of the traditional Transformer model, which has been the backbone of many recent advances in NLP. Unlike task-specific models, T5 casts every NLP problem as a text-to-text problem, where every task is framed in the same format: accepting text as input and producing new text as output. This simple yet powerful framing means that T5 can be used for translation (translating one language to another), summarization (condensing long text into a shorter version), text classification (assigning labels to text), and more, without any changes to the model's architecture.
- *Pre-training Techniques:* T5 diverges from earlier models by adopting a pre-training objective that is also text-to-text-based, the "span corruption" task. In this setup, random contiguous spans of text are replaced with a sentinel token, and the model is trained to predict the missing text. This pre-training task is more aligned with the downstream text-to-text tasks the model will eventually perform, unlike the more traditional MLM pre-training used by models like BERT, where individual tokens are masked for prediction.
- *Fine-Tuning T5 for Multiple Tasks:* Fine-tuning T5 is a streamlined process because the model inherently understands that all tasks require a text output. This is done by providing the model with task-specific prompts during training, which can be as simple as appending a task descriptor to the input text, like "translate English to French" or "summarize this article." T5's pre-training has endowed it with a broad understanding of language, so during fine-tuning, it rapidly learns the specifics of the task at hand.
- *Practical Examples of T5's Generalizability:* Several studies and real-world applications have demonstrated T5's versatility. For instance, Google has used T5 for its search engine to understand and generate snippets of relevant information. In academic research, T5 has been fine-tuned for tasks ranging from answering questions based on scientific papers to generating creative

fiction. The beauty of T5 is that all these diverse tasks use the same model, fine-tuned with task-specific data.

- *T5's Impact on NLP:* The creation of T5 marks a significant milestone in the NLP field. By demonstrating that a single model can learn a variety of language tasks, it has encouraged a shift in how researchers and practitioners approach problem-solving with NLP. The implications are far-reaching, suggesting that in the future, we may move toward an era where specialized NLP models are the exception rather than the rule, and generalized models dominate the landscape.

5.6 Learning with Minimal Examples

In traditional ML, the performance of a model is often directly tied to the quantity and quality of available training data. However, the paradigm is shifting with the advent of learning frameworks that require minimal examples—zero-shot, few-shot, and one-shot learning. These methods challenge the conventional necessity for large datasets and offer a glimpse into a future where models can make accurate predictions with scant data, reflecting more closely how humans learn. Zero-shot, few-shot, and one-shot learning represent a significant step toward creating intelligent systems that can learn and adapt with an efficiency that begins to approximate human learning.

- *Zero-shot learning (ZSL):* Refers to the ability of a model to correctly perform a task it has never explicitly seen during training. It relies on the model's understanding of task descriptions or its ability to relate knowledge from seen categories to unseen ones.
- *One-shot learning:* Involves training a model to understand a concept or category from a single example. It is crucial in scenarios where data is scarce or expensive to obtain.
- *Few-shot learning:* Sits between zero-shot and one-shot, where the model learns from only a handful of examples. It necessitates models that can generalize well from very limited information.

These learning paradigms leverage transfer learning, where a model pre-trained on a vast corpus of data applies its acquired knowledge to new tasks with minimal additional input. Furthermore, meta-learning or "learning to learn" plays a pivotal role, wherein the model is trained on a variety of tasks in a way that enables it to pick up new tasks quickly with little data.

Advancements in NLP model architectures have been central to the success of minimal example learning. Transformer-based models, with their ability to capture complex patterns and dependencies in data, have proven especially adept at these tasks.

One of the most notable examples of ZSL in NLP is the GPT-3 model by OpenAI, which can perform tasks it was not explicitly trained to do, such as translation or question-answering, given just a task description. Few-shot learning has been effectively used in creating custom text classifiers for niche domains, where companies may not have large, annotated datasets. For example, a model could learn to identify industry-specific sentiment with a handful of examples. In the field of language generation, one-shot learning has enabled the creation of models that can write poems, generate code, or create content based on a single prompt or example, as seen with models like Codex. These learning techniques are not just academic pursuits; they are being used in fields ranging from healthcare, where they assist in rare disease identification, to customer service, and powering chatbots that can handle a wide variety of queries with minimal prior examples.

But these methods come with their own set of challenges, such as the model's over-reliance on prior knowledge which can lead to biases, and the difficulty in choosing the right prior knowledge to generalize from. Ensuring diversity and representativeness in the training data is also a key factor.

5.7 Neuro-Symbolic Approaches

Neuro-symbolic approaches in NLP aim to combine the strengths of neural networks (neuro) and symbolic reasoning (symbolic) to create systems that can both understand and reason about language in a human-like manner. Neural networks are excellent at processing and learning from large datasets, capturing patterns and nuances in data. In contrast, symbolic reasoning deals with structured logic, rules, and relationships, providing the ability to reason, infer, and explain decisions systematically.

Neuro-symbolic approaches in NLP have a broad spectrum of use cases and applications, significantly enhancing the capabilities of language processing systems. In question answering, these approaches are invaluable, as they not only extract pertinent information from text but also apply reasoning to deliver precise, context-sensitive answers. This dual capability ensures that responses are not just based on data retrieval but also on an understanding of the question's deeper context and intent. In semantic parsing, neuro-symbolic systems shine by converting natural language into structured, formal representations of its meaning. They achieve this by blending neural networks' ability to parse complex language patterns with symbolic AI's capacity to interpret and organize these patterns logically, providing a robust understanding of linguistic structure and semantics. Furthermore, in the realm of automated reasoning, neuro-symbolic approaches empower machines to solve logical problems, prove theorems, or make informed decisions autonomously. By integrating the empirical learning from neural networks with the rule-based logic of symbolic reasoning, these systems can navigate complex problem spaces, offering solutions that are both data-informed and logically sound. Through these applications, neuro-symbolic approaches are setting a new standard for what is achievable in natural language understanding and processing, marrying the raw power of neural networks with the nuanced logic of symbolic AI.

5.7.1 Techniques in Neuro-Symbolic NLP

Neuro-symbolic approaches in NLP leverage the strengths of both neural networks and symbolic AI to create advanced systems capable of understanding and processing human language more effectively. Here's how these techniques manifest in real-world applications:

- *Integrated Models:* Integrated models in neuro-symbolic NLP blend the fluid, data-driven processing capabilities of neural networks with the structured, rule-based logic of symbolic reasoning. For example, a neural network might process text to understand its general content and sentiment, identifying key phrases, entities, and emotions. This raw understanding is then passed to a symbolic logic layer, which uses predefined rules and knowledge bases to perform deductive reasoning, generating explanations or decisions based on the combined information. For example, in a legal analysis tool, a neural network could be used to parse and preliminarily interpret legal documents, identifying relevant laws and precedents. Then, symbolic reasoning could apply legal rules to these findings to argue for or against certain interpretations, constructing legally sound arguments or identifying potential legal outcomes.
- *Hybrid Architectures:* Hybrid architectures maintain distinct neural and symbolic components that interact to solve complex problems. In these systems, the neural part typically manages tasks involving pattern recognition, data processing, and language understanding—areas where neural networks excel due to their ability to learn from vast amounts of data. The symbolic part, on the other hand, handles tasks requiring logical reasoning, structured decision-making, and rule-based processing. For example, in a diagnostic medical tool, neural components could analyze patient data and medical literature to identify symptoms and possible conditions, while symbolic reasoning could then apply medical rules and diagnostics criteria to formulate a diagnosis or recommend a treatment plan, ensuring that the conclusions follow established medical protocols.
- *Neural-Symbolic Cognitive Agents:* Neural-symbolic cognitive agents are designed to operate in dynamic environments, learning from interactions and

making decisions based on a combination of empirical learning and logical reasoning. These agents use neural networks to perceive their environment and learn from experiences, building a knowledge base that symbolic AI components use to make reasoned decisions and solve problems. For example, in an autonomous navigation system, the neural network component could process sensor data to understand the environment and detect obstacles, while the symbolic component uses this information to make decisions based on navigation rules, safety protocols, and destination objectives, dynamically adjusting the route in real time.

In all these cases, the goal of neuro-symbolic NLP is to create systems that not only understand language at a surface level but can also reason about it in a human-like manner, combining the adaptability and learning power of neural networks with the clear, logical reasoning of symbolic AI. This combination holds the promise of creating more intelligent, versatile, and reliable NLP systems that can tackle a wide range of language understanding and processing tasks with improved accuracy and efficiency.

Neuro-symbolic approaches in NLP bring a set of distinct advantages that make them particularly appealing. First, they enhance interpretability; by melding symbolic reasoning with neural networks, these systems can provide more transparent and understandable explanations for their decisions, fostering trust and reliability. This blend of logic and learning offers enhanced flexibility, enabling the handling of a wide range of tasks from intricate pattern recognition to complex logical reasoning, thus offering a holistic solution to language understanding and problem-solving. Furthermore, the robustness of neuro-symbolic systems to data scarcity is notable; the symbolic part of the system can operate effectively using rules and logic, even when data is limited, effectively complementing the data-hungry nature of neural networks.

However, these advantages come with their own set of challenges. The integration of neural and symbolic systems can be complex, demanding sophisticated mechanisms for their interaction and information exchange, which can be a technical hurdle. Scalability is another issue; while symbolic reasoning provides powerful logical capabilities, it can become computationally intensive with increased logic complexity, especially when coupled with large-scale neural models. Additionally, crafting data and knowledge representations that are conducive to both neural processing and symbolic reasoning poses a significant challenge. These representations must be rich and flexible enough to capture the diversity and complexity of human language and knowledge, bridging the gap between structured logic and the fluid, pattern-based learning of neural networks.

Knowledge Checkpoint 7

Multiple-Choice Questions (MCQs)

1 What is the main advantage of LSTM networks over traditional neural networks?
  A Faster computation
  B Ability to handle long-term dependencies
  C Lower memory requirements
  D Simpler architecture

2 Which model is known for introducing the self-attention mechanism?
  A LSTM
  B GPT
  C BERT
  D Transformer

3 What does transfer learning allow NLP models to do?
  A Predict the next word in a sequence more accurately
  B Learn from a small amount of data by applying knowledge from a related task
  C Translate languages with perfect accuracy
  D Perform speech recognition without training

Match the Following

1 Match the following concepts with their correct descriptions:
  A LSTM
  B Attention mechanism
  C Neuro-symbolic models
  D Transfer learning

2 Utilizes both neural networks and symbolic reasoning for enhanced language processing.

3 A method that improves model performance by allowing it to focus on relevant parts of the input.

4 Enables models to remember information over long intervals of time.

5 Involves adapting a pre-trained model for a new, but related, task.

True/False Statements

Indicate whether the following statements are true or false:

1 GRUs and LSTMs are exactly the same in terms of architecture and functionality. (True/False)

2 The Transformer model processes input data in a strictly sequential manner. (True/False)

3 Pre-trained models like BERT can be fine-tuned to improve performance on specific NLP tasks. (True/False)

4 Few-shot learning requires large amounts of labelled data to achieve high accuracy. (True/False)

5 Memory and recall models in NLP are designed to process information without considering its sequence or context. (True/False)

6

Fundamental Language Processing Techniques

Each step and concept we've previously covered serves as a stepping stone to deeper and more intricate text analyses. This chapter introduces a range of advanced techniques that probe deeply into text analysis. Each section is a thread in the intricate tapestry of NLP, revealing patterns and meaning beyond the surface of text.

6.1 Topic Modelling and Subject Identification

Language, in its evolving digital attire, has become an increasingly expansive domain of data. With millions of bytes of textual content being produced every day, the challenge lies not just in managing this massive data but also in extracting meaningful patterns from it. Enter Topic Modelling and Subject Identification—techniques that offer a bird's-eye view of extensive textual data, letting us identify the essence and overarching themes present within.

At its core, topic modelling is about discovery. It is a type of statistical model used to uncover abstract topics within a collection of documents. The beauty of topic modelling lies in its simplicity and power: it doesn't require detailed annotation by human readers but instead uses the co-occurrence of words within documents to reveal the hidden thematic structure. One can imagine a library with thousands of unlabelled books. Topic modelling is akin to a diligent librarian who, after reading through each book, begins to notice patterns: certain words like "king," "throne," and "crown" frequently appear together, while others like "neuron," "synapse," and "axon" cluster in a different set. From these observations, the librarian can infer the presence of topics such as "medieval history" and "neuroscience." Fig. 6.1 shows the conceptual diagram for topic modelling in text analysis.

While topic modelling offers a high-level view of the latent structures in a large text corpus, subject identification narrows down to the essence of a single document or a smaller collection. It is about extracting the main subject or theme from

Language Intelligence: Expanding Frontiers in Natural Language Processing, First Edition. Akshi Kumar.
© 2025 The Institute of Electrical and Electronics Engineers, Inc. Published 2025 by John Wiley & Sons, Inc.

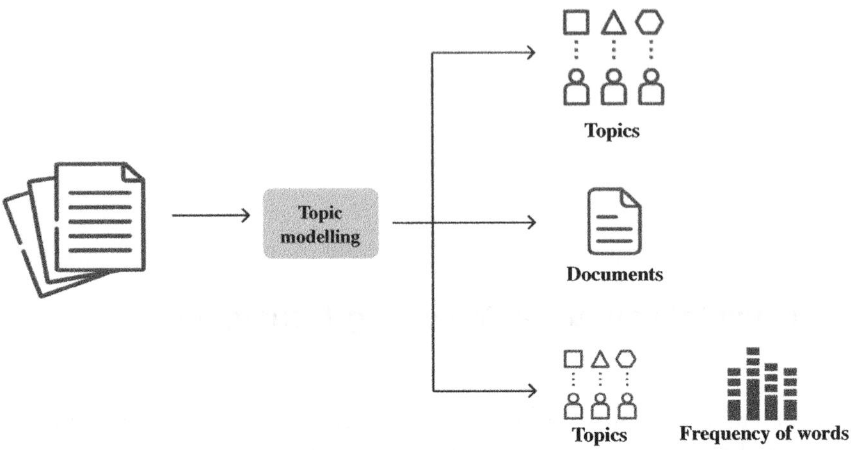

Figure 6.1 Schematic Representation of Topic Modelling Process.

a piece of text. Take, for instance, a tweet that mentions "Tesla," "stock price," and "quarterly earnings." A subject identification algorithm may categorize this as "Financial News" related to "Tesla." To do this effectively, the algorithm might leverage methods such as keyword extraction, where "Tesla" is identified as the main subject due to its prominence and relevance within the text.

6.1.1 Topic Modelling Methods

Topic modelling is a rich field with various methods developed to extract topics from large volumes of text. Each method comes with its own assumptions, advantages, and limitations. Here's a list of popular topic modelling methods:

- *Latent Dirichlet Allocation (LDA):* LDA is the most well-known topic modelling technique. It is a generative probabilistic model that assumes each document is a mixture of topics and a topic is a mixture of words.
- *Non-Negative Matrix Factorization (NMF):* This is based on linear algebra. It factorizes the given document-term matrix into two lower-dimensional matrices—one representing the documents and the other representing the terms. The non-negative constraint ensures interpretability.
- *Latent Semantic Analysis (LSA):* LSA, sometimes called Latent Semantic Indexing (LSI), is based on singular value decomposition (SVD). It reduces the dimensions of the term-document matrix, capturing the underlying structure in the data and helping in identifying patterns, thereby allowing for topic discovery.
- *Correlated Topic Model (CTM):* While LDA assumes topics are independent of each other, CTM relaxes this assumption and allows topics to be correlated.

- *Guided LDA:* This is a variant of LDA wherein users can define seed words for topics, which guides the algorithm to align topics as per the seeds.
- *Dynamic Topic Model (DTM):* DTM captures the evolution of topics in a sequential collection of documents. It's especially useful for understanding how certain topics have changed over time.
- *Hierarchical Dirichlet Process (HDP):* It's an extension of LDA but doesn't require the number of topics to be specified in advance. HDP can determine the number of topics based on the data.
- *Structured Topic Model (STM):* STM incorporates metadata into the topic modelling process, allowing for richer interpretations of topics.
- *Biterm Topic Model (BTM):* Unlike LDA, which works on the document level, BTM models topics based on word co-occurrence patterns, making it more suitable for short texts.
- *Author-Topic Model:* This is a variant designed to capture the topics associated with authors. It's particularly useful for academic publications where discerning author-specific topics can be insightful.
- *Pachinko Allocation:* This method allows topics to have a hierarchical structure, rather than the flat structure seen in models like LDA.
- *TART:* Stands for "Topics-Authors-Recipients-Text model." It is designed to identify topics in communication patterns where sender-receiver information is vital, e.g., email datasets.
- *Deep Learning-based Approaches:* With the rise of neural networks and deep learning, newer topic modelling methods like Neural Variational Document Model (NVDM), ProdLDA, and TopicRNN have emerged. These models utilize the capabilities of neural architectures to capture intricate patterns in data for topic modelling.
- *Word Embedding-based Approaches:* Models like Word2Vec and fastText capture semantic relationships between words. By clustering word vectors, topics within documents can be inferred, bridging traditional topic modelling and modern word embeddings.

In conclusion, the choice of topic modelling method largely depends on the nature of the dataset, the granularity of topics required, the assumptions one is willing to accept, and the computational resources available. The landscape of topic modelling is vast, and researchers continually develop and refine these methods to cater to diverse textual datasets.

6.1.2 Use Cases and Applications of Topic Modelling and Subject Identification Across Industries

The utility of topic modelling extends across various industries and disciplines, proving to be an invaluable tool for organizing, analyzing, and deriving insights from large datasets of unstructured text. In Table 6.1, we explore a selection of

Table 6.1 A Snapshot of Topic Modelling Applications Across Various Sectors.

Industry/Sector	Use Case/Application	Description
Academic Research	Literature Review	Topic modelling helps in synthesizing vast amounts of academic papers and identifying prevailing themes and research gaps.
Publishing and Media	News Aggregation and Categorization	Automating the classification of articles into topics for easier navigation and recommendation.
Business and Marketing	Customer Feedback Analysis	Analyzing customer reviews and feedback to identify common themes or issues with products or services.
Healthcare	Medical Records Analysis	Grouping patient records by symptoms or diseases to identify patterns and inform treatments.
Legal	Legal Document Discovery	Sifting through legal documents to find those relevant to certain cases or topics.
Finance	Market Research and Competitive Analysis	Tracking financial reports, news articles, and analyst notes for trends impacting industries or stocks.
Government and Public Policy	Policy Document Analysis	Analyzing policy papers and legislation to identify frequently discussed topics and policy directions.
E-Commerce	Product Listing Categorization	Organizing product descriptions into coherent categories for improved search and recommendation systems.
Social Media Analysis	Trending Topics Identification	Identifying and tracking trending topics and discussions across various social media platforms.
Content Management	Tagging and Organization of Digital Content	Assigning topics as tags to articles, blogs, and other digital content for better management and retrieval.
Search Engines	Enhancing Search Relevance	Using topic signatures to improve the relevance of search results by understanding the document's broader context.
Education	Curriculum Development	Analyzing academic content to structure curriculum around central topics and learning outcomes.
Library Sciences	Archive and Repository Management	Categorizing and tagging archival materials for improved accessibility and discoverability.
Technology	User Experience Personalization	Personalizing user experiences on platforms by aligning content with identified interests/topics.
Human Resources	Resume and Job Description Analysis	Extracting key topics from job descriptions and resumes to match candidates with job openings.

use cases and applications, showcasing how topic modelling serves to enhance understanding, streamline processes, and uncover hidden thematic patterns within diverse fields of work and study.

Subject identification, while closely related to topic modelling, tends to be more granular, focusing on pinpointing the primary themes within a single document or a more narrowly defined collection of texts. Table 6.2 illustrates the applications of subject identification and its impact on operational efficiency, targeted content delivery, and strategic insights in various industry sectors.

6.1.3 Tools and Software Packages for Topic Modelling and Subject Identification

For **topic modelling**, a prevalent method is the **Latent Dirichlet Allocation (LDA)**. Libraries such as **Gensim**, a Python-based library, are specially designed to handle topic modelling using this algorithm. Another robust Java-based package, **MALLET**, offers extensive capabilities for statistical natural language processing (NLP), including LDA-based topic modelling. The Python library, **lda**, is specifically tailored to offer an implementation of LDA. Additionally, the **Non-Negative Matrix Factorization (NMF)** method, which works by factorizing the given document-term matrix, is an alternative to LDA for extracting topics. You can find NMF implementations in libraries like **Scikit-learn**. For those interested in **Latent Semantic Analysis (LSA)** or **Latent Semantic Indexing (LSI)**, Gensim provides a reliable implementation. R users might find the **tm package** valuable, as it is a comprehensive text mining framework that includes facilities for topic modelling. There's also **BigARTM**, an open-source platform specifically for topic modelling with a rich Web API and cloud support.

On the other hand, for **subject identification**, there are several specialized tools and frameworks. **TextRazor** stands out for its powerful subject extraction capabilities, employing deep learning and other advanced techniques. The Python library **spaCy**, though widely recognized for Named Entity Recognition (NER), can be tailored for subject identification using custom pipelines. **OpenNLP** comes equipped with a document categorizer tool that can be instrumental for subject extraction. For R enthusiasts, the **text package** offers utilities tailored for text mining that can be deployed for subject identification tasks. Another comprehensive toolkit for linguistic data processing is the **Natural Language Toolkit (NLTK)**, which, through its chunking and named entity functionalities, can serve purposes of subject identification. **FastText**, birthed from Facebook's AI Research (FAIR) lab, is renowned for word embeddings and text classification and is adaptable for categorizing texts into predefined subjects. In the realm of deep learning, transformer-based models like **BERT and its offshoots (RoBERTa, DistilBERT, and others)**, when fine-tuned appropriately, emerge as formidable tools for subject identification.

Table 6.2 Applications of Subject Identification Across Different Sectors.

Industry/ Sector	Application of Subject Identification	Description
Publishing and Media	Editorial Tagging and Categorization	Identifying the main subject in articles for tagging and categorization in digital libraries.
Search Engines	Query Intent Understanding	Determining the subject matter of search queries to improve result accuracy and relevance.
Academic Research	Research Focus Identification	Extracting the core subjects from research papers to facilitate subject-based classification.
Customer Service	Inquiry and Complaint Sorting	Classifying customer inquiries by subject to route them to the appropriate department.
Marketing	Brand Mention Contextualization	Understanding the subject in which a brand is mentioned for targeted marketing strategies.
Social Media Monitoring	Social Media Post Categorization	Identifying the subjects discussed in social media posts to track trends and public sentiment.
Content Creation	Content Strategy and Development	Guiding content creators by identifying popular subjects to focus on for engagement.
Education	Learning Material Categorization	Organizing educational content by subject matter for curriculum development.
Legal	Case and Precedent Relevance Identification	Determining the main subjects in legal cases to find relevant precedents and laws.
Healthcare	Patient Concerns and Symptoms Classification	Classifying patient narratives by the main subjects to assist in preliminary diagnostics.
Finance	Financial Reporting Analysis	Identifying key subjects in financial reports for investment insights and strategy.
Human Resources	Job Specification Analysis	Extracting key subjects from job descriptions to inform recruitment and role definitions.
Technology	User Feedback Theme Extraction	Pinpointing the main subjects in user feedback to guide product improvement.
Government and Policy	Public Opinion and Issue Extraction	Isolating primary subjects from public discourse to inform policy decisions.
Cultural Studies	Cultural Trend Mapping	Identifying prevalent subjects in cultural texts to trace the evolution of cultural trends.

6.1.4 Challenges and Considerations in Topic Modelling and Subject Identification

While topic modelling and subject identification have advanced significantly over the years, they remain intertwined with a series of challenges that demand careful consideration:

- *Ambiguity and Polysemy:* As mentioned, words can often have multiple meanings. For instance, "apple" could either refer to the fruit or the globally recognized technology company. The word "bank" serves as another example, representing a financial institution or the side of a river. Such ambiguity can lead to topics being inaccurately represented or subjects being misclassified. Resolving these requires contextual understanding, which can be complex for automated systems.
- *Nuances of Language:* Language is replete with intricacies. There's irony, where the literal meaning is opposite to the intended; sarcasm, where a statement may convey contempt through praise; and idiomatic expressions that may be incomprehensible if taken literally. For example, "It's raining cats and dogs" has nothing to do with animals but signifies heavy rain. Detecting and understanding these nuances can pose significant challenges to automated topic and subject identification systems.
- *Cultural References and Context:* Language often carries with it cultural baggage and references that might be clear to a local but utterly confusing to an outsider. For instance, the word "*bollywood*" might be immediately recognized by someone from India as referring to their film industry, but for someone unfamiliar with Indian cinema, it might just seem like a misspelling of "*hollywood*". Such cultural nuances can be pivotal in understanding the context and, therefore, the topic or subject.
- *Quality and Cleanliness of Data:* No model, irrespective of its sophistication, can produce quality results from poor-quality data. If the texts are rife with errors, inconsistencies, or spam, it's likely the topic modelling or subject identification process will be adversely impacted. For instance, online product reviews might contain irrelevant information, spam, or even URLs. Feeding such data directly into a model can skew the results.
- *Scalability Issues:* Handling large volumes of data or streaming data requires efficient processing capabilities. While a tool might work perfectly for a dataset of a few thousand documents, it might struggle or become impractically slow when faced with millions.
- *Language Specificity:* Many tools and models are optimized for English. When handling languages with unique script systems or morphological complexities, challenges can emerge. For instance, Hindi, with its Devanagari script, possesses its own linguistic idiosyncrasies and nuances. While English uses the

word "*friend*", Hindi has multiple words based on gender and formality, such as "*dost*" for a casual male friend or "*saheli*" for a female friend. A model trained predominantly on English data might find it challenging to capture the nuance in a Hindi sentence like "*वह मेरी सहेली है*" which translates to "*She is my friend*" but carries the added layer of specifying the gender of the friend.
- *Temporal Evolution of Topics:* Over time, the importance and interpretation of topics can change. A topic that's relevant today might be obsolete in a few years. Conversely, new topics emerge, and models need to be updated to recognize them. For instance, a decade ago, the term "cryptocurrency" might not have been recognized as a significant topic, but today, it dominates many financial discussions.

Addressing these challenges often demands a combination of advanced modelling techniques, domain expertise, and iterative refining of the processes. As the field continues to advance, it remains essential to be vigilant and adaptive to ensure that the derived insights are both relevant and accurate.

6.2 Named Entity Recognition

In the expanding field of NLP, NER stands out as a fundamental task that has gained substantial attention in the core linguistic analytics domain. As a subtask of information extraction, NER is designed to locate and classify named entities mentioned in unstructured text into predefined categories such as the names of persons, organizations, locations, expressions of times, quantities, monetary values, and percentages, etc.

NER is the process of identifying entities that have a proper name and are of specific importance within a text. By parsing through the text, a NER system highlights words or phrases that are indicative of entities. This seemingly straightforward task involves sophisticated linguistic analysis because it must discern the context in which a word is used to ascertain whether it is a named entity. For instance, in the sentence "Apple announced a new release of their iPhone in California," a robust NER system should identify "Apple" as an organization, "iPhone" as a product, and "California" as a location. These entities are crucial for understanding the content's essence and for various applications like search engines, recommendation systems, content summarization, and more. Fig. 6.2 illustrates the application of NER in identifying and categorizing entities within a text passage, such as persons, locations, titles, dates, policies, and campaigns.

The term "Named Entity" was first coined during the 6th Message Understanding Conference (MUC-6) in 1996. The objective was to introduce a shared task where systems could identify and classify names of persons, organizations, and

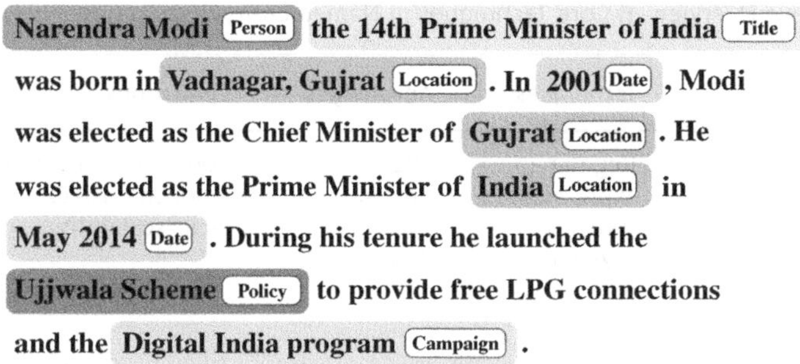

Figure 6.2 Example of Named Entity Recognition (NER) Annotations in a Text Passage.

locations from newswire text. Since then, the definition of named entities has expanded to include a broader range of categories like dates, times, and numerical quantities.

Initial approaches to NER were rule-based, relying on a set of human-crafted rules. These systems performed well on structured documents but were brittle in the face of the variability found in natural language. With the rise of statistical methods, machine learning (ML) approaches, particularly those using Conditional Random Fields (CRFs) and Hidden Markov Models (HMMs), became popular. These approaches consider context and sequence information, making them more robust across different text domains. Today, NER systems have been revolutionized by the advent of deep learning. Models such as Recurrent Neural Networks (RNNs), Long Short-Term Memory networks (LSTMs), and more recently, Transformer-based models like BERT (Bidirectional Encoder Representations from Transformers) have set new benchmarks for NER tasks.

6.2.1 Core Techniques in Named Entity Recognition

When exploring the landscape of NER, we dive into a myriad of techniques each marked by its unique methodologies, advantages, and challenges. These core techniques form the backbone of NER systems and are critical to understanding the evolution and capabilities of entity identification in various texts. Table 6.3 succinctly encapsulates these techniques, laying a comparative foundation for anyone looking to understand or work within the realm of NER.

6.2.2 Applications of Named Entity Recognition

NER is not just a fundamental component of NLP; it is a pivotal element that finds its utility across a wide range of applications, from enhancing search engine capabilities to powering recommendation systems. The versatility of NER is

Table 6.3 Comparative Overview of Core Techniques in Named Entity Recognition (NER).

Approach	Principle	Techniques	Advantages	Limitations
Rule-based NER	Creation of hand-crafted rules based on linguistic patterns	Regular expressions, lexicons, gazetteers, pattern matching	High precision for specific domains	Poor generalization, labor-intensive, lacks scalability
Statistical NER	Statistical models that learn from labelled data	HMMs, Maximum Entropy Models, CRFs	Good generalization to new data	Complex feature engineering, struggles with large feature spaces
Machine Learning NER	Machine learning algorithms learn from data features	SVMs, Decision Trees, Random Forests	Flexibility, handles large feature sets	Requires significant labelled data, risk of overfitting
Deep Learning NER	Neural networks learn data representations	RNNs, LSTMs, GRUs, CNNs, Transformers	Learn complex patterns, no manual feature engineering needed	Requires large, annotated datasets and computational resources, lack of interpretability
Hybrid NER	Combination of different NER techniques	Mix of rule-based, statistical, and deep learning methods	Improved accuracy and robustness	Implementation complexity, requires careful tuning
Transfer Learning NER	Utilizes pre-trained language models fine-tuned on NER data	Fine-tuning BERT, GPT, or other transformers on NER datasets	Powerful representations from large data, less task-specific data needed	Sensitive to fine-tuning process, may suffer from catastrophic forgetting of previously learned knowledge

showcased in its deployment across various industries, transforming raw text into actionable insights and structured data. In Table 6.4, we present a detailed view of the multifaceted applications of NER, each illustrating the breadth and depth of this technology's impact on both industry-specific tasks and common everyday functionalities.

Table 6.4 Applications of NER: Diverse Domains and Functional Utilization.

Application Area	Use Case Scenario	Benefits	Examples
Content Classification	Organizing and categorizing large volumes of text data	Improves searchability and accessibility of information	Classifying news articles by the entities mentioned. Sorting research papers by the scientific terms and author affiliations identified.
Customer Support Automation	Identifying key entities in customer inquiries to route to the appropriate response or department	Streamlines support ticket handling and improves customer satisfaction	Automatically tagging support tickets with 'refund', 'technical issue', or "billing" based on the entities recognized. Chatbots identifying product names and service issues in customer chats.
Sentiment Analysis	Assessing public sentiment towards specific products, services, or public figures	Helps businesses and organizations in reputation management and market analysis	Analyzing social media mentions of a new product to gauge public sentiment. Evaluating responses to a political figure's speech or policy announcement.
Information Retrieval	Enhancing search algorithms by focusing on key entities in the search queries	Leads to more relevant and precise search results	A legal document retrieval system returning documents where "Microsoft" is a litigant. A job search platform highlighting listings where "Java Developer" is mentioned.
Knowledge Graph Construction	Building databases of entities and their relationships	Facilitates richer understanding and reasoning over text data	Creating a medical knowledge graph with diseases, symptoms, and treatments as entities. Assembling a corporate database with companies, CEOs, and industry types linked together.

(*continued*)

Table 6.4 (Continued)

Application Area	Use Case Scenario	Benefits	Examples
Financial Analysis	Extracting financial entities for market analysis and risk assessment	Enhances decision-making in finance with timely and accurate information	Identifying company names, stock symbols, and financial indicators in market news for investment analysis. Monitoring news for mentions of mergers, acquisitions, or leadership changes.
Compliance Monitoring	Scanning for person names, organizations, and locations to ensure compliance with regulations	Reduces the risk of non-compliance fines and sanctions	Detecting mentions of embargoed countries in communications. Ensuring no unauthorized disclosure of personally identifiable information (PII) in public documents.
Healthcare Data Management	Identifying patient names, conditions, treatments, and medications from healthcare records	Improves patient care coordination and health data analysis	Extracting diagnosis and medication information from electronic health records (EHRs) for clinical research. Automating patient triage by identifying symptoms and medical history from intake forms.
Event Extraction	Recognizing and classifying events such as natural disasters, political rallies, or product launches	Enables timely response and situational awareness for various organizations	News agencies aggregating reports on "earthquakes" and "hurricanes" for immediate broadcast. Marketing firms tracking "product launch" events for competitive analysis.

Resume Filtering	Extracting skills, company names, and educational qualifications from resumes	Streamlines the recruitment process by automating candidate shortlisting	HR software categorizing applicants based on "Python programming" or "MBA degree" mentioned in their resumes. Talent acquisition platforms matching job openings with candidate profiles by identified competencies.
Travel and Hospitality Services	Identifying location names, points of interest, and cultural events from travel-related content	Enhances personalized recommendations and service offerings	Travel websites suggesting itineraries based on "museums", "historic sites", or "music festivals" recognized in user queries. Hospitality services customizing guest experiences based on preferences for "beachfront", "mountain view", or "city center" locales.
Real-time Monitoring and Alerts	Detecting mentions of entities in real-time data streams like news tickers and social media	Allows immediate action or response to developing situations	Security agencies monitoring for mentions of "threats" or "attacks." Financial traders setting alerts for real-time mentions of their portfolio companies.
Language Learning and Translation	Identifying proper nouns and culturally specific references for language learners	Enhances the learning experience by providing contextual translations	Language learning apps teaching proper noun pronunciation and usage. Translation services accurately handling names of people, places, and institutions.

6.2.3 Tools and Best Practices in Named Entity Recognition

The field of NER has seen considerable growth, thanks in part to the proliferation of sophisticated **tools** and the establishment of best practices that amplify the capabilities and streamline the implementation of NER systems. This narrative aims to shed light on some of the prominent tools that have become staples in NER endeavors, as well as the best practices that guide their effective deployment.

In the toolkit for modern NER, **SpaCy** stands out as a free, open-source NLP library in Python, prized for its speed and user-friendliness. It comes equipped with pre-trained models supporting multiple languages and is adept at carrying out NER tasks immediately. SpaCy is a go-to tool in the industry for NLP applications where entity recognition is a crucial part of the workflow. Another significant contributor is the **Stanford NER**, also known as **CRFClassifier**, part of the larger Stanford NLP framework. This Java-based toolkit employs CRF models and is designed to handle texts in English, Chinese, German, and other languages. Its precision makes it a favored choice for academic research and for applications within a Java ecosystem.

The **NLTK** is a leading platform for Python-based programs that deal with human language data. Although its NER capabilities are more limited compared to others, NLTK's extensive libraries make it a popular choice for educational purposes and early-stage NLP prototyping. For those on the cutting edge of NLP research, **AllenNLP** is an invaluable asset. This PyTorch-based library includes a fine-grained NER model along with other advanced deep-learning NLP models, positioning it as an essential resource for NLP research. The **Hugging Face's Transformers** library represents a collection of pre-trained models for NLP tasks, including but not limited to BERT, GPT, and T5. These models are readily available and have been fine-tuned for NER tasks across various domains. Due to its robustness and scalability, the Transformers library is widely adopted for developing sophisticated NLP applications in the industry.

Apache OpenNLP, a machine learning-based toolkit for natural language text processing, also finds its use in NER. It allows for the training of custom models for specialized NER tasks and is particularly well-suited for integration within Java environments and the broader Apache software ecosystem. Last, **Flair** provides a straightforward framework for state-of-the-art NLP. Developed by Zalando Research, Flair's approach to NER combines traditional CRF models with advanced character-level LSTM language models. This renders Flair particularly effective in applications where the context-sensitivity of NER is of paramount importance, applicable in both academic and industrial contexts.

Adherence to best practices is crucial when implementing these tools. This includes careful data preparation, selection of appropriate models based on the task and language, rigorous training and fine-tuning with domain-specific datasets, continuous performance evaluation against benchmarks, and integration into broader NLP pipelines in a way that leverages the strengths of each tool. By navigating these practices, NER systems can achieve the precision and efficiency required for the complex task of entity recognition in natural language.

6.2.4 Challenges in Named Entity Recognition

NER stands as a critical task in the sphere of NLP, offering the promise of transforming unstructured text into data points that machines can understand and act upon. However, the road to effective NER is paved with a diverse array of challenges that stem from the intricacies of human language and the ever-evolving landscape of data. These challenges range from linguistic subtleties to technical constraints, each presenting hurdles that must be overcome to build robust and accurate NER systems. In this section, we will explore these challenges in depth, examining the obstacles that practitioners and researchers face in the pursuit of extracting meaningful entities from the vast sea of text.

- *Ambiguity:* Consider the sentence: "After working on the project, Jordan went to the Jordan to relax." In this case, "Jordan" first refers to a person's name and then to the country. An NER system must use the context provided by the surrounding words to disambiguate this word.
- *Variability:* The company "Apple Inc." might be mentioned in various ways, such as "Apple", "Apple Inc.", "Apple Computers", "the tech giant Apple", etc. An effective NER system must recognize that all these variants point to the same entity.
- *Domain-Specific Entities:* In the biomedical field, the term "CD40L" refers to a specific protein. However, outside of this domain, "CD40L" might not be recognized as an entity. A model trained on general news articles might not recognize "CD40L" as an entity, whereas a model trained on biomedical literature is expected to do so.
- *Cross-Language NER:* The name "George" in English is "Jorge" in Spanish, "Georges" in French, and "Георгий" in Russian. Multilingual NER systems must understand that these names refer to the same entity across languages, which is especially challenging without a robust multilingual dataset.
- *Complex Entity Identification:* Identifying entities like "the third Thursday in November" as a date requires the system to interpret the meaning beyond simple pattern recognition. Similarly, "the Big Apple" as a nickname for New York City is another complex entity that standard models may not easily classify as a location.
- *Entity Discontinuity:* In the phrase "the Nobel Prize-winning physicist", the entity is not contiguous; "Nobel" and "physicist" belong together but are

separated by "Prize-winning". Recognizing such discontinuous entities is a challenge for many NER systems.

- *Nested Entities:* The sentence "John Doe, the CEO of Doe Enterprises, announced a new venture" contains nested entities. "John Doe" is a person, and "Doe Enterprises" is an organization. Some entities like "the CEO of Doe Enterprises" include both a person and an organizational title, which are difficult for NER systems to parse and classify accurately.
- *Entity Evolution:* New entities emerge, and existing ones may change over time. "COVID-19", before the pandemic, would not have been recognized as an entity. Post-2020, it is a widely recognized disease entity. NER systems need to be updated to keep up with such evolving entities.

Each of these challenges represents a distinct obstacle that requires sophisticated linguistic understanding and adaptability on the part of NER systems. Overcoming these obstacles involves a combination of advanced machine learning techniques, comprehensive datasets, domain expertise, and iterative refinement of models. With ongoing research and development, NER systems continue to improve, making significant strides in accurately interpreting and classifying entities across various domains and languages.

6.3 Text Coherence and Cohesion

Text coherence and cohesion are fundamental aspects of NLP that assess how individual parts of a text come together to form a meaningful whole. Coherence refers to the logical flow and consistency of ideas, ensuring the narrative or argument structure is understandable. Cohesion, meanwhile, concerns the grammatical and lexical connections within the text, such as the use of connectives, pronouns, and lexical ties that aid in unifying the text.

- *Coherence in NLP:* Coherence is about the logical organization and how each part of the text contributes to the overall meaning. In NLP, ensuring coherence involves analyzing the text to see if it logically progresses from one sentence to the next and whether the overall structure makes sense. This aspect is crucial in applications like automated essay scoring, where the algorithm evaluates the logical flow of arguments, and content generation, where the goal is to produce text that is logical and consistent. Several techniques are used in NLP to analyze coherence:
  a) **Discourse Analysis:** This technique analyzes the structure of text to identify discourse relations, such as cause-effect, problem-solution, or general-specific information. For example, in an essay discussing environmental conservation, discourse analysis can identify passages that introduce

problems (like deforestation) and subsequent solutions (like reforestation programs), thereby assessing the logical flow of the essay.

b) **Topic Segmentation:** This involves dividing a text into sections based on the topics discussed. In a news article that initially discusses a political event and then shifts to its economic implications, topic segmentation would identify these as distinct sections, helping verify that each segment maintains its thematic focus.

c) **Latent Semantic Analysis (LSA):** LSA uncovers the relationship between terms in a text to ensure coherence. For instance, in a medical research paper, LSA can analyze the use of related terms like "diabetes," "insulin," and "glucose," to determine if the paper maintains thematic consistency throughout. Challenges in Coherence Analysis

Coherence analysis encompasses various challenges, particularly when dealing with the subtleties of contextual transitions and the variability across cultures and languages. For example, in a narrative text, a subtle transition might occur when the story shifts from a present scene to a character's memory without explicit markers, which can be difficult for algorithms to detect and interpret as a coherent flow of events. Similarly, cultural and linguistic variability adds complexity to coherence analysis. What constitutes a coherent text in one culture or language may not align with the standards or structures prevalent in another. For instance, the way stories are structured in English, with a clear beginning, middle, and end, might differ from the more cyclical or episodic storytelling common in Indigenous or Asian narratives. These nuances challenge NLP systems to adapt and accurately assess coherence in a diverse range of textual materials, highlighting the need for sophisticated, context-aware algorithms that can navigate the intricate dynamics of language and culture.

- *Cohesion in NLP:* Cohesion in text is about the grammatical and lexical elements that help the text stick together. It includes the use of connectives (like "however," "therefore"), pronouns (like "it," "they"), and lexical ties (repetitions of significant words, synonyms, antonyms). To analyze cohesion, NLP uses techniques such as:

  a) **Referential Analysis:** This technique tracks pronouns and other referential expressions to their antecedents to ensure clarity. For example, in the sentence "John visited his uncle. He was happy to see him," referential analysis helps to confirm that "He" refers to "John" and "him" refers to "his uncle."

  b) **Conjunction Analysis:** This examines how conjunctions and transitional phrases link sentences and ideas. In a complex narrative, conjunctions like "however," "furthermore," and "then" guide the reader through the argument or story, indicating shifts in reasoning or the sequence of events.

c) **Lexical Chain Analysis:** Identifying chains of related words ensures lexical consistency. In a technical document about computer hardware, terms like "processor," "motherboard," "RAM," and "hard drive" might form a lexical chain, establishing cohesion by consistently referencing parts of a computer system.

Cohesion analysis in NLP poses specific challenges, particularly with the ambiguity in referencing and the complexity of lexical ties. For instance, the sentence "After Sarah gave her sister the keys, she felt relieved" contains an ambiguous reference: "she" could refer to either Sarah or her sister, leading to potential confusion. Such ambiguity can make it difficult for NLP algorithms to understand and maintain the text's coherence. Moreover, the complexity of lexical ties adds another layer of difficulty. Words like "fast" and "rapid" are synonyms and should theoretically reinforce cohesion, but their appropriateness can vary greatly with context, affecting how well an NLP system can assess the text's cohesiveness.

Understanding text coherence and cohesion is crucial for various NLP applications. In essay scoring, for instance, automated systems rely on analyzing these elements to evaluate the quality of writing, providing essential feedback in educational settings. In the realm of summarization, the challenge is to produce concise summaries that retain the logical flow and essential meaning of the original text, ensuring that the resultant summary is both coherent and cohesive. Similarly, text generation tasks, especially those involving advanced language models, necessitate the production of text that is not only grammatically correct but also logically structured and easy to follow, thereby enhancing the overall readability and engagement of the generated content.

6.3.1 Text Summarization

Text summarization pertains to the process of distilling the most important information from a source text and presenting that information in a condensed form. This can be likened to the way a human might read a lengthy article and then explain the key points to someone else in a few sentences. It seeks to condense a longer piece of text into a concise summary that retains the original document's main points. Imagine skimming an article and extracting its essence, all without losing its core message. That's what automated text summarization aspires to achieve. The benefits range from creating short previews for long articles to summarizing transcripts of lengthy meetings. However, not all summarization tasks are the same. They can differ based on the type of input, the intended purpose, and the nature of the output generated. Table 6.5 provides a quick reference guide for understanding the various aspects of text summarization, from the nature of the input data to the purpose and the characteristics of the output. It can serve as

Table 6.5 Types of Text Summarization.

Classification	Sub-Type	Definition	Applications	Pros/Cons
Input Type	Single Document	Involves summarizing content from a single document.	Book summaries, news briefings, abstracts in research papers.	Simplicity in handling one document. Can be limited to the content and perspectives available in one source.
	Multi-document	Summarization that draws from multiple documents.	Aggregating news or reviews from various sources.	Can be rich and diverse in information but requires advanced algorithms to manage and synthesize diverse data.
Purpose	Informative	Aims to provide detailed and factual summaries that convey the main points.	Executive summaries, academic abstracts.	Comprehensive but might be lengthier than other summary types.
	Indicative	Intended to give an overview or hint, often without revealing all key details.	Search engine result descriptions, table-of-contents explanations.	Generally brief and intriguing but may lack detail.
	Critical	Entails evaluation, analysis, or expressing an opinion about the source content.	Book or movie reviews, evaluative research summaries.	Offers evaluative insights but may be subject to biases and varied interpretations.
Output Type	Extractive	Creates summaries by extracting sentences or fragments directly from the source text.	Highlights, quick facts.	High fidelity to original content, possibly lacking in cohesion or implicit themes.
	Abstractive	Generates summaries by understanding and rephrasing the source content, often creating new sentences.	Rewritten articles, paraphrased explanations.	Can create nuanced and fluent summaries, potential risk of inaccuracies and is computationally demanding.
	Hybrid	Utilizes a combination of both extractive and abstractive summarization techniques.	Advanced summarization tools, comprehensive news briefings.	Balances accuracy and fluency, might be complex to implement and can inherit the disadvantages of both methods.

a framework for selecting and designing summarization models, ensuring alignment with specific use cases and requirements.

The following sub-sections elaborate the two primary types of text summarization: extractive and abstractive.

- *Extractive Summarization:* It involves identifying the key sentences or phrases from the original text and stitching them together to create a summary. This form of summarization does not alter the original text but rather extracts parts of it as shown in Fig. 6.3.
  The method relies heavily on algorithms that can determine the importance of each sentence, often based on statistical methods, keyword frequency (e.g., TF-IDF), or more advanced techniques like graph-based representations of sentences.
  a) **Statistical Methods:** These are among the earliest approaches used in extractive summarization. They involve quantifying the significance of sentences based on statistical properties. A simple method might count the frequency of words, considering sentences that contain highly frequent words as important. The assumption is that if a word occurs often, it's likely to be central to the topic.
  b) **TF-IDF (Term Frequency-Inverse Document Frequency):** This technique goes a step further by evaluating how important a word is to a document in a collection or corpus. TF measures how frequently a term appears in a document, while IDF diminishes the weight of terms that occur very frequently across the corpus, valuing rarity. Sentences with high TF-IDF scores for their words are often considered important and thus selected for the summary.
  c) **Positional Methods:** Positional heuristics are based on the observation that the position of a sentence in a document often indicates its potential importance. For example, sentences at the beginning of a news article or a paragraph might be weighted more heavily under the presumption that they often introduce the main topic.

Figure 6.3 Extractive Summarization.

d) **Graph-Based Methods:** Advanced techniques such as TextRank create a graph where sentences are nodes connected by edges. The edges represent the similarity between sentences, which can be computed based on shared words or more complex semantic similarity measures. A weighted graph is then constructed, and a ranking algorithm (like PageRank) is applied to identify the most central sentences, which are then selected for the summary.
e) **Machine Learning Models:** With machine learning, features such as sentence length, term weights, thematic words, positional information, and even named entities can be used to train a model to score and select sentences. The model learns from annotated datasets to predict which sentences are likely to be included in a summary. Classifiers like support vector machines (SVMs), random forests, or neural networks can be utilized for this task.
f) **Cue Words and Named Entities:** Certain words or phrases in the text, known as cue words (e.g., "consequently," "importantly"), may signal that the sentence is summarizing or concluding a portion of the text and thus might be selected for the summary. Similarly, sentences containing named entities like people, organizations, or locations might be considered more information-dense and chosen more frequently.

The process usually involves pre-processing the text (tokenization, stemming, stop-word removal), followed by feature computation for each sentence. Once the features are computed, a selection algorithm or model ranks the sentences according to their perceived importance. The top-ranked sentences are then extracted and concatenated to form the final summary. This extraction is done while maintaining the original order of sentences to preserve coherence.
Examples of Extractive Summarization include News Summarization with algorithms that produce digests of news articles by extracting key sentences and research paper summarization tools like arXiv's Sanity Preserver that summarize academic papers for quicker consumption by extracting the most significant sentences. While extractive summarization systems are generally robust and preserve the factual accuracy of the original text, they can struggle with producing a coherent summary that smoothly transitions between extracted sentences. Since they are limited to using the exact sentences from the original text, the summaries may also include redundant information or miss nuances that could be captured by paraphrasing or generating new sentences, which is where abstractive summarization techniques shine. Despite these challenges, extractive summarization remains a popular choice due to its relative simplicity and the more interpretable nature of its process, which is an important consideration in applications where understanding the reasoning behind the system's decision is crucial.

- *Abstractive Summarization:* Abstractive summarization is an advanced form of summarization that generates a concise and coherent version of the original text

Figure 6.4 Abstractive Summarization.

by creating new phrases and sentences. Unlike extractive summarization, which simply selects portions of the original text, abstractive summarization interprets the main ideas and expresses them in a new, shorter form. This process closely mimics how humans summarize information, often synthesizing new expressions while maintaining the original meaning as shown in Fig. 6.4.

It involves generating new sentences that are not necessarily present in the source text but still capture its main points. This requires a deeper understanding of language and the ability to paraphrase and rephrase the essence of the text. It's a more complex process often relying on advanced machine learning models, like sequence-to-sequence models, that can generate coherent and contextually relevant summaries. The techniques in abstractive summarization include:

a) **Sequence-to-Sequence (Seq2Seq) Models:** These are neural network models that consist of two parts: an encoder and a decoder. The encoder reads and understands the entire text, encoding the information into a fixed-length vector. The decoder then uses this vector to generate a summary, one word at a time. This framework is often based on RNNs or LSTMs, which are types of networks capable of handling sequences of data.
b) **Attention Mechanisms:** Attention mechanisms were introduced to help seq2seq models focus on relevant parts of the input text while generating each word of the summary. This is akin to when humans write summaries; we re-read and focus on the parts of the source material that are most relevant to the part of the summary we are currently writing.
c) **Transformer Models:** Transformers are a type of model architecture that rely entirely on self-attention mechanisms without using sequence-aligned RNNs or convolution. Introduced by the paper "Attention Is All You Need" in 2017, transformers have proven to be more efficient and effective at handling long-range dependencies in text, which is essential for summarization.
d) **Pre-trained Language Models:** Large pre-trained models like BERT, GPT, and T5 have caused a paradigm shift in abstractive summarization. These models are trained on massive corpora of text in a self-supervised manner and

then fine-tuned for specific tasks such as summarization. They have a high level of understanding of language nuances, which allows them to generate more fluent and accurate summaries.

e) **Fine-Tuning with Summarization Datasets:** Fine-tuning involves taking a pre-trained model and training it further on a dataset specifically for summarization. This allows the model to adapt its general language understanding capabilities to the specific task of generating summaries.

f) **Controlled Generation and Conditional Language Models:** Recent advances also include models that can be controlled for various aspects of the generated summaries, such as length, style, or inclusion of specific keywords, by conditioning the model's outputs on these factors.

The process typically starts with the input text being pre-processed and tokenized into a format that the model can understand. The neural network then encodes this information, often considering the entire context of the input text. The generation phase is iterative, with the model predicting the next word in the sequence given the previous words, continually referring back to the input text's encoded representation. Abstractive summarization models must overcome significant challenges such as ensuring the factual accuracy of the generated summaries, maintaining coherence across the entire text, and avoiding repetition. They also require more computational resources to train and run than extractive models.

Abstractive summarization systems are becoming increasingly capable, producing summaries that are often more readable and concise than those produced by extractive systems. As NLP technology continues to advance, these systems are expected to get even better at generating high-quality summaries that are indistinguishable from those written by humans. Examples of Abstractive Summarization include:

- *GPT-3:* By providing a prompt to the model that includes instructions for summarization, GPT-3 can generate summaries that are not constrained to using sentences from the original text.
- *T5:* Google's T5 treats summarization as a text-to-text problem, where the model is given a task description (e.g., "summarize:") followed by the text to summarize, and it outputs a summary.

6.4 Stylistic Analysis

Stylistic analysis in NLP intricately examines how language is used across different texts, focusing on elements like word choice, sentence structure, rhetorical devices, and overall text organization. This methodical examination is pivotal in revealing the author's stylistic fingerprint and aids in authorship attribution, literary analysis, and content marketing strategy.

In the context of **authorship attribution**, stylistic analysis is instrumental. For example, when analyzing the Federalist Papers, experts have employed stylistic cues to distinguish between writings attributed to Alexander Hamilton and James Madison, focusing on aspects like lexical choice and sentence complexity. This type of analysis has been crucial in making informed guesses about the authors of historical texts based on their unique stylistic features. In **literary studies**, stylistic analysis provides profound insights into the elements that characterize different genres or the works of specific authors. The use of iambic pentameter by Shakespeare, for instance, not only defines the rhythmic pattern of his works but also contributes significantly to the emotional and thematic depth of his plays and sonnets, offering a richer understanding of his literary genius. For **content marketing**, understanding stylistic nuances is key to engaging the target audience effectively. Analyzing the style of successful marketing campaigns, like the emotive and concise language used in Apple's advertising, can reveal how certain stylistic choices resonate with the audience, helping content creators craft messages that strike the right chord with consumers.

Stylistic analysis is also becoming increasingly important in **mental health analysis**. Variations in an individual's writing style, such as an increased use of negative emotion words or a sudden shift in narrative style, can signal changes in mental health. Psychologists and researchers might analyze text from therapy sessions or social media posts to detect these subtle linguistic indicators of mental well-being. In the realm of **sensational content monitoring**, stylistic analysis helps in identifying texts that aim to provoke or manipulate readers. News outlets or articles that employ a sensationalist style, characterized by exaggerated headlines, or emotionally charged language, can be detected and analyzed for their potential to mislead or create unwarranted hype.

Through these applications, stylistic analysis in NLP bridges the gap between the quantitative mechanics of language processing and qualitative, interpretive understanding, providing a comprehensive toolkit for dissecting the complex interplay of written communication in various domains.

6.4.1 Techniques for Stylistic Analysis

In stylistic analysis, a variety of techniques are employed to decipher and interpret the nuanced use of language within texts. These methods provide insights into the distinctive features that characterize different styles of writing.

- *Feature Extraction:* Feature extraction targets specific elements that signify the style of a text, including lexical richness, syntactic complexity, and the

prevalence of phrases or idioms. For example, examining the works of Edgar Allan Poe might show a preference for complex sentence structures and a unique lexicon, highlighting his gothic style. This technique is vital in applications such as literary analysis, where understanding the stylistic elements of a text can lead to deeper interpretations of its content and context.
- *Machine Learning Models:* Machine learning models like SVMs or neural networks are used to analyze these stylistic features to categorize texts or deduce authorship. Training these models on a dataset with known authorial styles allows them to identify the probable author of a given text based on its stylistic attributes. For example, machine learning can help in distinguishing between contemporary authors' styles, aiding in authorship attribution and literary scholarship by analyzing patterns such as word usage, narrative structure, and rhetorical devices.
- *N-Gram Analysis:* N-Gram analysis involves studying the frequency of consecutive word sequences to detect stylistic patterns characteristic of authors or genres. This technique can reveal, for instance, the repetitive use of certain phrases or sentence structures that are emblematic of an author's writing style. In crime fiction, the frequent use of suspense-building n-grams might be identified, showcasing how this literary device is woven into the narrative. N-Gram analysis is instrumental in stylometry, helping scholars and analysts quantify and compare stylistic elements across various texts, thus uncovering the underlying stylistic fingerprints that differentiate one writer's work from another.

Stylistic analysis in NLP faces several challenges, primarily due to the complex and subjective nature of language and style. One significant challenge is the inherent variability in an author's writing style; authors may vary their style based on context, genre, or over time, making it difficult to establish a consistent stylistic signature. Additionally, stylistic elements are often subtle and nuanced, requiring sophisticated algorithms to detect and interpret them accurately. The subjectivity of stylistic interpretation also poses a problem, as different readers—or algorithms—may perceive and analyze a text's style differently. Furthermore, large and diverse datasets are needed to train machine learning models effectively, but such datasets are often difficult to compile, especially for less-studied languages or genres. Last, distinguishing between stylistic features and content-specific elements can be challenging, as certain word choices or syntactic structures might be more related to the topic of the text rather than the author's unique style. These challenges necessitate ongoing research and development to refine the tools and methods used in stylistic analysis, ensuring they are robust, adaptable, and capable of handling the intricate layers of language use.

6.5 Semantic Role Labelling

Semantic Role Labelling (SRL) is a critical process in NLP that involves assigning labels to words or phrases within a sentence to identify their semantic roles in relation to the main verb or action. This process clarifies the structure of actions and relationships, delineating who is performing the action (the agent), who is receiving the action (the patient), and other elements like the location or instrument involved in the action. For instance, in the sentence "The chef (agent) cooked (verb) the meal (patient) in the kitchen (location) with a stove (instrument)," SRL helps in identifying not just the action but also the roles played by each entity in the sentence. This elucidation is crucial in various NLP applications.

In information extraction, SRL is employed to transform unstructured text into a structured format that clearly defines the relationships between entities, facilitating the retrieval of specific information. For example, from business news articles, an SRL system can extract who acquired whom, for how much, and when, turning unstructured text into valuable, actionable data.

In question-answering systems, SRL enhances the machine's understanding of natural language queries, thereby improving its ability to generate relevant and accurate answers. By understanding the semantic roles within a query, the system can pinpoint the exact information needed. For example, if someone asks, "Who wrote 'Hamlet'?" the system recognizes "wrote" as the action and "Hamlet" as the object, leading to the identification of "Shakespeare" as the agent or the author. Moreover, in machine translation, SRL aids in ensuring that the translated text preserves the meaning of the original by accurately translating the semantic roles from one language to another. This process is vital for maintaining the sentence's integrity and ensuring that the translation conveys the same message as the source text. SRL can discern the narrative structure of sensational content, highlighting how subjects, objects, and actions interrelate to create a biased or sensational narrative. Understanding these roles can reveal the underlying mechanisms of how such content manipulates reader perception and emotions, aiding in the development of more effective content moderation strategies.

SRL, therefore, not only deepens the understanding of linguistic structures but also enhances the functionality of NLP systems in processing and interpreting human language, making it a fundamental technique in the development of intelligent language processing applications.

6.5.1 Techniques for Semantic Role Labelling

Understanding the intricacies of language and its functional components is crucial in NLP. Various techniques have been developed to analyze and interpret these components effectively, each with its specific methodology and use cases. Here's how some of these techniques work:

- *Predicate-Argument Structures:*
  a) **How It Works:** Predicate-Argument Structures focus on the verb (predicate) in a sentence and the entities (arguments) that participate in the action or event described by the verb. This method helps in identifying the relationship between different parts of a sentence, establishing who did what to whom.
  b) **Example:** In the sentence "The cat (agent) chased (predicate) the mouse (patient)," "chased" is the predicate indicating the action, "the cat" is the argument performing the action (agent), and "the mouse" is the argument affected by the action (patient).
  c) **Use Case:** This technique is widely used in syntactic parsing and information extraction. For instance, in an NLP system designed for legal document analysis, understanding the agent and patient can help in extracting relevant facts like who committed a crime and who was the victim.
- *Supervised Learning Models:*
  a) **How It Works:** Supervised learning models in NLP are trained on annotated corpora where the semantic roles of words or phrases in sentences are already labeled. By learning from these annotations, the models can predict the roles of entities in new, unseen sentences.
  b) **Example:** In a training dataset, the sentence "John (agent) donated (predicate) money (theme) to the charity (recipient)" would be annotated with labels indicating the semantic roles. A supervised learning model trained on such data could then learn to identify these roles in similar sentences.
  c) **Use Case:** This method is essential in building systems for question answering where the model needs to understand the roles different entities play in a text to accurately answer questions about it. For instance, in a customer service chatbot, identifying who is providing a service and who is receiving it can help in generating correct and contextually relevant responses.
- *Deep Learning Approaches:*
  a) **How It Works:** Deep learning approaches in semantic role labelling utilize complex neural network architectures, often with attention mechanisms, to process the input text. These models can understand the broader context and the nuanced relationships between words, beyond simple predicate-argument structures.
  b) **Example:** Using a model like BERT (Bidirectional Encoder Representations from Transformers) equipped with attention mechanisms, a deep learning system can effectively capture the semantic relationships in the sentence "After saving for years, Lisa (agent) bought (predicate) a car (theme) from the dealership (source)."
  c) **Use Case:** Deep learning models are pivotal in creating advanced NLP systems that require a nuanced understanding of text, such as in machine translation. Here, capturing the subtle semantic nuances in the source language and accurately mapping them to the target language is crucial for producing

high-quality translations. For example, ensuring that the subject's actions and the objects of these actions are correctly translated preserves the sentence's meaning across languages.

SRL too faces several challenges that stem from the complexity and diversity of human language. One of the primary challenges is the inherent ambiguity in linguistic expressions; the same sentence structure can imply different semantic roles in different contexts, making it difficult for algorithms to consistently identify roles accurately. Moreover, languages vary greatly in their syntactic and semantic structures, which complicates the development of universal SRL models that can handle multiple languages effectively. Another significant challenge is the need for large, annotated corpora to train SRL models, as creating these datasets is time-consuming and requires expert linguistic knowledge. Additionally, sentences with complex or implicit meanings, idiomatic expressions, and nested or coordinated structures present substantial difficulties in parsing and role assignment. These challenges necessitate advanced machine learning models and comprehensive, diverse training data to improve the accuracy and reliability of SRL systems in capturing the nuanced dynamics of language use.

Knowledge Checkpoint 8

Mixed Worksheet

1 What is the main objective of topic modelling in NLP?
A To correct grammatical errors in a text
B To uncover abstract topics within a collection of documents
C To translate text from one language to another
D To summarize texts into shorter versions

2 Which technique is often used for Semantic Role Labelling (SRL)?
A Latent Dirichlet Allocation
B Conditional Random Field
C Term Frequency-Inverse Document Frequency
D Non-Negative Matrix Factorization

3 ______________ is the process of identifying the main subject or theme from a piece of text.

4 In Named Entity Recognition (NER), "Apple" identified as an organization is an example of a(n) ______________ entity.

5 Latent Semantic Analysis (LSA) is used for correcting spelling errors in text. (True/False)

6 Guided LDA allows users to define seed words for topics, guiding the topic modelling process. (True/False)

7 Cohesion analysis in NLP involves examining how grammatical and lexical ties create unity in a text. (True/False)

8 If an NLP model needs to identify specific financial terms within market analysis reports, it is likely using:
A Text Summarization
B Named Entity Recognition
C Topic Modelling
D Sentence Splitting

9 In analyzing a large collection of historical documents to uncover common themes over centuries, the best NLP technique would be:
A Semantic Role Labelling
B Named Entity Recognition
C Topic Modelling
D Text Summarization

10 A system designed to assess the sentiment expressed in customer reviews about a new product uses:
A Sentence Splitting
B Text Coherence Analysis
C Topic Modelling
D Sentiment Analysis

11 An NLP tool that breaks down a legal document into who (agent), what (action), and whom (beneficiary) is primarily performing:
A Text Summarization
B Named Entity Recognition
C Semantic Role Labelling
D Topic Modelling

12 A chatbot that can understand and manage user inquiries by identifying keywords and their purpose is employing:
A Text Summarization
B Named Entity Recognition
C Subject Identification
D Semantic Role Labelling

7

Natural Language Processing for Affective, Psychological, and Content Analysis

In the ever-evolving landscape of digital communication, NLP has become an indispensable tool for resolving the complex web of human emotions, behaviors, and cognitive patterns. This chapter explores the multifaceted ways in which NLP intersects with the nuanced realms of human affect, cognition, and social interaction. From the detailed detection of sentiment and emotion in text to the nuanced understanding of humor, irony, and sarcasm, this narrative examines how advanced computational techniques reveal the subtleties of psychological expression. Furthermore, we navigate the critical domains of psychometric analysis, identifying distress signals in textual data, uncovering learning disabilities, and navigating the ethical considerations of digital content moderation. This comprehensive exploration not only clarifies the sophisticated mechanisms behind affective NLP but also underscores its transformative potential in enhancing our understanding of the intricate dynamics of human communication and psychological well-being.

7.1 Sentiment Analysis: *Dissecting Text for Opinion Mining*

Sentiment analysis, also known as opinion mining, is the process of discerning and quantifying the emotional tone and polarity conveyed within a piece of text. Rather than merely categorizing text as positive, negative, or neutral, sentiment analysis now extends to identifying complex emotional states and nuances, offering a richer understanding of textual sentiment. The foundation of sentiment analysis lies in the amalgamation of NLP techniques and machine learning models. These algorithms act as linguistic detectives, scrutinizing linguistic cues such as word choice, sentence structure, and contextual information to classify the text's sentiment. Consider a customer review as a typical use case. In a positive sentiment

Language Intelligence: Expanding Frontiers in Natural Language Processing, First Edition. Akshi Kumar.
© 2025 The Institute of Electrical and Electronics Engineers, Inc. Published 2025 by John Wiley & Sons, Inc.

Figure 7.1 Example of Sentiment Analysis.

review, the text might exclaim, *"This product is amazing! I love the features, and it exceeded my expectations."* Conversely, in a negative sentiment review, the tone could be drastically different: *"This product is terrible. It's poorly designed, and it didn't work at all."* Sentiment analysis algorithms meticulously analyze the words employed, the structure of sentences, and the overarching context to accurately categorize these sentences as positive and negative, respectively (Fig. 7.1).

The sentiment analysis process is a structured workflow designed to systematically analyze and interpret sentiments expressed in text data. It begins with data collection, where textual information is gathered from various sources, such as social media, reviews, or news articles. Once collected, the data undergoes a preprocessing phase, which includes tasks like text cleaning, tokenization, and removing stop words to prepare the text for analysis. The next crucial step involves sentiment lexicons, dictionaries, or machine learning models. In the lexicon-based approach, each word in the text is assigned a sentiment score based on pre-defined sentiment dictionaries. These scores are aggregated to compute an overall sentiment for the document. Alternatively, machine learning models can be employed, where algorithms are trained on labelled data to predict sentiment labels (positive, negative, or neutral) for text segments.

Fig. 7.2 depicts a classification hierarchy for sentiment analysis methods, breaking them down into Lexicon-Based, Machine Learning, Hybrid, and Other Approaches, each with various specific techniques such as Naïve Bayes, Neural Networks, and LSTM.

When exploring the domain of sentiment analysis, it's crucial to understand the range of techniques available for effectively processing and analyzing subjective information. Each technique offers a unique approach to interpreting the sentiments embedded within text data. To aid in the comprehension of these diverse methodologies, Table 7.1. shows the categories of sentiment analysis techniques, outlines the specific methods within each category, and provides a concise description of each method's core characteristics.

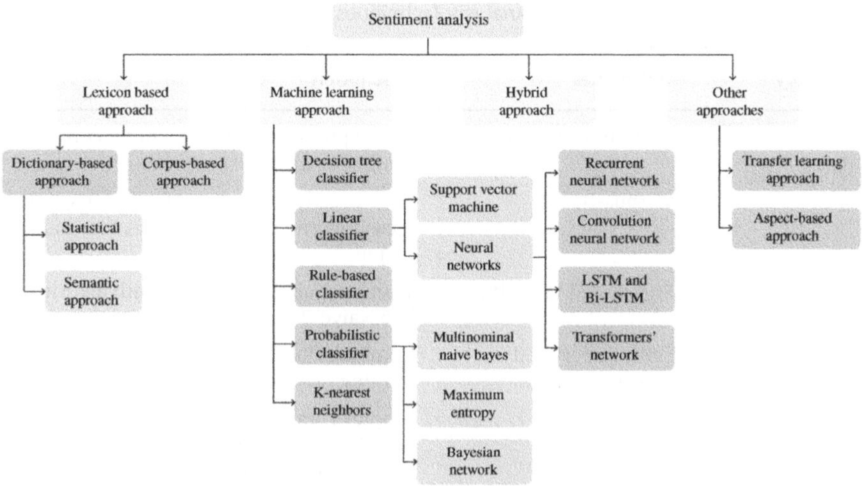

Figure 7.2 Overview of Sentiment Analysis Techniques.

7.1.1 Modern Tools and Techniques

In the realm of sentiment analysis, the recent advances in NLP have ushered in an era of unprecedented sophistication and accuracy. This section explores the cutting-edge tools and techniques that have transformed sentiment analysis into a nuanced and versatile discipline.

- *Transformers and Pre-trained Models:* The advent of transformer-based models, such as BERT (Bidirectional Encoder Representations from Transformers) and GPT-3 (Generative Pre-trained Transformer 3), has revolutionized sentiment analysis. These models, pre-trained on massive amounts of text data, exhibit a profound understanding of context and semantics, allowing them to capture subtle sentiment nuances.
- *Fine-tuning:* Researchers and practitioners fine-tune pre-trained models like BERT for specific sentiment analysis tasks. This transfer learning approach significantly enhances model performance on sentiment analysis tasks in diverse domains.
- *Aspect-based Sentiment Analysis:* Traditional sentiment analysis primarily focuses on overall sentiment. However, the latest techniques explore aspect-based sentiment analysis, where sentiment is evaluated concerning specific aspects or features within a text. This level of granularity offers valuable insights, particularly in product reviews or user feedback analysis.
- *Multimodal Analysis:* Combining textual analysis with other modalities like audio and visual cues has become increasingly prevalent. Multimodal sentiment

Table 7.1 Overview of Sentiment Analysis Techniques and Their Description.

Category	Techniques	Description
Lexicon-Based	Dictionary-Based	Uses a pre-defined list of words with sentiment scores.
	Corpus-Based	Derives sentiment scores from statistical measures and word co-occurrences in a corpus.
Machine Learning	Supervised Learning	Trains on labelled datasets with algorithms like Naive Bayes, SVM, etc.
	Semi-Supervised Learning	Combines labelled and unlabelled data for training.
	Deep Learning	Employs neural networks (CNNs, RNNs, LSTMs, Transformers) to capture deeper language structures.
Rule-Based	Manual or Automated Rules	Uses a set of predetermined rules to identify sentiment.
Hybrid Approaches	Combination	Integrates lexicon-based and machine learning methods for better performance.
Aspect-Based	Aspect-Level Analysis	Determines sentiment toward specific aspects of a product or service.
Transfer Learning	Pre-Trained Models (BERT, GPT, etc.)	Adapts models pre-trained on large datasets for sentiment analysis tasks.
	Feature Extraction	
	Bag of Words (BoW)	Represents text as an unordered collection of words.
	TF-IDF	Weighs word frequency against its document frequency.
	Word Embeddings (Word2Vec, GloVe)	Provides a dense, meaningful representation of words.
	Sentence Embeddings (BERT, GPT)	Offers context-aware representation of sentences.

analysis provides a holistic understanding of sentiment by considering tone of voice, facial expressions, and textual content.

- *Transfer Learning and Zero-Shot Learning:* Sentiment analysis models now leverage transfer learning to adapt to various domains. Zero-shot learning techniques enable models to classify sentiments for classes that were not seen during training, enhancing adaptability and generalization.

In the rapidly growing field of sentiment analysis, several commercial tools and platforms have emerged to provide businesses and organizations with powerful sentiment analysis capabilities. Tools like IBM Watson Natural Language Understanding, Microsoft Azure Text Analytics, and Amazon Comprehend offer sentiment analysis as part of their broader natural language processing (NLP) services. These platforms leverage machine learning algorithms and pre-trained models to accurately detect sentiment in text data, enabling businesses to gain insights into customer feedback, social media chatter, and product reviews. They often provide sentiment scoring, sentiment classification, and entity recognition features, allowing users to not only gauge sentiment but also identify specific aspects or entities driving sentiment. These tools are user-friendly, scalable, and integrate seamlessly with other data analysis and visualization tools, making them valuable assets for businesses seeking to understand and respond to customer sentiments effectively.

7.1.2 Applications of Advanced Sentiment Analysis

The applications of advanced sentiment analysis are as diverse as they are impactful, extending across various industries and domains. These applications underscore the versatility and significance of advanced sentiment analysis across a multitude of industries. By harnessing the power of sentiment analysis, businesses and organizations can gain deeper insights into customer sentiment, market trends, and public opinion, thereby making more informed decisions and staying responsive to evolving demands and expectations.

- ***Financial Markets:*** *Industry: Finance*
  a) *Challenge:* Financial institutions operate in a complex and ever-changing market environment where sentiment can significantly impact investment decisions. They require accurate insights into market sentiment to manage portfolios effectively and make informed investment choices.
  b) *Solution:* Advanced sentiment analysis is leveraged to gauge market sentiment by analyzing diverse data sources, including news articles, social media chatter, and expert opinions. Sophisticated sentiment analysis models and algorithms process this data to identify trends and shifts in market sentiment. Financial institutions use these insights to make more informed investment decisions, anticipate market movements, and mitigate risks. Real-time monitoring of social media and news allows for proactive adjustments to investment strategies.
  c) *Impact:* This application enables financial institutions to gain a competitive edge by leveraging sentiment analysis to respond swiftly to market changes and capitalize on opportunities. It provides a data-driven foundation for investment decisions, portfolio management, and risk mitigation.

- ***Healthcare:*** *Industry: Healthcare*
  a) *Challenge:* Healthcare providers aim to offer patient-centric care and continuously improve patient satisfaction. They require a systematic approach to analyze patient feedback and reviews to identify areas for enhancement.
  b) *Solution:* Sentiment analysis is employed to analyze patient feedback and online reviews. By applying advanced sentiment analysis techniques to textual data, healthcare providers gain valuable insights into patient sentiments. These insights enable providers to assess patient satisfaction levels, pinpoint specific areas where improvements are needed, and enhance the overall quality of care. Sentiment analysis also helps in identifying common issues and trends across patient feedback.
  c) *Impact:* The use of sentiment analysis in healthcare contributes to an improved patient experience, increased patient loyalty, and enhanced healthcare services. Healthcare providers can address concerns promptly, allocate resources more efficiently, and maintain a positive reputation within the healthcare sector.
- ***Entertainment:*** *Industry: Media and Entertainment*
  a) *Challenge:* In the competitive entertainment industry, engaging audiences effectively is essential. Content creators and distributors need to understand audience preferences to tailor their content and recommendations accordingly.
  b) *Solution:* Sentiment analysis is employed to gauge audience reactions to movies, TV shows, and music. By analyzing social media chatter, reviews, and audience comments, entertainment companies gain insights into audience sentiments. These insights inform content recommendations, content creation strategies, and marketing efforts. For example, if an audience overwhelmingly expresses excitement for a particular genre, entertainment platforms can prioritize content in that category.
  c) *Impact:* Sentiment analysis enhances audience engagement, content personalization, and audience satisfaction. It allows the entertainment industry to respond swiftly to changing audience preferences and deliver content that resonates with viewers.
- ***Customer Experience:*** *Industry: Various*
  a) *Challenge:* Businesses across industries must actively collect and analyze customer feedback to enhance customer satisfaction and improve their products and services. Extracting actionable insights from a large volume of customer feedback can be challenging.
  b) *Solution:* Advanced sentiment analysis is employed to gain a deeper understanding of customer opinions. By applying sentiment analysis to customer feedback and reviews, companies can categorize sentiments and identify specific aspects or issues that customers appreciate or find problematic. These

insights empower companies to make data-driven improvements, prioritize product enhancements, and refine customer interactions.

c) *Impact:* This application of sentiment analysis strengthens customer relationships, fosters customer loyalty, and drives business growth. Companies can respond effectively to customer needs, address concerns promptly, and align their products and services with customer expectations.

- ***Social Media Monitoring:*** *Industry: Marketing, Brand Management*
  a) *Challenge:* Brands and organizations must actively monitor their online presence and reputation across social media platforms. Social media provides a platform for customers to express opinions and share experiences, making real-time monitoring crucial.
  b) *Solution:* Brands and organizations employ advanced sentiment analysis tools to track brand sentiment across social media channels. These tools analyze social media posts, comments, and mentions to assess brand sentiment and identify emerging trends. By monitoring social media sentiment in real time, companies can promptly respond to customer feedback, manage their brand's online reputation, and engage effectively with their audience.
  c) *Impact:* Social media monitoring through sentiment analysis enables proactive reputation management, crisis mitigation, and responsive engagement with customers. It helps companies maintain a positive online presence, build brand loyalty, and drive customer satisfaction.

These applications highlight the versatility and significance of advanced sentiment analysis in diverse industries, enabling organizations to harness the power of data-driven decision-making and stay responsive to evolving market dynamics and customer preferences.

7.1.3 Datasets for NLP-Based Sentiment Analysis

Having access to high-quality datasets is essential for training and evaluating sentiment analysis models. Here are some popular datasets commonly used for sentiment analysis tasks:

- **IMDb Movie Reviews Dataset:**
  a) **Description:** This dataset contains movie reviews from the Internet Movie Database (IMDb). Reviews are labelled as positive or negative based on the sentiment expressed.
  b) **Source:** http://ai.stanford.edu/~amaas/data/sentiment/
- **Amazon Product Reviews Dataset:**
  a) **Description:** Amazon provides datasets of product reviews in various categories, including electronics, books, and more. Reviews are labelled with star ratings and can be used for sentiment analysis.
  b) **Source:** https://registry.opendata.aws/amazon-reviews/

- **Twitter Sentiment Analysis Dataset:**
  a) **Description:** Twitter datasets consist of tweets along with sentiment labels (positive, negative, neutral). Researchers often collect and annotate tweets for sentiment analysis studies.
  b) **Source:** You can collect Twitter data using the Twitter API or find pre-annotated datasets on platforms like Kaggle.
- **Yelp Review Dataset:**
  a) **Description:** Yelp provides a dataset of user reviews and ratings for businesses. The dataset includes text reviews and star ratings, making it suitable for sentiment analysis.
  b) **Source:** https://www.yelp.com/dataset
- **MovieLens User Ratings Dataset:**
  a) **Description:** The MovieLens dataset contains user ratings and reviews of movies. While it primarily serves movie recommendation purposes, the text reviews can be used for sentiment analysis.
  b) **Source:** https://grouplens.org/datasets/movielens/
- **SST-2 (Stanford Sentiment Treebank):**
  a) **Description:** SST-2 is a widely used benchmark dataset for binary sentiment classification. It contains sentences from movie reviews labeled as positive or negative.
  b) **Source:** https://nlp.stanford.edu/sentiment/
- **Financial News Sentiment Analysis Dataset:**
  a) **Description:** This dataset consists of financial news articles labeled with sentiment scores related to the stock market's impact. It's suitable for sentiment analysis in the finance domain.
  b) **Source:** https://www.kaggle.com/ankurzing/sentiment-analysis-for-financial-news
- **Multi-Domain Sentiment Dataset (Multi-Domain Sentiment Dataset II):**
  a) **Description:** This dataset covers multiple domains, including electronics, books, DVDs, and kitchen appliances. It is designed for domain adaptation in sentiment analysis.
  b) **Source:** https://www.cs.jhu.edu/~mdredze/datasets/sentiment/

When working with sentiment analysis datasets, it's crucial to preprocess the text data, perform feature engineering, and choose an appropriate machine learning or deep learning model based on your specific task and dataset characteristics. Additionally, consider the data's licensing terms and ethical considerations when using it for research or applications.

7.1.4 Challenges and Innovations in Sentiment Analysis

In the ever-evolving landscape of sentiment analysis, persistent challenges and ongoing research efforts shape its trajectory. Despite remarkable progress, several enduring challenges persist, casting a spotlight on the need for continuous innovation:

- *Contextual Understanding:* Grasping the full context remains a paramount challenge in sentiment analysis. The interpretation of phrases like "not bad" hinges on the surrounding context, demanding a profound understanding to determine whether they convey a positive or negative sentiment accurately.
- *Handling Sarcasm and Irony:* Detecting sarcasm and irony within text remains an intricate puzzle. While transformer models have contributed to improved performance, this challenge endures due to the subtleties and nuances inherent in these forms of expression.
- *Multilingual Analysis:* As sentiment analysis transcends geographical boundaries, the management of multiple languages introduces complexities tied to linguistic nuances and cultural differences. Tools must adeptly recognize sentiment nuances across diverse languages to ensure accurate analysis on a global scale.
- *Data Privacy and Ethics:* Responsible utilization of sentiment analysis, especially concerning user data privacy and potential biases in analysis, stands as a prominent concern. The establishment of ethical guidelines and safeguards is essential to address these sensitive issues.

In parallel, the future of sentiment analysis brims with promise, driven by ongoing research and emerging trends that seek to overcome these challenges and expand the capabilities of sentiment analysis:

- *Context-aware Models:* Researchers are actively pioneering context-aware sentiment analysis models that integrate broader contextual information. This advancement enhances the accuracy of sentiment analysis, enabling a more profound understanding of complex sentences and the nuances of sarcasm.
- *Cross-lingual Models:* The development of cross-lingual sentiment analysis models aims to dismantle language barriers, facilitating precise sentiment analysis across multiple languages. This cross-cultural perspective enhances the global applicability of sentiment analysis.
- *Emotion Recognition Integration:* The integration of emotion recognition techniques with sentiment analysis is gaining momentum. This synergistic approach provides a deeper understanding of the emotional states conveyed in text, enriching the insights derived from sentiment analysis.

- *Explainable AI:* Efforts are underway to make sentiment analysis models more transparent and interpretable. The pursuit of explainable AI ensures that sentiment analysis models elucidate their decision-making processes, fostering trust and accountability in their application.

Sentiment analysis, driven by the latest tools and techniques, stands as a pivotal domain within NLP, enabling a nuanced understanding of textual sentiments. Its applications span various industries, from finance and healthcare to entertainment and customer service. While challenges persist, ongoing research and advancements promise to make sentiment analysis even more accurate, adaptable, and responsible in the future, revolutionizing our capacity to glean insights from textual data and facilitating more informed decision-making across sectors.

7.2 Emotion Recognition: *Beyond Polarity*

Emotion recognition in text represents a deeper and more nuanced level of affective computing. It goes beyond merely categorizing text as positive, negative, or neutral, aiming to identify the specific emotions conveyed by the author. This endeavor is vital in fields like mental health, customer service, and social media analysis, where understanding the underlying emotional state of individuals can unlock valuable insights.

Emotions, the intricate and multifaceted facets of human existence, introduce a captivating layer of complexity to the realm of NLP. Unlike sentiment analysis, which places text into broad sentiment categories, emotion recognition seeks to unveil a spectrum of emotions, including joy, anger, sadness, fear, surprise, and more. To accomplish this, emotion recognition models draw upon a fusion of NLP techniques and machine learning algorithms. They take into account a multitude of factors, including word choice, sentence structure, and contextual cues, all in pursuit of making precise determinations about the emotional state of the author. Consider the following text: *"I am ecstatic about the news! I can't contain my excitement!"* In this instance, an emotion recognition model would discern the emotion as "ecstasy" by analyzing the words chosen and the intensity of the expressed emotion.

7.2.1 Emotion Recognition versus Sentiment Analysis

To grasp the complexity of emotion in NLP, it's crucial to differentiate between emotion recognition and sentiment analysis. As discussed in the previous section, Sentiment analysis is a fundamental component of affective computing, and focuses on the classification of text into broad sentiment categories. This classification typically includes determining whether a piece of text expresses a positive, negative, or neutral sentiment. Sentiment analysis plays a vital role in various applications, from gauging customer satisfaction and tracking brand sentiment to analyzing public sentiment during elections or assessing the overall sentiment of product reviews. Consider the following example:

Example 7.1 ***Review for a Restaurant***
"The food at this restaurant is fantastic, and the service is impeccable!"

In sentiment analysis, this review would be categorized as "positive" due to the use of positive descriptors like "fantastic" and "impeccable." While sentiment analysis is invaluable for obtaining a general sense of public sentiment or customer feedback, it operates at a surface level, not delving into the specific emotions underlying the text.

Emotion recognition, on the other hand, seeks to unravel the intricate spectrum of emotions conveyed within text. Rather than limiting the analysis to broad sentiment categories, it aspires to identify specific emotions that individuals express, which can range from basic emotions like happiness and anger to more complex and nuanced emotional states. To achieve this, emotion recognition models navigate a complex interplay of linguistic cues, contextual information, and cultural nuances. Let's explore an example:

Example 7.2 ***Social Media Post***
"I just received some unexpected, good news, and I'm over the moon!"

In emotion recognition, this text would be analyzed to discern the specific emotion of "ecstasy" or "elation" due to the intensity of the expressed emotion and the use of phrases like "over the moon." This granular analysis goes beyond sentiment analysis by pinpointing the exact emotional state of the author, offering a deeper understanding of the affective content within the text.

7.2.2 Complexity of Emotion Recognition

Emotion recognition in text introduces a layer of complexity that extends beyond the capabilities of sentiment analysis. This nuanced approach adds layers of complexity as it requires models to decode the intricate interplay of words, sentence structures, and contextual cues to pinpoint the underlying emotional states. This complexity arises from several key factors:

- *Nuanced Emotional States:* Human emotions are not confined to simple positive or negative categories. Emotions encompass a vast and intricate spectrum, including not only basic emotions but also a myriad of nuanced emotional states. Recognizing and categorizing these nuanced emotions require a more sophisticated approach. Consider the following example:

Example 7.3 ***Text Message Conversation***
Person A: *"I'm feeling a bit under the weather."*
Person B: *"I'm so sorry to hear that. Is there anything I can do to help?"*

In this exchange, emotion recognition would go beyond a simple positive or negative sentiment assessment. It would discern that Person A is expressing a state of "*discomfort*" or "*sickness,*" and Person B is conveying "*empathy*" or "*concern.*" Recognizing these nuanced emotional states adds depth to the analysis and enhances the understanding of the emotional dynamics within the conversation.

- *Contextual Dependency:* Emotions are highly context-dependent. The same text can convey different emotions based on the surrounding context. For example, the phrase "I can't believe this happened" can express joy in a positive context or disbelief in a negative one. Understanding these contextual nuances is a daunting task for emotion recognition models.

Example 7.4 ***Social Media Comment***
"I can't believe they won the championship!"

In this instance, the emotional context is crucial for accurate recognition. If this comment appears in the context of a fan celebrating their favorite team's victory, it conveys "joy" and "excitement." However, if it surfaces in the context of a rival team's supporter expressing disbelief at their victory, it reflects "disappointment" or "shock." Deciphering these contextual nuances is a complex task that emotion recognition models must grapple with.

- *Cultural and Linguistic Variations:* Cultural and linguistic variations introduce yet another layer of complexity in emotion recognition. Different cultures and languages have unique ways of expressing emotions, which may not directly align with one another. Idiomatic expressions, cultural norms, and emotions that lack direct translations in other languages further compound this challenge. Here's an example that highlights these variations:

Example 7.5 ***Hindi Cultural Expression***
"अतिथि देवो भव:" (Atithi Devo Bhava)

This Hindi phrase translates to *"The guest is God"* and reflects the cultural value of treating guests with utmost respect and hospitality. Emotion recognition models need to understand the emotional connotations embedded in such cultural expressions to accurately recognize emotions in texts from Hindi-speaking communities. In this context, the emotion of "hospitality" or "respect" is implicit within the phrase and may not have a direct translation in other languages, illustrating the challenges of accounting for cultural and linguistic variations in emotion recognition.

- *Subjectivity and Individual Differences:* Emotions are inherently subjective and can vary greatly among individuals. Personal experiences, beliefs, and cultural backgrounds significantly influence how people interpret and express emotions. What one person perceives as "excitement," another may interpret as "anxiety" or "nervousness." This subjectivity adds another layer of complexity, making it challenging to develop one-size-fits-all emotion recognition models. An example illustrates this point:

Example 7.6 ***Response to a Surprise Party***
Person A: *"I can't believe you all did this! I'm overwhelmed with joy!"*
Person B: *"I can't believe you all did this! I'm overwhelmed with anxiety!"*

In this scenario, the same surprise party elicits entirely different emotional responses from Person A and Person B. While Person A experiences *"joy,"* Person B feels *"anxiety."* Recognizing and respecting these individual differences in emotional interpretation is a critical consideration in the development of emotion recognition models.

In essence, emotion recognition ventures into the intricate terrain of human emotions, offering a deeper understanding of the affective content in text. While sentiment analysis serves as a valuable tool for gauging general sentiment, emotion recognition aims to uncover the complex and diverse emotional landscape that underlies human communication, making it a vital component in the evolving field of affective computing within NLP.

Table 7.2 offers an at-a-glance understanding of the breadth of emotion recognition techniques, which are more diverse due to the need to process different types of data, such as facial expressions, voice intonations, textual content, and physiological signals. Each technique's description gives insight into how these approaches are used to capture the complexity of human emotions.

7.2.3 Applications of Emotion Recognition

Emotion recognition in text serves as a powerful tool with a diverse range of applications, each harnessing its unique ability to unravel the intricate nuances of emotional expression within written communication:

Table 7.2 Summary of Emotion Recognition Techniques and Their Descriptions.

Category	Techniques	Description
Facial Expression Analysis	Feature-based Methods	Extracts facial features and analyzes them to determine emotions.
	Deep Learning (CNNs, RNNs)	Uses neural networks to process raw image data of facial expressions to classify emotions.
Voice Analysis	Prosodic Features Extraction	Analyzes vocal features such as pitch, tone, and speed to identify emotions.
	Speech Recognition	Converts spoken language into text and uses language models to determine emotion.
Text Analysis	Rule-Based NLP	Uses a set of rules to detect emotion based on word choice and sentence structure.
	Machine Learning (SVM, Random Forests)	Trains on labelled datasets to classify text into different emotions.
	Deep Learning (LSTMs, Transformers)	Uses advanced neural network architectures to capture emotional context within text.
Physiological Signals Analysis	Feature Extraction	Gathers and processes physiological signals like heart rate and skin conductance to identify emotions.
	Machine Learning Classifiers	Utilizes classifiers to interpret the extracted features from physiological data.
Multimodal Emotion Recognition	Data Fusion	Integrates data from facial, vocal, textual, and physiological sources to improve accuracy in emotion recognition.
	Deep Multimodal Learning	Uses deep learning techniques to combine and analyze data from multiple modalities.

- *Mental Health:* Within the realm of mental health, emotion recognition takes on a pivotal role. It enables mental health professionals to assess an individual's emotional state based solely on their written communication. This transformative technology empowers therapists and counsellors to provide support that is not only more targeted but also profoundly empathetic, ultimately fostering a more compassionate approach to mental healthcare.

Example: A mental health chatbot equipped with emotion recognition can detect signs of emotional distress in a user's text messages and offer immediate support and resources.

- *Customer Service:* Within customer service interactions, discerning the emotional state of customers is paramount. Emotion recognition empowers customer service representatives to customize their responses, addressing the unique emotional needs of customers, and thereby enhancing the overall service experience. This personalized approach elevates the quality of customer interactions, leading to increased customer satisfaction and loyalty.
  Example: An airline's customer service team can use emotion recognition to identify frustrated customers in their written inquiries and provide extra assistance to turn their experience around.
- *Social Media Analysis:* Social media platforms, rich sources of emotional expression, greatly benefit from emotion recognition. It facilitates insights into user sentiment and emotions, enabling the identification of trending topics, monitoring user engagement, and proactively detecting potential crises. Social media managers leverage this technology to craft communication strategies that are not only effective but also adaptive, maintaining a positive online presence even amidst turbulent digital waters.
  Example: A social media management tool can use emotion recognition to assess user reactions to a brand's posts, allowing companies to fine-tune their content strategy.
- *Education:* Emotion recognition extends its influence into the realm of education, offering an invaluable tool to gauge student engagement and emotional well-being. Through the analysis of written assignments and communication, educators gain profound insights into their students' emotional states. Armed with this information, teachers can refine and customize their teaching methods, creating an educational environment that is not only conducive but inherently supportive.
  Example: An educational platform can employ emotion recognition to identify students who may be struggling emotionally and connect them with appropriate support resources.
- *Virtual Assistants:* The integration of emotion recognition into virtual assistants endows these digital entities with an unparalleled capacity to provide empathetic and supportive interactions. Virtual therapists and chatbots, fortified with emotion recognition capabilities, extend individuals a more personalized and emotionally attuned form of support.
  Example: A virtual therapist can detect signs of distress in a user's messages and provide immediate coping strategies and resources.

7.2.4 Text-only Datasets for NLP-Based Emotion Recognition

Here are some text-only datasets specifically designed for emotion recognition in NLP tasks:

- **Friends TV Show Transcripts (Emotion Recognition):**
  a) **Description:** This dataset contains transcripts from the TV show "Friends" and is labelled with emotional categories corresponding to the characters' lines in the show, making it suitable for emotion recognition tasks.
  b) **Source:** Available on various platforms, including Kaggle.
- **SemEval-2018 Task 1: Affect in Tweets:**
  a) **Description:** This dataset consists of tweets annotated with emotion labels, including anger, joy, sadness, surprise, and others. It was part of a shared task in the SemEval-2018 workshop, specifically designed for emotion recognition.
  b) **Source:** http://saifmohammad.com/WebPages/EmotionIntensity-SharedTask.html
- **EmoReact:**
  a) **Description:** EmoReact is a dataset of Facebook reactions to news articles and their associated comments, with emotions categorized into like, love, wow, haha, sad, and angry.
  b) **Source:** https://github.com/ducminhnguyen/EmoReact
- **Friends TV Show Scripts (EmoReact Extension):**
  a) **Description:** An extension of the Friends TV show dataset, this dataset is labelled with emotions specifically for use in the EmoReact project, providing a larger set of labelled textual data.
  b) **Source:** https://github.com/ducminhnguyen/EmoReact
- **DailyDialog Dataset:**
  a) **Description:** The DailyDialog dataset contains daily conversation data with emotion labels, making it suitable for emotion analysis in everyday conversations.
  b) **Source:** https://www.aclweb.org/anthology/I17–1099/

7.2.5 Challenges in Emotion Recognition and Future Directions

Emotion recognition in text, despite its tremendous potential, confronts several noteworthy challenges. These challenges encompass various dimensions:

- *Contextual Understanding:* One of the intricate challenges is grasping the emotional context of text. Emotions are often nuanced and can depend on subtle cues, context, and cultural differences. A phrase that conveys one emotion in a particular context may have an entirely different emotional interpretation in another setting.

- *Multimodal Data:* The integration of text with other modalities such as audio and video can enhance the accuracy of emotion recognition by considering additional sensory information. However, this approach introduces additional layers of complexity in data processing and model integration, requiring advanced techniques for multimodal analysis.
- *Subjectivity:* Emotions are inherently subjective, and individuals may express them in diverse and idiosyncratic ways. This subjectivity poses a formidable challenge in developing universal emotion recognition models that can effectively account for the vast range of individual emotional expressions.
- *Data Privacy:* Emotion recognition often requires access to personal data, including text messages and speech recordings, which raises legitimate concerns about data privacy and ethics. Safeguarding the responsible and ethical use of emotion recognition technology is imperative to protect individuals' privacy and rights.

On the horizon, the future of emotion recognition in text is teeming with promise. Advancements in deep learning, coupled with the proliferation of large emotion-labelled datasets, are steadily enhancing the accuracy and robustness of emotion recognition models. Moreover, the integration of text analysis with other modalities such as speech and facial expression promises to furnish a more comprehensive understanding of human emotions, providing a more holistic view of affective computing. In the ever-evolving landscape of affective computing, emotion recognition is poised to become an increasingly indispensable tool for deciphering the intricate tapestry of human feelings expressed in text. These advancements are set to not only address the existing challenges but also open new avenues for applications that benefit from a deeper understanding of human emotions in natural language text.

7.3 Irony and Sarcasm Detection: *Between the Lines*

In the rich tapestry of human communication, irony and sarcasm stand out as complex linguistic phenomena that often serve as a stress test for the capabilities of NLP systems within the realm of affective computing. Unlike straightforward emotional expressions, irony and sarcasm involve a sophisticated interplay of context, tone, shared knowledge, and often, intent to convey the opposite of what is being explicitly stated. When a person says, "*What a beautiful day!*" in the middle of a hurricane, they are clearly not referring to the weather's beauty but rather commenting sarcastically on the situation. Detecting such nuances in written text presents NLP with a set of challenges that push the boundaries of affective computing.

Before diving into the complexities of detecting irony and sarcasm in text, it is essential to understand their definitions and the theoretical frameworks that underlie their study. Irony, at its core, is a figure of speech where the intended meaning is opposite to the literal meaning. Sarcasm, often considered a form of irony, is characterized by sharp, bitter, or cutting expressions or remarks; it is irony designed to convey contempt or ridicule.

Linguistically, both irony and sarcasm are often studied under the umbrella of pragmatics—the branch of linguistics concerned with language use in context and the ways in which context contributes to meaning. Pragmatics is essential for understanding how the same sequence of words can convey different meanings based on the speaker's intentions and the listener's perceptions.

The linguistic features that signal irony or sarcasm can be subtle and diverse. They can include hyperbolic language, where an exaggerated term is used to imply the opposite sentiment, or understatement, where a phrase is deliberately downplayed to indicate a larger significance. Other features might include jarring juxtaposition, contradictory statements, or a marked incongruity between the context and the literal meaning of the words. These linguistic cues require careful analysis since the same phrase might be genuine in one context and ironic in another. Therefore, computational models must be sensitive to a wide array of linguistic signals and the contexts in which they are used to accurately detect irony and sarcasm.

7.3.1 Challenges in NLP for Irony and Sarcasm Detection

The detection and interpretation of irony and sarcasm in text bring several challenges to the forefront of NLP:

- *Lack of Prosodic and Non-verbal Cues:* In spoken language, intonation, pauses, and stress on certain words can signal irony or sarcasm. In written text, these prosodic cues are absent, making it harder for NLP systems to discern the intended tonality.
  Example: "*You're standing on my foot,*" said without emphasis might be a simple statement. In contrast, "*You're standing on my foot,*" said with heavy stress on "*my,*" could indicate irritation and be construed as sarcastic in spoken language. An NLP system might struggle to infer sarcasm from "*You're standing on my foot*" without these prosodic cues.
- *Contextual Dependency:* The meaning of sarcastic or ironic remarks often depends on the context—both immediate and broader situational context—that may not be captured in the text.
  Example: "*What a fantastic way to ruin my day!*" can be a sincere statement if found in a review for a bad movie. However, if this line follows a text describing

an unforeseen pleasant event, it would be sarcastic. NLP systems need to analyze not just the statement but also the preceding text to catch the sarcasm.

- *Common Knowledge and Cultural References:* Irony and sarcasm frequently rely on the assumption of shared knowledge or cultural references, which an NLP system might not be privy to.
  Example: *"Great, another 'wonderful' episode of that show tonight."* This might be sarcastic if there is a widely known opinion that the show is terrible. An NLP system must have access to such cultural sentiments to interpret the sarcasm correctly.
- *Polysemy and Ambiguity:* Words with multiple meanings or ambiguous constructs can be deliberately used to create ironic or sarcastic statements, further complicating detection.
  Example: The word *"cool"* can mean either positive ("fashionably attractive or impressive") or literally low in temperature. So, *"I love how the weather is cool in the summer here,"* could be sarcastic in a place known for its scorching summers. Detecting sarcasm here involves recognizing the ambiguity and polysemy in the word "cool."
- *Variability of Expression:* People express sarcasm and irony in various ways, some being more subtle than others. This variability can confuse algorithms that look for specific patterns.
  Example: One person might express sarcasm very overtly, like *"Oh, brilliant, it's raining again,"* while another might be subtler, saying, *"Just what I needed, a bit of water with my coffee,"* when caught in the rain. NLP systems need to learn the vast spectrum of sarcasm expressions, which requires extensive and varied training data.

In tackling the complexities of detecting irony and sarcasm in text, researchers have carved out a range of computational strategies. Fig. 7.3 outlines the computational approaches for detecting sarcasm and irony, highlighting key strategies such as analyzing linguistic and contextual cues, sentiment incongruity, pragmatic analysis, and the fine-tuning of pre-trained models for domain-specific data.

One foundational method involves examining lexical and syntactic cues, searching for specific words, phrases, or sentence structures commonly associated with ironic or sarcastic tones. A contrasting approach focuses on sentiment incongruity, looking for mismatches between the expressed sentiment and the context it appears in, which often flags the use of irony or sarcasm.

Machine learning, particularly through deep learning paradigms, has become a cornerstone in this domain. These models are trained on vast corpora of text that have been meticulously annotated for irony and sarcasm, enabling them to discern intricate patterns that may indicate such tones. The leap forward with techniques

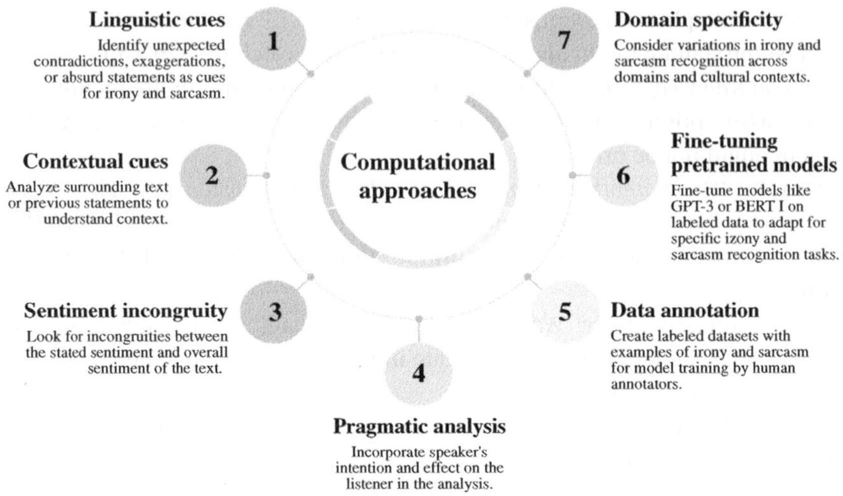

Figure 7.3 Computational Approaches for Sarcasm and Irony Detection.

like BERT and GPT offers even greater promise, as these models generate contextual embeddings that can grasp the nuances of language on a more profound level, thus enhancing the accuracy of irony and sarcasm detection.

Additionally, incorporating insights from pragmatics and discourse analysis allows for a more holistic view, taking into account the flow of conversation and the relationships between speakers. This knowledge is crucial, as it helps systems to better interpret the subtleties inherent in human communication, especially when it comes to the nuanced realm of ironic and sarcastic expressions.

7.3.2 Datasets for NLP-Based Irony and Sarcasm Detection

Several datasets have been compiled to aid in the development and testing of NLP systems, particularly for tasks like irony and sarcasm detection. These datasets often consist of text from social media platforms, forums, and other online sources where such tones are frequently used. Here are examples of publicly available datasets for irony and sarcasm:

- *SemEval Datasets:*
  a) **SemEval-2018 Task 3:** A dataset provided for "Irony detection in English tweets." It includes a collection of tweets specifically annotated for the presence of irony.
  b) **SemEval-2019 Task 5:** Multilingual detection of hate speech against immigrants and women on Twitter (HatEval), which contains instances where sarcasm and irony are used.

- *Reddit Sarcasm Dataset:*
  A dataset compiled from Reddit comments, specifically annotated for sarcasm. The platform's/**s** tag, used by authors to indicate sarcasm, has been especially useful for creating this dataset.
- *The Sarcasm Corpus V2 (SARC):*
  A large-scale self-annotated corpus for sarcasm, sourced from Reddit. This dataset is notable for its size and for containing both sarcastic and non-sarcastic responses in the same threads, allowing for context analysis.
- *FigLang2020 Shared Task on Figurative Language:*
  A shared task that includes a sarcasm detection dataset with annotated tweets. The task was designed to identify various forms of figurative language, including sarcasm.
- *Twitter Irony Corpus (TWITTER-IRONIC):*
  A dataset consisting of ironic and non-ironic tweets manually annotated by experts. It focuses on capturing different types of irony, including situational irony and sarcasm.
- *IAC (Internet Argument Corpus):*
  While not solely focused on sarcasm, this dataset includes argumentative posts from online forums, with some annotated for sarcasm. This allows the study of sarcasm in the context of online debates and arguments.
- *IronyDB:*
  A multilingual irony detection dataset with sentences labelled for irony, collected from various sources like Twitter and review websites.
- *SarCasm ANnotated Corpus (SARCASM-V2):*
  Another dataset originating from Twitter, providing instances of tweets where sarcasm is present, along with context and user interaction data.

These datasets have been instrumental in the development of NLP models capable of detecting irony and sarcasm. They provide a variety of linguistic expressions, contexts, and uses of language, which are critical for training robust algorithms. The continual creation and refinement of such datasets are vital as language evolves and new forms of expression emerge.

Irony and sarcasm detection is a dynamic field that sits at the crossroads of computational linguistics, machine learning, and cognitive psychology. It challenges us to build models that understand not just the literal meaning of words but also the subtleties of human communication. As the field progresses, it holds the potential to enrich human-computer interaction and open up new avenues for understanding the complexity of human language. Beyond the technical aspects, the detection of irony and sarcasm in text also brings ethical and cultural considerations to light. Sarcasm detection algorithms, for example, could be used in moderating online content, but they must be applied with care to avoid misinterpreting or censoring legitimate communication. Cultural sensitivity is also vital, as what may be considered sarcastic in one culture might be interpreted differently in another.

7.4 Humor Identification in Text: *Tapping into Textual Tickle*

The quest to decode humor through text within the field of NLP is a pursuit that treads the fine line between computational linguistics and the intrinsic subtlety of human mirth. Unlike other affective computing tasks, humor identification isn't just about discerning an emotional state; it requires the algorithm to grasp the essence of wit, satire, and the social context that makes a statement humorous.

Humor in text is a multifaceted phenomenon—it is deeply rooted in cultural semantics, reliant on linguistic creativity, and often hinges on the unexpected deviation from a logical discourse. Identifying humor involves not only detecting the presence of jokes, wordplay, or comical anecdotes but also understanding the situational irony, subtle cues, and the timing inherent in the text that's intended to amuse.

7.4.1 Computational Linguistics of Humor

Computational approaches to humor identification often need to tackle a series of linguistic gymnastics. One of the primary tasks is to decipher wordplay, such as puns, which hinge on the multiple meanings of words or similar-sounding words with different meanings. Another is recognizing hyperboles, where exaggeration is used for comic effect. Table 7.3 encapsulates the various computational techniques used in humor identification, offering a snapshot of their methodologies and where they can be practically applied. Each technique provides a unique approach to unravelling the complexities of humor within text.

7.4.2 Applications of Humor Identification

Humor plays a pivotal role in human interactions, transcending mere entertainment to affect how information is communicated, perceived, and remembered. In the digital age, humor identification through affective computing has burgeoned into an area with far-reaching applications. By leveraging NLP and machine learning, systems can now detect and generate humor, enriching user experience, enhancing content, and facilitating more natural social interactions.

Table 7.3 Overview of Computational Linguistics Techniques for Humor Identification.

Technique	Description	Example Applications
Rule-Based Methods	Utilize predefined patterns to detect common joke structures like setups and punchlines or specific stylistic features of humor.	Identifying joke formats in text, enhancing chatbots with humor detection
Statistical Models	Apply machine learning to discover humor patterns within large text corpora, learning from examples rather than explicit rules.	Content filtering, sentiment analysis in social media
Semantic Analysis	Focus on detecting semantic incongruities where the literal meaning is nonsensical or absurd, indicating humor.	Enhancing natural language understanding systems
Template Recognition	Look for well-known humor schemas or formats, making it easier to spot conventional types of jokes.	Curation of themed joke collections, automated joke generation

- *Entertainment and Media:* One of the most obvious applications is in entertainment and media. Comedy shows, humorous articles, and funny podcasts often use algorithms to gauge audience preferences and tailor content accordingly. An example is the recommendation algorithms of streaming services like Netflix, which analyze user reactions to comedic content to suggest new titles.
- *Social Media and Advertising:* In social media, humor is a currency of engagement. Platforms like Twitter and Facebook employ humor identification to highlight trending memes or funny posts, enhancing user engagement. Advertisers, too, use these insights to craft campaigns that are likely to resonate and spread organically. For instance, Wendy's use of humorous clapbacks on Twitter has become part of their brand identity, endearing them to younger demographics.
- *Customer Service and Chatbots:* In customer service, chatbots equipped with humor identification capabilities can provide a more engaging experience. When a chatbot recognizes a joke from a customer, responding with humor can defuse tension and build rapport. For example, Amtrak's virtual assistant, Julie, incorporates a level of humor to make interactions feel more personal and less mechanical.
- *Education and Learning:* Humor is also a potent tool in education. E-learning platforms use humor identification to create enjoyable learning experiences. Duolingo, a language learning app, occasionally includes humorous sentences in its exercises, making the learning process more entertaining and memorable.

- *Mental Health and Well-being:* Applications extend to mental health, where humor identification can help in the analysis of social media posts for signs of distress. In this context, understanding when a person uses humor to cope with stress or mask other emotions can be critical. Therapy chatbots like Woebot use conversational AI to interact with users, employing humor at appropriate times to support users' emotional well-being.
- *Workplace Communication:* In the corporate world, humor is integral to creating a pleasant work environment. Slack and other communication tools could integrate humor detection to facilitate icebreakers or lighten the mood during stressful periods, fostering a more cohesive team dynamic.
- *Cultural Exchange and Language Learning:* For language learners, understanding humor is often seen as a high level of proficiency. Platforms dedicated to language exchange can use humor identification to highlight idiomatic expressions and cultural jokes, aiding in cultural understanding and language acquisition.

7.4.3 Challenges of Humor Identification

Addressing the challenges of humor identification in text through affective computing and NLP presents a multifaceted puzzle. The very attributes that make humor a uniquely human trait—its cultural rootedness, layered meanings, and dynamic evolution—pose significant hurdles for computational systems. Here, we explore the intricacies of these challenges with examples:

- *Cultural and Contextual Relativity:*
  The nuances of humor are deeply embedded within cultural and social fabrics. A satirical comment about a political figure, for example, can be hilarious in one society but completely misunderstood or even offensive in another. Consider a British comedy show steeped in dry wit and understatements—it might not resonate with an audience accustomed to the more overt humor styles found in American sitcoms.
  NLP systems face the monumental task of not just translating language, but also crossing cultural divides. For example, "hasya kavita" (humorous poetry) is a popular form in Hindi literature that combines wit, satire, and puns, often dealing with social and political issues in a light-hearted manner. Consider a "hasya kavita" that plays on the words "चलती का नाम गाड़ी" (Chalti ka naam gaadi). Literally translated, it means "that which moves is called a vehicle." However, this phrase is often used humorously in Hindi to comment on something that barely functions but is still going—much like saying "it's held together with spit and bailing wire" in English. A non-Hindi speaking algorithm trained on English humor would miss the humor entirely, not only because it's a linguistic pun but also because it requires cultural context to understand that the humor derives

from the colloquial use of the phrase. Similarly, humor that relies on wordplay such as puns may be untranslatable across languages due to differing phonetic and lexical structures.

- *Subtlety and Complexity:*
  Humor often operates on an intricate interplay of language, requiring a deep understanding of irony, sarcasm, metaphor, and the bending of social norms. A quip such as *"I'd agree with you but then we'd both be wrong"* exemplifies humor that is not only a play on words but also a subtle social commentary.
  For an algorithm, parsing the layers within such a statement, recognizing the subtle inversion of expected agreement, and classifying it as humor is a formidable challenge. Current NLP systems might catch the contradiction in the statement but understanding that it is humorous rather than confrontational is a nuanced distinction that often eludes computational methods.
- *Evolving Nature of Humor:*
  Humor is a living, breathing aspect of human interaction that evolves with time and social change. What was funny a decade ago might now be considered inappropriate or stale. Memetic humor, which is highly prevalent on social media, morphs at internet speed, with new formats and references constantly emerging. For example, an NLP model trained on meme humor from the early 2010s might be perplexed by the absurdist, often context-less humor seen in today's meme culture. The constant influx of new public figures, technologies, and societal changes generates new material for humor, which means that algorithms need to be updated regularly to keep up with these trends. Otherwise, they risk becoming outdated, misinterpreting or missing the humor in current texts altogether.

Addressing these challenges requires a dynamic approach to NLP, one that incorporates continuous learning, cross-cultural understanding, and a sensitivity to the subtleties of human expression. It demands a combination of large, diverse, and up-to-date datasets, sophisticated models capable of deep semantic analysis, and perhaps an incorporation of user feedback loops to fine-tune the humor detection capabilities in line with evolving trends and societal norms.

7.4.4 Datasets for NLP-Based Humor Detection

For humor detection specifically, datasets tend to focus on jokes, funny quotes, or other forms of comedic content. Here are examples of datasets tailored for humor detection:

- *The Humicroedit Dataset:*
  Created for the SemEval-2020 Task 7, it involves editing headlines to make them humorous. Researchers can request access to the dataset for academic purposes.

- *One Million Reddit Jokes:*
  This dataset consists of jokes scraped from various Reddit threads like "r/Jokes". It is a popular source for training NLP models to recognize humor.
- *Short Jokes Dataset:*
  Available on Kaggle, this dataset contains a collection of over 200,000 short jokes collected from various websites.
- *The Puns Dataset:*
  Another Kaggle dataset that includes a list of puns, which are a common form of humor based on wordplay.
- *The Jester Jokes Dataset:*
  As mentioned earlier, the Jester Dataset is not only useful for collaborative filtering but also for humor detection, containing a large number of user-rated jokes.
- *The STAND-UP Joke Dataset:*
  This is a dataset that was specifically curated for humor recognition, composed of jokes that are meant to be understandable by children with complex communication needs.
- *The HAHA (Humor Analysis based on Human Annotation) Dataset:*
  Released during the HAHA challenge, it includes a collection of tweets in Spanish that were labelled based on whether they were humorous or not.

7.5 Psychometric NLP

The intersection of psychology and technology heralds a transformative era in understanding the human mind—specifically, how it manifests through language. Psychometric NLP stands at this crossroads, aiming to decipher the intricacies of human communication to infer psychological attributes, predict behavior, and identify potential cognitive shifts. As a subfield of NLP, psychometric NLP utilizes computational linguistics to analyze human language data and extract psychometric properties from the text. The implications of psychometric NLP are profound and far-reaching. From improving mental health diagnostics to tailoring educational programs to an individual's learning needs, from enhancing the recruitment process by identifying personality fit to pioneering preventive measures in mental health, psychometric NLP paves the way for an unprecedented understanding of the human psyche through the lens of language. This section explores two principal applications of psychometric NLP: personality trait estimation and learning disabilities detection.

7.5.1 Personality Trait Estimation

Personality, in essence, refers to the distinctive patterns of thinking, feeling, and behaving that arise from a combination of inherent temperaments, inclinations, and external factors such as environments and experiences. Personality traits serve as tangible psychometric measures for explaining human behavior. There are numerous personality traits that collectively make up an individual's unique personality. These traits influence how people think, feel, and behave in various situations. Personality trait estimation is a domain of psychometric NLP that focuses on discerning individual psychological characteristics from linguistic behavior. In a world increasingly transcribed into digital text through emails, social media, and instant messaging, the words we use—and how we use them—provide fertile ground for the analysis of personality.

7.5.2 Theoretical Frameworks in Personality Psychology and Psychometric Assessment

The Big Five traits, the extraversion-introversion spectrum, and the MBTI typology represent three distinct but complementary frameworks for understanding human personality. These models offer a rich tapestry for psychometric assessment, providing valuable insights into individual differences in behavior, emotion, and cognition. Here we examine each framework and their significance in personality psychology.

- *The Big Five Personality Traits (OCEAN Model):* The Big Five personality traits, also known as the OCEAN model, are the most empirically supported framework for assessing personality. It posits that there are five broad dimensions of personality:
  a) **Openness to Experience**: This trait features characteristics such as imagination and insight, and those high in this trait also tend to have a broad range of interests. It is associated with curiosity, creativity, and a preference for novelty and variety.
  b) **Conscientiousness**: High levels of thoughtfulness, good impulse control, and goal-directed behaviors are markers of this trait. Conscientious individuals are organized and mindful of details.
  c) **Extraversion**: Extraverts are energetic, talkative, and assertive. They are sociable and tend to gain energy from social interaction, as opposed to introverts who feel more energized by solitary pursuits.
  d) **Agreeableness**: This personality dimension includes attributes such as trust, altruism, kindness, affection, and other prosocial behaviors. High agreeableness is associated with a strong concern for others and a desire for social harmony.
  e) **Neuroticism**: Individuals who score high on neuroticism are more likely to experience emotions such as anxiety, anger, or depression. They respond worse to stressors and are more likely to interpret ordinary situations as threatening.

These traits have been found to be relatively stable throughout an individual's life and have been shown to have genetic underpinnings. They are used extensively in various settings, from clinical psychology to career counselling, and have been adapted into numerous self-report inventories and questionnaires.

- *Extraversion-Introversion Spectrum:* While extraversion is one of the Big Five traits, the extraversion-introversion spectrum is often highlighted in personality psychology due to its apparent manifestation in social behavior. This spectrum reflects a person's preference for certain social environments and energy management. Introverts tend to feel drained after socializing and regain their energy by spending time alone, while extroverts obtain energy from interacting with others. Ambiverts are individuals who exhibit qualities of both introversion and extraversion and can adapt to a variety of social situations. Understanding where an individual falls on this spectrum is crucial for personal development, interpersonal relationships, and workplace dynamics.
- *MBTI Typology:* The Myers-Briggs Type Indicator (MBTI) is a personality framework that categorizes individuals into 16 distinct personality types based on four dichotomies:
  a) **Extraversion (E)/Introversion (I)**—This scale involves the preference for focusing on the outer world or one's own internal world.
  b) **Sensing (S)/Intuition (N)**—This dichotomy pertains to the preference for gathering information through five senses or interpreting it in a more abstract way.
  c) **Thinking (T)/Feeling (F)**—It indicates whether a person tends to make decisions based on logic and consistency or based on people and special circumstances.
  d) **Judging (J)/Perceiving (P)**—This scale relates to one's approach to dealing with the outside world, whether it is in a structured or spontaneous way.

  While not as empirically validated as the Big Five, the MBTI remains popular in the business world and among the general public for its approachable and applicable personality categories. It is often used for team building, career counselling, and personal development.

These frameworks are not mutually exclusive and can be integrated for a comprehensive understanding of personality. The Big Five traits provide a broad, scientifically grounded outline of personality, while the MBTI adds a layer of specific personality types that people find intuitive and actionable. The extraversion-introversion spectrum serves as a common thread between these models, emphasizing the social dimension of personality that is evident in day-to-day life.

In psychometric assessments, a combined approach allows for a nuanced profile that can accommodate the richness of human personality. Researchers and practitioners can draw from the strengths of each model, using them to complement one another rather than in competition, for a well-rounded understanding of individual differences.

7.5.3 Linguistic Indicators of Personality Traits

Language, as a vehicle of human expression, carries an abundance of subtle cues about a speaker's or writer's personality. NLP allows us to decode these cues by analyzing linguistic indicators. By examining how individuals express themselves, we can harness NLP to offer insights into the core traits that govern behavior, thought, and emotion. Different aspects of linguistic analysis used to infer personality traits include:

- *Lexical Choices and Personality Inference:* Lexical choices refer to the specific words and phrases that individuals select in communication. These choices can reveal significant information about one's personality. NLP tools can be designed to recognize and interpret these lexical patterns.
  a) **High-Frequency Words**: Certain words are used more commonly by people with specific personality traits. For instance, individuals high in extraversion might frequently use words like "party," "friends," and "exciting," while those with high agreeableness may use "team," "together," and "help."
  b) **Word Categories**: Linguistic Inquiry and Word Count (LIWC) is a widely used tool in psycholinguistics that categorizes words into psychologically meaningful categories. It has been employed in studies to correlate these categories with personality traits.
  c) **Emotionally-Charged Words**: The use of affective language, including emotionally charged words, can be indicative of neuroticism or openness, depending on the context and valence of the emotions expressed.
  d) **Novelty and Variety in Language**: People who score high on openness are likely to use a broader vocabulary and more unique language structures, suggesting creativity and a willingness to explore.
- *Syntax and Semantic Patterns in Relation to Personality:* Beyond individual words, the way sentences are constructed—syntax—and the meanings they convey—semantics—provide deeper insights into personality.
  a) **Complexity of Sentence Structure:** More complex sentence structures can indicate higher levels of education or intellect, which can correlate with certain traits like openness to experience.
  b) **Narrative Style:** The tendency to tell stories or relate experiences in a certain way can be a rich source of personality information. For example, conscientious people might describe tasks or events in a more organized and detailed manner.

c) **Use of Pronouns:** Pronoun usage can reveal focus on the self (higher usage of "I," "me," "my") typically seen in people with certain traits such as neuroticism or introversion, whereas extraverts may have a more outward focus, reflected in more frequent use of "we" or "us."

- *The Role of Metadata in Textual Analysis:* Metadata is data about data, and in the context of textual analysis, it can provide contextual clues that are not found within the text itself but can be crucial for accurate personality assessment.

a) **Temporal Patterns:** The time of day when messages are posted can signal certain traits; for example, night-time activity might correlate with certain aspects of openness or neuroticism.
b) **Interactivity Metrics:** The frequency of interactions, such as replies, likes, or shares on social media, can be indicative of extraversion or agreeableness.
c) **Editing and Revision Patterns:** The way people edit their messages, the use of spellcheck, or their attentiveness to grammatical correctness might hint at conscientiousness.

In summary, linguistic indicators in text—be they lexical, syntactic, semantic, or meta-textual—offer a multi-dimensional view of personality. Through the lens of NLP, these subtle nuances can be systematically identified, quantified, and interpreted, transforming the art of personality assessment into a data-driven science.

Table 7.4 presents a synthesis of linguistic indicators used by NLP algorithms to detect the Big Five personality traits, assess the extraversion-introversion spectrum, and align language usage with the MBTI typology. It highlights specific language usage patterns and gives examples of their detection in text-based communication. These insights not only enhance our understanding of personality but also pave the way for more personalized and efficient psychological assessments.

This table combines the theoretical aspects of personality traits with practical examples of how NLP can be used to detect and assess these traits in real-world textual data. The examples provide a clear illustration of how various NLP tools and techniques can be applied to language to estimate a person's position within these personality frameworks.

7.5.4 NLP Methodologies for Personality Estimation

In the domain of psychometric NLP, methodologies for personality estimation have evolved from simple lexical analyzes to sophisticated machine learning and deep learning models, each providing nuanced insights into the complexities of human personality as expressed through language. Text mining serves as the bedrock of this process, involving meticulous data collection across diverse sources like social media and spoken transcripts, followed by rigorous preprocessing to cleanse the text from extraneous elements and extract salient linguistic

Table 7.4 NLP Indicators for Personality Trait Assessment.

Trait	NLP Indicators	Detection Examples
	Big Five Traits	
Openness	Diverse vocabulary, complex structures	Creative language in blogs, abstract ideas in surveys
Conscientiousness	References to goals/plans, organized language	Structured lists in apps, goal-oriented professional emails
Extraversion	Frequent social words, positive emotions	Social media analysis, speech content in public talks
Agreeableness	Positive emotions, cooperative language	Politeness in emails, empathetic language in customer service
Neuroticism	Language of anxiety/sadness, negative emotions	Diaries for distress, forums for worry signs
	Extraversion-Introversion Spectrum	
Extraversion	Energetic language, group-oriented discussions	Active tweets, engagement in speeches
Introversion	Reflective, solitary activity discussions	Self-focused emails, low social media presence
Ambiversion	Combination of extroverted/introverted patterns	Language variation in different social contexts
	MBTI Typology	
I/E	Introverted versus extraverted content	Social media content type and activity
S/N	Sensing (factual) versus intuitive (theoretical) language	Forum and article content categorization
T/F	Thinking (logical) versus feeling (empathetic) language	Styles in debates and forum arguments
J/P	Judging (structured) versus perceiving (flexible) language	Planner use versus social media spontaneity

features. Within this spectrum, sentiment analysis and emotion detection emerge as pivotal components, distilling the subtle attitudes and emotional undercurrents woven into the fabric of language, which are often indicative of underlying personality traits. The polarity of sentiments in textual content, assessed through sophisticated algorithms, can, for instance, hint at the neurotic tendencies of a writer, while the presence of specific emotion-laden words and their contextual interpretation can elucidate aspects of their temperament.

Advancing further, machine learning models have brought a predictive edge to personality detection, capitalizing on labelled datasets to discern intricate patterns associated with known personality profiles and paving the way for accurate trait predictions. The dichotomy of supervised and unsupervised learning within machine learning leverages both known personality constructs and the innate structure within data to classify and predict personality types. The accuracy of these models is meticulously evaluated through statistical measures, refining their predictive prowess. The advent of deep learning, with its multi-layered neural networks, has heralded a new era in computational personality psychology. Recurrent Neural Networks (RNNs), for instance, are particularly adept at processing the sequential nature of text, capturing nuances over longer stretches of discourse, while Convolutional Neural Networks (CNNs) and Transformer models, like BERT, have been adapted from their triumphs in image processing to extract complex patterns in text data, offering contextual depth to the personality inference process. The fine-tuning of such pre-trained models to the specific task of personality estimation has yielded unprecedented accuracy, enabling the nuanced capture of personality traits from linguistic patterns with relatively minimal training data.

Integrating these varied NLP methodologies, from foundational text mining to advanced deep learning constructs, offers a comprehensive approach to personality estimation. It balances the breadth of feature extraction with the depth of contextual understanding, ensuring a more accurate and holistic profile of an individual's personality through the prism of their language use. This integration signifies a transformative leap in the field of personalized services, mental health, and the broader understanding of human behavior, making psychometric NLP an indispensable tool in the modern era.

7.6 Learning Disabilities Detection

Learning disabilities are neurologically based processing problems that can interfere with learning basic skills such as reading, writing, or math. They can also hinder higher-level skills such as organization, time planning, abstract reasoning, long or short-term memory, and attention. It is important to note that learning disabilities can occur in individuals of all intelligence levels and are not indicative of intellectual disabilities. Learning disabilities are intrinsic to the individual and can vary greatly in their manifestations and intensity. They are often identified in school-aged children when there is a significant gap between a student's potential and actual achievement. Common types of learning disabilities include:

- *Dyslexia:* Difficulty with reading due to problems identifying speech sounds and learning how they relate to letters and words (decoding).
- *Dysgraphia:* Difficulty with writing, which may include problems with spelling, grammar, punctuation, and handwriting.
- *Dyscalculia:* Difficulty with math, particularly with concepts like time, measurement, and spatial reasoning.
- *Auditory and Visual Processing Disorders:* Difficulty in understanding and retaining information through auditory or visual means.
- *Non-Verbal Learning Disabilities:* Trouble with nonverbal cues, such as coordination and body language, often leading to social challenges.

7.6.1 Traditional versus NLP-Based Detection Methods

Traditional methods of detecting learning disabilities have long been the standard in educational and psychological evaluations. These methods often involve a combination of standardized testing, detailed observations in classroom settings, interviews and questionnaires involving parents and teachers, as well as thorough reviews of a student's educational and health history. While these techniques are invaluable for providing a comprehensive view of a student's learning abilities and challenges, they are not without drawbacks. They can be time-consuming, resource-intensive, and occasionally subjective, relying heavily on the interpretations of professionals.

In contrast, the advent of NLP-based approaches to detect learning disabilities presents a range of advantages that can complement, and in some cases, enhance traditional methods. NLP tools are capable of processing vast amounts of language data swiftly, providing insights at a speed that manual evaluations cannot match. This rapid analysis allows for the possibility of earlier interventions, which is critical in mitigating the impacts of learning disabilities. Moreover, NLP algorithms offer a level of objectivity that can sometimes be difficult to achieve through human observation and assessment alone. Another key benefit of NLP-based detection is accessibility. Once set up, these tools can be used by educators with minimal need for specialist intervention, making it a more readily available resource in educational settings. Additionally, NLP enables continuous and real-time monitoring of a student's progress, which traditional methods cannot offer due to logistical limitations. The quantitative data generated by NLP can be tracked over time, providing invaluable information on a student's development or highlighting areas where they might be regressing. Customization is another area where NLP shines, as algorithms can be tailored to identify specific patterns and errors that are unique to each learner, thus allowing educational interventions to be more personalized.

7.6.2 Harnessing NLP in the Detection of Learning Disabilities

The integration of NLP techniques into the detection of learning disabilities signifies a transformative leap forward in educational diagnostics. These computational methods offer multifaceted analyses of linguistic elements, which can reveal subtle but telling signs of various learning challenges. Table 7.5 encapsulates the multifaceted role of NLP in the early detection and analysis of learning disabilities. By scrutinizing various aspects of language use, from word choice to sentence structure and speech patterns, these techniques can reveal inconsistencies and

Table 7.5 Applications of NLP Techniques in the Detection of Learning Disabilities.

NLP Technique	Application in Learning Disabilities Detection	Examples
Lexical Analysis	Examines word usage and vocabulary. Detects a reduced lexical variety that could suggest difficulties in word retrieval.	A student might use "get" for various actions instead of more specific verbs like "fetch," "grab," or "purchase."
Syntactic Analysis	Analyzes sentence structure. Identifies overly simple or grammatically incorrect sentence construction.	A student may consistently write fragments instead of full sentences, or struggle to use complex sentences.
Semantic Analysis	Assesses understanding and use of meaning in language. Flags narratives that lack logical progression or veer off-topic.	A student's essay might drift into unrelated subjects, or they may provide definitions that are incorrect or too broad.
Discourse Analysis	Evaluates coherence and the ability to maintain a topic in conversation or writing.	A student's story may have no clear beginning, middle, or end, or they might repeat points multiple times.
Acoustic Analysis	Analyzes speech for phonetic inconsistencies or articulatory difficulties.	A student may mispronounce sounds, such as saying "wabbit" instead of "rabbit," or exhibit unusual speech rhythm.
Machine Learning	Identifies patterns of errors and changes in language use over time, supporting early detection.	Algorithms might recognize a student's consistent reversal of letters, like "d" for "b," or frequent spelling errors that mirror pronunciation.

anomalies that may indicate underlying challenges in language acquisition and processing. These insights enable educators and clinicians to intervene more effectively at early stages.

Machine learning, a subset of NLP, is particularly adept at identifying the hallmark patterns of dyslexia in written language. These algorithms can be trained to recognize classic dyslexic errors in writing samples, such as letter transpositions or phonetic spelling mistakes. A dyslexic student might write "brite" instead of "bright" or persistently mix up "b" and "d." Machine learning algorithms can sift through vast amounts of text data to identify these recurrent patterns, providing a quantitative assessment that can support early detection and intervention.

The application of machine learning algorithms doesn't stop at text analysis. They also enable the early detection of learning disabilities by tracking the evolution of a student's language use over time. For example, a student may begin with rich, varied language in their written work, but as coursework becomes more challenging, they may start to exhibit telltale signs of dyslexia or another language-based learning disability. Machine learning models can alert educators to these shifts, often long before the student's performance significantly declines.

Together, these NLP techniques converge to offer a powerful diagnostic toolkit. By harnessing the precision and efficiency of NLP, educators, and psychologists can gain deeper insights into students' unique challenges and strengths, paving the way for tailored educational strategies that could vastly improve learning outcomes for students with disabilities.

7.6.3 Challenges and Limitations of NLP in Learning Disability Detection

While the use of NLP in the detection of learning disabilities offers innovative approaches and has considerable potential, it is not without its challenges and limitations. Understanding these is crucial for the development of more effective diagnostic tools and for setting realistic expectations for what NLP can achieve in this field. Here's an elaboration on some of these challenges and limitations:

- *Language Variation and Complexity:* Language is inherently complex and variable. Dialects, slang, multilingualism, and individual linguistic idiosyncrasies can all affect how language is used, making it challenging for NLP systems to accurately interpret and categorize language use, particularly in diverse educational settings.
- *Contextual Nuances:* The subtleties of context can dramatically alter the meaning of language. NLP algorithms may struggle to discern context, especially when analyzing speech or text that contains irony, sarcasm, or humor, which are often used by children and can be misinterpreted by these systems.

- *Over-Reliance on Textual Data:* Many NLP techniques rely heavily on written text for analysis. However, not all learning disabilities are readily apparent from writing alone. For instance, conditions that primarily affect verbal skills may not be detected through text-based analysis.
- *Standardization of Data:* The effectiveness of NLP algorithms often depends on having large, standardized datasets for training. However, educational data can be highly varied, and privacy concerns may limit the availability of such data for creating comprehensive NLP systems.
- *Misdiagnosis and Overdiagnosis:* The risk of false positives and false negatives can never be fully eliminated. NLP systems may identify language use patterns that resemble those of a learning disability, but which actually result from other factors, leading to misdiagnosis or overdiagnosis.
- *Ethical Considerations:* The application of NLP in educational settings raises significant ethical questions, particularly regarding the privacy and consent of students. There is also the potential for bias in the algorithms, which could unfairly affect certain groups of students if not carefully monitored and addressed.
- *Need for Human Expertise:* NLP can assist with the detection of learning disabilities, but it cannot replace the nuanced understanding and professional judgment of educators and psychologists. Relying solely on NLP could overlook the individual circumstances of each student.
- *Technology Integration:* Integrating NLP tools into existing educational and psychological assessment practices can be challenging. Schools and clinics may lack the resources or technical expertise needed to implement and maintain such systems effectively.
- *Continuous Learning and Adaptation:* Language evolves rapidly, and educational methodologies change. NLP systems must be designed to learn and adapt continuously, which requires ongoing development and investment.
- *User Trust and Acceptance:* Gaining the trust of educators, parents, and students in NLP technology is critical. Scepticism or resistance to technological solutions can hinder the adoption of NLP tools, regardless of their potential benefits.

Despite these challenges, the intersection of NLP and learning disability detection remains a promising area of research and application. Overcoming these limitations will require interdisciplinary collaboration, transparent methodologies, and the development of NLP systems that are as dynamic and adaptable as the learners they aim to support.

7.7 Textual Indicators of Distress: *Addressing Depression, Anxiety, and Beyond*

The advent of social media and online communities has brought about a paradigm shift in the way we communicate and express ourselves. These platforms have transcended physical boundaries, allowing for instant sharing of thoughts and emotions. However, this digital landscape is also rife with expressions of personal distress, such as depression, anxiety, and other mental health challenges. Recognizing and responding to such indicators of distress through digital content moderation has become imperative for platform providers to ensure the well-being of their users.

7.7.1 Understanding Distress in Textual Form

In an increasingly interconnected world, individuals turn to online platforms not just for social interaction but also for emotional support. The veil of anonymity and the reach of digital communities provide a unique avenue for people to express feelings they might otherwise suppress. A troubling consequence is the online manifestation of psychological distress, which, if unnoticed, can have dire repercussions. Digital content moderators are tasked with the challenging responsibility of detecting and managing these signals of distress to mitigate potential harm.

Distress manifests in various forms and degrees of intensity. The linguistic markers of psychological distress are as diverse as the individuals who experience it. They can range from explicit statements of despair to subtle shifts in tone or language use.

- *Depression:* Depression, as one of the most prevalent mental health issues globally, poses a significant challenge for digital content moderation. The textual indicators of depression in online platforms are not always overt. Users might not directly state their emotional state but may exhibit patterns in their language that hint at depressive symptoms. This subtlety requires sophisticated NLP tools to uncover. The linguistic markers of depression can vary but typically include:
  a) **Lexical choices:** An increased use of words related to sadness, loneliness, and negativity. For example, frequent use of words like "empty," "tired," or "alone" can be indicative.
  b) **Self-focused language:** Pronoun usage can be telling, with a higher frequency of singular first-person pronouns (I, me, my) as opposed to second (you, your) or third person (he, she, they) pronouns.
  c) **Decreased temporal focus:** Linguistic analysis may show less future tense, which could indicate a lack of optimism or planning for the future.
  d) **Sentiment analysis:** Machine learning models trained for sentiment analysis can classify texts into negative, neutral, or positive sentiments, with depressive content tending toward the negative.
  e) **Cognitive process words:** Depressive language might also include more words related to cognitive processes, especially those indicating certainty (e.g., "always," "nothing") and those suggesting causal relationships (e.g., "because," "therefore"), which can reflect a deterministic or pessimistic worldview.

- *Anxiety:* Anxiety, like depression, often leaves a textual trail, albeit one that might be less distinguishable. The online discourse of a person experiencing anxiety may be peppered with uncertainty and an overemphasis on problematic situations. Features suggestive of anxiety that can be discerned from text include:
  a) **Uncertainty markers:** Frequent use of modal verbs like "might," "could," or "should," which indicate a sense of uncertainty and concern.
  b) **Hypervigilance to threat:** Language that suggests an acute awareness of potential danger or preoccupation with worrying scenarios.
  c) **Physical or mental response descriptions:** References to physiological or psychological responses to stress, such as "palpitations," "sweating," or "overthinking."
- *Beyond Depression and Anxiety:* Beyond depression and anxiety, there are other forms of distress that can emerge in digital communication, such as expressions of trauma, stress, and suicidal ideation. These may be signalled by disruptions in narrative coherence, abrupt topic shifts, and mentions of trauma-related content. Moreover, indicators of suicidal ideation might include direct or indirect references to self-harm or a fascination with death. The linguistic indicators can vary widely but may include:
  a) **Narrative disruptions:** A lack of coherence in storytelling, which might signal trauma or cognitive fragmentation.
  b) **Abrupt topic changes:** Sudden shifts in conversation topics could reflect a tumultuous inner experience.
  c) **Direct or coded speech:** Explicit mentions or coded language related to self-harm or suicidal thoughts require immediate attention.

7.7.2 Utilizing NLP to Identify Indicators of Mental Distress in Online Communications

In the realm of digital content moderation, one of the most nuanced challenges is identifying and responding to online textual manifestations of mental distress. NLP offers a suite of techniques that, when adeptly applied, can discern subtle cues indicative of mental health issues such as depression, anxiety, and a range of other psychological conditions. This task is complicated by the need to balance technological intervention with ethical considerations such as user privacy and consent. Table 7.6 presents a synthesis of how NLP techniques align with the linguistic indicators associated with various mental health challenges, reflecting the current state of research and application in this critical domain. It provides a structured perspective on the intersection of computational linguistics and mental health in the context of social media and online interactions, paving the way for a responsive and responsible approach to content moderation.

Table 7.6 Comparative Analysis of NLP Techniques for Detecting Linguistic Indicators of Depression, Anxiety, and Broader Mental Health Issues.

Mental Health Issue	Linguistic Indicators	NLP Techniques	Tools/Algorithms
Depression	• Persistent sadness	• Sentiment Analysis	• Support Vector Machines (SVM)
	• Loss of interest	• Topic Modelling	• Latent Dirichlet Allocation (LDA)
	• Decline in self-esteem	• Machine Learning Classifiers	• Neural Networks (CNNs, RNNs)
	• Negative affect words	• Syntax and Semantic Analysis	• Recursive Neural Networks (RecNNs)
	• Self-deprecatory language		• Linguistic Inquiry and Word Count (LIWC)
	• Feelings of worthlessness or hopelessness		
Anxiety	• Language conveying worry and restlessness	• Contextual Analysis	• Long Short-Term Memory Networks (LSTMs)
	• Preoccupation with future concerns	• Deep Learning	• Word Embedding Models (Word2Vec, GloVe)
	• Hypervigilance to threat	• Psycholinguistic Dictionaries	• LIWC
	• Uncertainty markers (modal verbs like might, could, should)		• BERT (for context-aware analysis)
Broader Issues	• Disruptions in narrative coherence (trauma, stress)	• Pattern Recognition	• Clustering Algorithms (k-means, hierarchical)
	• Abrupt topic shifts	• Alert Systems	• Anomaly Detection Algorithms
	• References to self-harm or death (suicidal ideation)	• Crisis Intervention Protocols	• Decision Trees
	• Coded speech related to distress		• Automated Reporting Systems

This table provides an overview of how different NLP techniques and tools can be applied to various mental health issues based on the linguistic indicators present in textual content. It serves as a comparative framework for researchers, practitioners, and developers in the field of digital content moderation. Each entry in the table represents a convergence of problem-specific linguistic indicators, applicable NLP techniques, and the corresponding tools or algorithms that facilitate the identification and analysis of distress within textual data. As we traverse from conventional machine learning models to more sophisticated deep learning architectures, it becomes evident that the field is rapidly evolving to address the complexities inherent in human language and emotional expression. The effectiveness of these NLP applications in real-world scenarios is contingent upon continuous refinement and ethical governance, ensuring that such technologies serve to support and protect online communities.

7.8 Digital Content Moderation using NLP

The dawn of the internet brought with it a new epoch of human interaction and knowledge sharing, unprecedented in scale and scope. Today, social media platforms, forums, and comment sections of websites have become the town squares of the digital age—a place where opinions are voiced, ideas are exchanged, and communities are formed. Amidst this vast exchange of digital communication lies a significant challenge that has emerged as a defining issue of our times: digital content moderation. Every second, users around the globe upload content that ranges from the undisruptive and mundane to the innovative and awe-inspiring. Yet, this same capability also opens the floodgates to potential misuse. Users can disseminate hate speech, engage in cyberbullying, spread misinformation, and fake news, incite extremism and radicalization, and even express intentions of self-harm or suicidal ideation. Such content can have dire consequences: it can influence public opinion, shape political landscapes, endanger vulnerable individuals, and in some cases, even lead to real-world violence.

As this user-generated content proliferates, it becomes increasingly crucial for platforms to monitor and manage this content to ensure that it does not violate community standards or legal regulations. Therefore, digital content moderation has become an imperative for platform providers—not only as a moral responsibility but often as a legal one. The task is huge, given that every minute, vast swathes of new text, images, and videos are uploaded to the internet. Human moderation alone cannot keep pace with this influx, leading to the adoption of automated systems, particularly those driven by NLP, to supplement human efforts. NLP, an interdisciplinary domain that intersects computer science, artificial intelligence, and linguistics, aims to give computers the ability to understand text and spoken words in much the same way human beings can. Within the context of content moderation, NLP systems are trained to parse, comprehend, and make decisions about the appropriateness of textual content at scale—a formidable task given the nuances of human language.

7.8.1 Hate Speech and Cyberbullying Monitoring

In the digital age, the pervasiveness of hate speech and cyberbullying poses significant challenges to online communities, platforms, and individual users. The rise of social media has provided a medium where such behavior can proliferate and remain, impacting individuals and groups long after the initial act. The implications of hate speech and cyberbullying can be profound, leading to psychological trauma, social division, and in extreme cases, physical harm. The monitoring and moderation of such content are thus not merely regulatory requirements but also moral imperatives for digital platforms. The integration of NLP into content moderation processes is crucial in addressing these challenges at scale.

- *The Phenomenon of Hate Speech:* Hate speech, a term with many layers, is broadly understood as public speech that expresses hate or encourages violence toward a person or group based on something such as race, religion, sex, or sexual orientation. Here's a closer examination of the different types of hate speech, accompanied by examples for better comprehension. Hate speech is defined as any form of communication that disparages a person or a group on the basis of some characteristic such as race, color, ethnicity, gender, disability, sexual orientation, nationality, religion, or other characteristic. It ranges from blatant statements of bigotry to subtle insinuations designed to provoke disdain or discrimination. While hate speech is protected under freedom of speech in some countries, it can also be restricted by law in others, particularly when it incites violence, discrimination, or hatred. Understanding hate speech involves looking at specific examples, which may vary in blatancy and intention:

  a) *Direct Hate Speech:*
     - Explicit statements like "All [members of a religious group] are terrorists," which incites prejudice and hostility against that group.
     - Use of derogatory racial slurs intended to belittle or dehumanize a partic ular racial group.

  b) *Indirect Hate Speech:*
     - Code words or phrases that are culturally understood to have hateful connotations, like referring to immigrants as "invaders" or "aliens," suggesting they are a hostile force or non-human.
     - Dog whistles, which are statements that on the surface appear normal but are intended to signal and mobilize support from those with hateful ideologies.

Hate speech can further be classified into various types. Explicit hate speech is characterized by direct language that clearly expresses hate or advocates violence, such as making derogatory statements about an entire ethnicity. Implicit hate speech conveys hate or bias in a less overt manner, requiring an understanding of context to recognize, like using racially charged terms to indirectly refer to a minority group. Incidental hate speech occurs when statements not meant to spread hate are perceived as offensive, often due to ignorance or misunderstanding, such as using phrases that inadvertently trivialize serious issues. Insidious hate speech might seem harmless initially but subtly reinforces harmful stereotypes or narratives, like memes that negatively stereotype religious groups under the guise of humor. Micro aggressive hate speech consists of subtle expressions of bias that convey derogatory implications, often surprising due to the speaker's background or perceived abilities. This nuanced categorization in the table helps in grasping the breadth of hate speech manifestations in digital environments.

- *Landscape of Cyberbullying Behavior:* Cyberbullying involves the use of digital technologies to harm, intimidate, and harass others. Unlike traditional bullying, it does not require physical presence; it can be persistent, permanent, and hard to notice. It can include posting rumors or gossip to damage a person's reputation, harassment, threats, sexual remarks, and victimization based on one's race, religion, sexuality, or other personal characteristics. Examples of cyberbullying are wide-ranging and can have serious implications for the mental health and well-being of victims.

  Cyberbullying represents a complex and multifaceted issue in the digital age, transcending traditional bullying's physical and temporal boundaries to invade the lives of individuals through their screens. With the rise of social media, online forums, and instant messaging, the avenues for such harassment have expanded, leading to a pressing need for effective identification and intervention strategies.

  Cyberbullying can take various forms, each with distinct characteristics and behaviors. Trolling involves provoking others online to cause disruption or distress, often through repeated provocative engagement across different platforms. Defamation is the act of spreading false, harmful information about someone, and systematically targeting individuals to damage their reputation. Fraping occurs when someone uses another's social media account without permission, posting content that harms the account owner's reputation. Catfishing involves deceiving others with a fake identity, leading to emotional manipulation and exploitation. Denigration, or "dissing," harms an individual's reputation through public derogatory postings, ensuring wide visibility and often amplification by others. Trickery involves gaining trust to acquire sensitive information, and then betraying that trust by sharing the information publicly. Exclusion is the intentional act of leaving someone out of an online group, creating exclusive circles and repeatedly excluding the same individuals. Flaming includes engaging in hostile online exchanges, often escalating to personal attacks and abusive language. Cyber threats involve threatening harm to someone, which can escalate and connect with offline behaviors. Happy slapping is the sharing of videos depicting physical bullying, showing premeditation through the act of recording and distributing the content. Image shaming involves circulating embarrassing or edited images to ridicule someone, while doxing is the act of publicly revealing someone's private information, often to intimidate or incite harassment. Each of these forms of cyberbullying exhibits specific patterns of behavior that contribute to the toxic environment experienced by victims in virtual spaces.

- *Challenges in Combating Hate Speech and Cyberbullying: Shared and Specific Issues:* In the digital expanse, the interwoven challenges of hate speech and cyberbullying present a formidable frontier for content moderation. This sub-section explores the complex terrain, considering how the ambiguity of language, the cloak of online anonymity, and the ever-changing online lexicon complicate the detection of harmful content. At the same time, this section probes into the distinct obstacles specific to each category: the varying regional sensitivities to hate speech and the pervasive, often cross-platform nature of cyberbullying. By unpacking these issues, we set the stage for more nuanced, context-sensitive interventions that balance the essential principle of free expression with the need for digital safety and civility.

a) **Common Challenges in Monitoring Hate Speech and Cyberbullying**

- Linguistic Nuances:
  i) **Shared Challenge:** Both hate speech and cyberbullying involve complex nuances of language that can be context-dependent and laden with implied meanings, making automatic detection difficult.
  ii) **Example:** Phrases like "You wouldn't want to do that," could be a simple suggestion or a veiled threat, depending on context.
- Evolving Language:
  i) **Shared Challenge:** The dynamic nature of online language with new slang, memes, and coded messages makes it hard for algorithms to keep up with the latest trends in both hate speech and cyberbullying.
  ii) **Example:** An expression like "OK boomer" may start as a trendy dismissal but can be used in a derogatory manner.
- Scale of Data:
  i) **Shared Challenge:** The sheer volume of online interactions is overwhelming for manual review, necessitating automated systems that can struggle to accurately interpret every post or message.

ii) **Example:** Millions of comments on a viral social media post need to be analyzed rapidly, with some containing subtle hate speech or cyberbullying.

- Anonymity:
  i) **Shared Challenge:** The cloak of anonymity online emboldens users to engage in both hate speech and cyberbullying with little fear of repercussion.
  ii) **Example:** Users hiding behind pseudonyms launch ad hominem attacks or spread hate speech against certain groups.
- Legal and Ethical Considerations:
  i) **Shared Challenge:** Balancing the need to curb harmful content while respecting freedom of speech is a tightrope walk faced in both areas.
  ii) **Example:** Policies around what constitutes a banable offense can vary, leading to content being treated differently across platforms.

b) **Specific Challenges in Monitoring Hate Speech**

- Hate Speech Variance by Region:
  i) **Specific Challenge:** Definitions and social norms regarding hate speech can vary significantly from one region to another, requiring region-specific moderation approaches.
  ii) **Example:** A term derogatory in one country may be inoffensive in another, making global standards for moderation complex.
- False Equivalences:
  i) **Specific Challenge:** Differentiating between genuine hate speech and content that exposes or discusses hate speech for educational or journalistic purposes.
  ii) **Example:** A news article quoting a hate speech incident for reporting purposes being flagged by an algorithm.

c) **Specific Challenges in Monitoring Cyberbullying**

- Behavioral Patterns:
  i) **Specific Challenge:** Cyberbullying is often characterized by repeated behavior rather than one-off remarks, requiring algorithms to identify patterns over time.
  ii) **Example:** Repeatedly targeting a specific user with negative comments across various posts may indicate cyberbullying.
- Multi-platform Dynamics:
  i) **Specific Challenge:** Cyberbullying often spans across multiple digital platforms, necessitating a cross-platform approach to monitoring.
  ii) **Example:** A user bullied on a gaming platform may also face harassment from the same users on social media.

By understanding both the shared and unique challenges of hate speech and cyberbullying, developers and researchers can create more refined NLP tools. These tools need to be flexible enough to handle common issues while also being specialized to address the challenges peculiar to hate speech and cyberbullying. Such an approach can help platforms enforce their community standards more effectively and contribute to safer online spaces.

- *Techniques in NLP for Hate Speech and Cyberbullying Monitoring:* The surge in online communication has led to a corresponding rise in the need for effective content moderation. Within the arsenal of digital content moderation, NLP provides an array of techniques to combat hate speech and cyberbullying. These techniques harness machine learning, natural language understanding, and feature extraction to not only flag but also understand the nuanced expression of undesirable content. The application of these techniques serves as a testament to the sophistication possible in contemporary NLP, offering a multi-faceted approach to a pressing societal issue.

  a) **Machine Learning Models:** Machine learning remains the backbone of automated content moderation, employing a range of models to discern patterns indicative of hate speech and cyberbullying.
     - **Supervised Learning:** At its core, supervised learning involves training models on a dataset where the "right answers" (labels) are known. For hate speech and cyberbullying, these labels could indicate whether a text is offensive or benign. Classical machine learning algorithms like Support Vector Machines (SVM), Naïve Bayes, and Random Forests have been effectively employed, often as part of an ensemble that leverages the strengths of various models for better accuracy.
     - **Deep Learning:** The rise of deep learning has revolutionized NLP. Neural networks, particularly CNNs and RNNs, are adept at capturing the intricate patterns within text data. They are capable of learning hierarchical representations and can be particularly powerful when dealing with the sequential nature of language found in social media posts and conversations.

  b) **Natural Language Understanding:** The subtlety of language use in hate speech and cyberbullying necessitates advanced understanding that goes beyond simple keyword matching:
     - **Sentiment Analysis:** By determining the tone behind words, sentiment analysis models can assist in identifying content that carries a negative or hostile tone, which may be indicative of cyberbullying or hate speech.
     - **Semantic Analysis**: This involves decoding the meaning of text to catch instances of hate speech that may be subtle or nuanced. It helps distinguish between harmful content and similar, non-harmful expressions.
     - **Contextual Analysis**: Advanced models like BERT (Bidirectional Encoder Representations from Transformers) and GPT (Generative Pre-trained Transformer) are designed to understand the context in which

words are used. This is vital in content moderation, as the intent and meaning of words can change significantly with context.

c) **Feature Extraction:** Effective feature extraction can significantly enhance model performance by isolating the attributes of text most relevant to the task:
   - **Bag-of-Words**: This method, while simplistic, offers a starting point for analysis. It involves treating text as a collection of individual words, disregarding grammar and even word order, but preserving multiplicity.
   - **Word Embeddings**: Techniques like Word2Vec or GloVe provide a more sophisticated approach, representing words in a continuous vector space. These embeddings capture semantic and syntactic nuances, thereby enabling models to discern subtler forms of hate speech and cyberbullying.

d) **Transfer Learning:** Leveraging pre-existing knowledge can save time and resources:
   - **Models Pre-Trained on Large Datasets**: Transfer learning involves taking a model that has been pre-trained on a large corpus of data and fine-tuning it on a more specific task, such as hate speech detection. This allows the model to adapt to the nuances of a platform's unique communication style and user base.

e) **Anomaly Detection**: Detecting the abnormal to catch what's typically missed:
   - **Unsupervised Learning Algorithms**: Anomaly detection techniques are used to identify unusual patterns or outliers within data. These can be indicative of new, emerging trends in hate speech or cyberbullying that supervised methods may not catch.

f) **Human-in-the-Loop:** The human element remains irreplaceable:
   - **Integrating Human Reviewers**: No matter how sophisticated algorithms become, there will always be a need for human judgment. Human-in-the-loop systems allow for the nuanced understanding that algorithms might miss, ensuring that complex cases of hate speech and cyberbullying are dealt with the necessary sensitivity and discernment.

Despite these techniques, the field faces the constant challenge of improving accuracy while minimizing false positives and false negatives. Privacy must be balanced with enforcement, and transparency in how models make decisions is increasingly demanded by both users and regulators. Continuous development in NLP, including more sophisticated models for understanding context and the rapid identification of emerging patterns of speech, is key. Active learning, where models learn on-the-job from the actions of human moderators, promises to refine the accuracy of these systems. The ultimate goal is a dynamic, responsive system that protects individuals from harm without impinging on free expression, all the while respecting cultural and linguistic diversity. The task is complex, with social, technical, and ethical dimensions, but the promise of NLP in creating safer online communities remains a compelling motivation for ongoing research and development.

7.8.2 Misinformation and Fake News Analysis

In today's interconnected world, the digital landscape has been significantly defined by the rapid spread of various forms of misinformation. From innocent slip-ups that result in the spread of false information to calculated campaigns of deception, the internet has become fertile ground for the proliferation of content that can mislead, misinform, and manipulate. Fig. 7.4 shows a range of concepts related to the spread of unreliable or false information, often referred to collectively as "information disorders."

- *Misinformation:* This refers to false or inaccurate information that is spread, regardless of intent to deceive. Misinformation can be the result of an honest error, misunderstanding, or the misrepresentation of facts. *Example:* A viral social media post during a natural disaster falsely claims that drinking bleach can purify any contaminated water. This information, shared in a state of panic, may not be intended to cause harm but is inaccurate and potentially dangerous.
- *Fake News:* A type of misinformation that consists of deliberate falsehoods or fabrications presented as news, often designed to mislead for financial, political, or other gains. *Example:* An online article headline reads, "Celebrity X endorses Product Y," despite no such endorsement occurring. The article is intentionally crafted to generate ad revenue through sensationalism, exploiting the fame of the individual for clicks and shares.

Figure 7.4 Spectrum of Online Information Disorders.

- *Rumors:* These are unverified pieces of information or stories that are spread informally, typically by word of mouth. Rumors may not have malicious intent but can contribute to misinformation if they turn out to be false. *Example:* Amidst a global pandemic, a rumor starts circulating through instant messaging platforms that a nationwide lockdown will be imposed within the next 48 hours, causing a surge in panic buying. The rumor, while not grounded in official communication, spreads quickly due to public anxiety.
- *Propaganda:* Propaganda is information, especially of a biased or misleading nature, used to promote a political cause or point of view. It often involves the use of emotional appeal, selective facts, and repetitive messaging to influence public opinion. *Example:* A state-sponsored news outlet repeatedly publishes stories highlighting the supposed failures of a rival country's government while suppressing any positive news or external criticisms of its state. The content is systematically designed to shape public sentiment in favor of the home country.
- *Disinformation:* It is a form of misinformation that is intentionally created and disseminated to deceive and mislead others. It is often designed to create confusion, sow distrust, or undermine opposition. *Example:* A coordinated campaign is launched on social media platforms where bots and trolls disseminate false information about a political candidate, claiming they have a hidden criminal past. The intent is to discredit the candidate in the eyes of voters.
- *Hoaxes:* A hoax is a deliberately fabricated falsehood made to masquerade as truth. It is often designed to prank or provoke the public but can also have more serious implications if believed and acted upon. *Example:* An elaborate story surfaces online, complete with fake photographs and testimonials, claiming the discovery of a new insect species in a well-known city park that can transmit a dangerous virus to humans. The hoax is designed as a practical joke but leads to unwarranted public concern and a waste of public health resources.

The nuances in the types of misinformation reflect the complexity and pervasiveness of the issue, affecting everything from personal decisions to global politics. Rumors and propaganda can be seen as catalysts or even forms of misinformation and disinformation. Rumors may begin innocently but can transform into more malicious forms if they are weaponized or politicized. Propaganda, on the other hand, is typically crafted with intent, using rumors, misinformation, and even disinformation as tools to shape public perception toward a desired end.

- *Dynamics of Misinformation and Fake News:* The dynamics of misinformation and fake news involve a complex interplay of psychological, technological, and social factors:
  a) *Cognitive Biases:* Human susceptibility to confirmation bias, where individuals favor information that confirms their pre-existing beliefs, and the Dunning-Kruger effect, a cognitive bias in which people with low ability

at a task overestimate their ability, plays a significant role in the spread of misinformation.

b) *Echo Chambers:* Online platforms often create echo chambers, where users are exposed predominantly to viewpoints that align with their own. This environment facilitates the spread of misinformation and fake news, as contradictory evidence is either not seen or readily dismissed.

c) *Social Networks:* The structure and nature of social networks contribute to the rapid spread of misinformation. Information cascades occur when individuals see others sharing a piece of information and follow suit, often without verifying its authenticity.

d) *Manipulation Tactics:* Those who create and disseminate fake news and disinformation often exploit emotional triggers. Stories that evoke fear, anger, or excitement are more likely to be shared, increasing their reach.

e) *Technological Facilitation:* Algorithms governing search results and newsfeeds on social media tend to prioritize engaging content, not accuracy, inadvertently promoting misinformation.

f) *Psychological Impact of Hoaxes:* Hoaxes can be particularly psychologically impactful because they often exploit trust and can lead to significant emotional or physical responses.

- *Foundational Techniques in NLP for Identification of Misinformation:* In the ceaseless struggle against misinformation, NLP serves as a sentinel at the gates of truth. By harnessing semantic classification, NLP meticulously sifts through the digital narrative, distinguishing fact from fiction, while its incisive analysis of emotional tone and bias cuts through the subtext to reveal the true colors of the content. Factual inconsistency checks further fortify this defence, ensuring that each piece of information aligns with the bedrock of established truth. The following table, Table 7.7 presents a concise overview of the core strategies employed in the detection and analysis of fake news and misinformation, each illuminated with an illustrative example:
- *Advanced NLP Techniques in NLP for Content Moderation:* In an ever-evolving digital landscape where misinformation can spread with viral speed, advanced detection mechanisms powered by NLP have become indispensable tools in the fight against fake news. These cutting-edge techniques leverage the full spectrum of AI's analytical prowess to peel back the layers of complexity and deceit that often shroud false narratives. Table 7.8 summarizes these advanced mechanisms, each accompanied by a relevant example to illustrate their application in real-world scenarios.
- *Challenges in Combating Misinformation and Fake News:* Combating misinformation and fake news is a daunting task that encompasses various challenges. These challenges range from technical difficulties in detecting nuanced language to the broader implications of censorship and freedom of expression.

Table 7.7 NLP Strategies for Fake News and Misinformation Detection.

Strategy	Description	Example
Semantic Classification for Veracity Assessment	Involves NLP models classifying content into "verified," "unverified," or "false" based on a pre-annotated corpus of text.	**Verified**: "UN passes a new resolution on climate change." **Unverified**: "Potential life discovered on Venus!" **False**: "Dinosaurs were spotted in the Amazon rainforest."
Emotional Tone and Bias Detection	Analyzes the sentiment of the text to determine if content is crafted to elicit emotional responses or push a biased agenda.	**Positive Bias**: "This miracle cream cures all skin problems overnight!" **Negative Bias**: "Eating carrots invariably leads to poor eyesight."
Factual Inconsistency and Anomaly Recognition	Detects when content contains factual inaccuracies or presents data that is at odds with established truths.	**Inconsistency**: "Celebrity X wins an Oscar in 2023" when no Oscars were held that year. **Anomaly**: "A new planet in our solar system has been named after a famous soda."

Table 7.8 Advanced NLP Mechanisms in the Identification of Misinformation.

Mechanism	Description	Example
Neural Linguistic Modelling for Deception Identification	Deep learning models that are proficient in discerning the intricate linguistic cues indicative of deceptive language.	**Example**: An article uses complex scientific terminology to claim a breakthrough in cancer treatment without any substantial evidence or peer-reviewed research backing it.
Factuality Networks and Verification	Systems that link claims to a dynamic network of verified data, checking for congruence with established facts.	**Example:** A viral tweet stating a celebrity's death is disproven by checking against recent public appearances and official press releases.
Contextual and Network Analysis	Analytical processes that consider the broader context of content dissemination, evaluating patterns and source credibility to pinpoint misinformation campaigns.	**Example:** A flood of similar posts and memes from dubious accounts coinciding with a political event, suggesting a coordinated effort to mislead or sway public opinion.

As NLP and other technologies continue to develop, they face an array of obstacles that make the war against digital falsehoods particularly complex.

a) *Rapid Evolution of Misinformation Tactics:* One of the main challenges is the adaptability and inventiveness of those who produce misinformation. As NLP tools become more adept at identifying and filtering out false narratives, the creators of such narratives evolve their strategies to circumvent these new defences. This creates a dynamic battleground where techniques and algorithms must constantly evolve to keep up. *Example:* Creators of fake news might switch from text-based articles to memes and videos, which are harder for text-based NLP systems to analyze. As algorithms improve in detecting fake news on one platform, perpetrators move to another, less moderated platform, exploiting its algorithms and user base.
b) *Language Nuances and Context:* The subtleties of human language present significant hurdles. Sarcasm, satire, and parody are particularly challenging to distinguish from genuine misinformation because they often mimic the latter's tone and stylistic features intentionally. Additionally, context is critical; the same statement could be true in one context and misleading in another. *Example:* A satirical article from "The Onion" could be mistaken for true news by an NLP system not attuned to satirical cues. Meanwhile, genuine news that seems outrageous or unexpected may be incorrectly flagged as fake.
c) *Scale and Volume of Data:* The sheer volume of content that must be monitored is overwhelming. Millions of articles, posts, and messages are created every day across various platforms. NLP algorithms must process and analyze this vast amount of data in real time, which requires immense computational resources and sophisticated models. *Example:* During an election, there might be a surge in political content across social media. NLP systems might struggle to keep pace with the volume, potentially allowing some misinformation to slip through the cracks due to the sheer amount of data to process.
d) *Mislabelling and Bias:* Machine learning models, including those used in NLP, are only as good as the data they are trained on. If the training data is biased or contains errors, the model may mislabel content, leading to false positives or negatives. Ensuring that the training data is representative, unbiased, and accurate is a significant challenge. *Example:* If an NLP model is trained predominantly on a dataset containing news from a specific political bias, it may disproportionately flag content from the opposing viewpoint as misinformation, reflecting the bias present in its training data.
e) *Balancing Act Between Moderation and Censorship:* Content moderation can sometimes be perceived as censorship, raising concerns about freedom of expression and the role of tech companies in regulating speech. Finding the

right balance between removing harmful misinformation and preserving free speech is an ongoing debate with no easy solutions. *Example:* A platform might aggressively target and remove misinformation related to vaccines, leading to accusations of censorship from groups who perceive their legitimate concerns or alternative views as being suppressed.

f) *Multilingual and Cultural Diversity:* Misinformation is a global issue that crosses linguistic and cultural boundaries. Developing NLP systems that can effectively operate in multiple languages and understand cultural contexts is a complex task that requires not only advanced technology but also cultural knowledge and sensitivity. *Example:* A rumor spreads on social media in Hindi about a celebrity's death. An NLP system trained primarily on English content might fail to detect and address this misinformation, allowing it to spread within the Hindi-speaking community.

g) *User Behavior and Education:* Technology alone cannot solve the problem of misinformation; user behavior plays a crucial role. Educating the public about media literacy and critical thinking is vital. Users must be able to question the content they encounter and verify information through credible sources. *Example:* A well-crafted piece of fake news about a natural disaster may be shared by thousands before fact-checkers can debunk it, showing that user education on critical evaluation of sources is as crucial as technological solutions.

h) *Legal and Ethical Considerations:* There are legal and ethical dimensions to content moderation. For instance, different countries have different laws regarding speech, and an NLP system may need to be tailored to comply with these regulations. Ethically, there's a responsibility to ensure that NLP tools do not infringe on privacy and that they treat all users and viewpoints fairly. *Example:* In Europe, the General Data Protection Regulation (GDPR) might restrict how an NLP system can be used to monitor or store user data, affecting the way content moderation can be legally conducted.

i) *Platform Ecosystems:* Each social media platform has its unique ecosystem and user behavior patterns. Misinformation strategies that work on one platform may not be effective on another. NLP tools must be customized for the specific characteristics of each platform, which multiplies the complexity of the moderation task. *Example:* Misinformation about health remedies may thrive on a platform like Instagram through visually appealing but misleading infographics, while conspiracy theories might spread more easily through Facebook's groups and sharing mechanisms.

j) *Combating Deepfakes and Synthetic Media:* The rise of deepfakes and synthetic media poses a new frontier in the fight against misinformation. These highly convincing fake videos and audio recordings can be used to create false narratives that are difficult to debunk. NLP must work in concert with other technologies to detect and mitigate these sophisticated forms of misinformation. *Example:* A deepfake video of a political leader appears to show them making inflammatory statements they never actually made. This synthetic media is so well-crafted that it requires a combination of NLP, video analysis, and human fact-checking to debunk.

NLP provides a powerful toolset for fighting misinformation and fake news, but the challenges it faces are multifaceted and continually evolving. Addressing these issues requires not only technological innovation but also cross-disciplinary collaboration, public education, and thoughtful consideration of the ethical and societal implications of content moderation.

- *Advanced NLP Techniques for Identification of Misinformation:* Specialized tools powered by NLP are increasingly critical in the ongoing battle against misinformation and fake news. These tools are not just preventative measures; they are integral to the real-time analysis and assessment of content, enabling responses to the rapid spread of false information. Here we elaborate on the specific tools designed to address various aspects of misinformation.
  a) *Automated Verification Systems:*
  Automated verification systems stand at the forefront of technological responses to misinformation. These systems integrate with vast, continuously updated databases containing verified facts, scientific data, and news records. When a piece of content is disseminated online, the verification system analyzes it in real time, checking the veracity of its claims against this database. Should a claim not be substantiated by evidence or be directly contradicted by reliable sources, the system flags it for further human review or public annotation. This immediate feedback loop is vital, as it helps prevent the entrenchment of false narratives before they can take hold in the public consciousness.
  For instance, if an online article claims that a public figure has made a controversial statement, the automated verification system can immediately compare this claim against a database of recorded speeches, interviews, and public records. If the statement cannot be found, or if the context differs significantly from what is reported, the system can flag the article as potentially misleading.
  b) *Argumentation Mining for Bias and Stance Detection:*
  Argumentation mining is a sophisticated application of NLP that deconstructs the text to its fundamental arguments. It examines the premises put forth, follows the logical progression to the conclusions drawn, and evaluates the soundness of the reasoning involved. This granular analysis is particularly adept at uncovering bias and detecting the stance of a given text. If the argumentation within a piece of content is found to be fallacious

or heavily biased, it could be indicative of an attempt to mislead or distort the truth.

Take, for example, a blog post that presents a controversial issue. Argumentation mining would dissect the post's arguments, assessing the strength and relevance of each point. If the post relies heavily on ad hominem attacks or appeals to emotion rather than factual evidence, it may be flagged as presenting a biased viewpoint, potentially misleading readers.

c) *Linguistic Forensics for Authenticity Analysis:*

Linguistic forensics is a field that applies the principles of forensic science to language. It looks at the style, syntax, and other linguistic characteristics to profile the author and assess the authenticity of the text. By analyzing these features, linguistic forensics can detect when a piece of writing doesn't match the known characteristics of an alleged author or contains the stylistic fingerprints commonly associated with disinformation, such as sensationalism or unfounded assertiveness.

An example of this could be a social media account claiming to belong to a reputable news agency, but which publishes posts with exaggerated language that is not characteristic of the agency's verified communications. Linguistic forensics tools can compare these suspect posts to a corpus of authentic posts, highlighting the stylistic discrepancies and supporting the identification of the account as a purveyor of fake news.

Together, these specialized NLP tools form an essential part of the infrastructure necessary to maintain a semblance of truth and trustworthiness in the digital information ecosystem. They work in concert to identify, analyze, and counteract the spread of misinformation and fake news, though they also raise questions about privacy, the potential for overreach, and the definition of truth in a complex world.

7.8.3 Extremism and Radicalization Identification

In an age where the digital ecosystem is as integral to societal discourse as the spoken word, the shadows cast by extremism and radicalization grow longer and more pervasive. These are not new phenomena; however, their manifestation in the digital sphere presents unique challenges and dangers. To understand the gravity of these challenges and to effectively combat them, we must first scrutinize the concepts of extremism and radicalization, acknowledge the role that digital platforms play in amplifying such content, and explore the ways in which NLP can serve as a powerful tool in the moderation of online content.

- *Defining Extremism and Radicalization:* Extremism refers to attitudes, actions, or ideologies that lie at the far end of the political spectrum, far removed from the mainstream. Extremist views are typically characterized by their support for radical changes in society, often advocating for the use of violence or the imposition of stringent ideologies on others. Extremism is not confined to any single ideology, region, or belief system; it manifests across a broad spectrum of political, religious, and social landscapes. It can be found in the ultra-nationalist rhetoric of a political group that advocates for ethnic cleansing to "purify" the nation, much like the harrowing narratives that fuelled the Rwandan genocide in the 1990s. It can also be seen in the actions of religious zealots like those of ISIS, who espouse a perverted interpretation of Islam to justify their campaign of terror and their goal of establishing a theocratic state.

On the other end of the spectrum, extremism can emerge from ideologies that purport to fight oppression, such as the radical left-wing militancy of groups like the Red Brigades in Italy during the 1970s and 1980s, which sought to create a revolutionary state through violence and intimidation. In the United States, white supremacist ideologies espoused by groups like the Ku Klux Klan, which advocate for racial segregation and the subjugation of non-white populations, are another grim example of extremism.

Radicalization, the process leading to extremism, often unfolds in a series of stages. It may begin with an individual's exposure to extremist propaganda online, perhaps through a seemingly innocuous forum post or a targeted recruitment video on a social media platform. For example, an individual may come across content that blames societal woes on a particular ethnic group or political faction, feeding into their pre-existing biases or grievances. As they descend into this rabbit hole, they may find themselves in more extreme online communities that echo and amplify these sentiments. The story of how young men and women from around the world were radicalized into joining ISIS through savvy social media campaigns and messaging apps is a cautionary tale of radicalization in the digital age. Radicalization can also occur through influential figures, such as the radical cleric Anwar al-Awlaki, whose speeches and writings have been implicated in inspiring several terrorist attacks in the West. His content, widely disseminated online even after his death, provides a blueprint for how charismatic figures can utilize digital mediums to radicalize followers.

The process of radicalization is complex and multifaceted, typically involving an interplay of personal, social, and political factors. Individuals may become radicalized through personal grievances, identity crises, or a desire for change. Social factors include the influence of peers, communities, and networks that endorse extremist ideologies. Politically, radicalization can be fuelled by perceived or real injustices, both at a local and global level. The pathway to radicalization is often marked by a deepening engagement with extremist content, leading to a solidification of extreme beliefs, and, in the worst cases, culminating in the decision to commit acts of violence. The journey from a passive consumer of extremist content to an active participant in extremist activities underscores the insidious nature of radicalization.

In this digital era, a tweet, a blog post, or a viral video can be the catalyst for radicalization, as seen in the 2011 Norway attacks, where the perpetrator was heavily influenced by extremist content he consumed online. The Boston Marathon bombing in 2013 is another tragic example, where the perpetrators were believed to have been self-radicalized through jihadist material accessed on the internet.

The digital world has become a petri dish for extremist content, providing an unparalleled platform for its dissemination. The inherent features of online platforms, such as anonymity, instant global reach, and algorithmic amplification, have created an environment in which extremist views can not only survive but thrive and proliferate. Content that, in the past, would have been confined to the fringes of society can now find its way into the mainstream with alarming ease. Algorithms designed to capture user attention can inadvertently promote extremist content, which often elicits strong emotional reactions and, consequently, high levels of engagement. This digital echo chamber effect bolsters radical ideologies, as users are continuously fed content that reinforces their existing beliefs, pushing them further toward the extremes. Moreover, the virality of digital content means that messages of hate and division can spread rapidly, crossing geographical, political, and social boundaries in moments.

Fig. 7.5 presents a pyramid diagram illustrating the process of radicalization and the potential interventions at various stages. It highlights the importance of a multifaceted approach that includes prevention, intervention, and reintegration strategies, which are critical for effective counter-radicalization efforts.

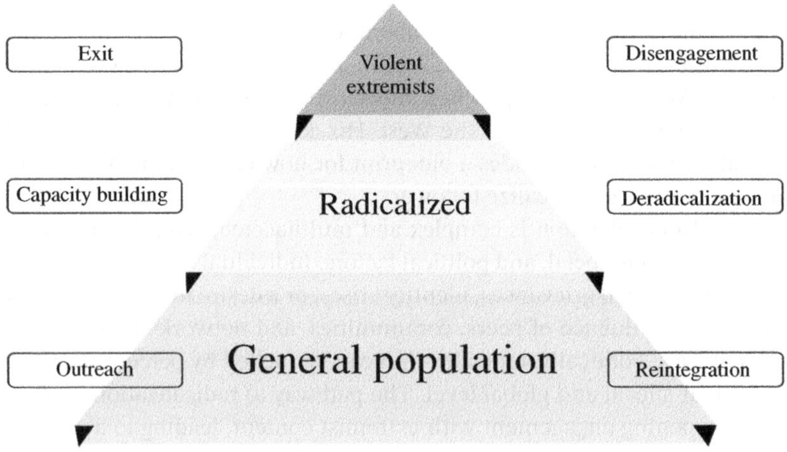

Figure 7.5 Aarhus Model Showing How Violent Extremism Can Be Mitigated.

Here's a detailed breakdown of what each level represents:

a) *General Population (Green Layer):* This is the base of the pyramid and represents the broader society. Most people belong to this layer and are not involved in extremist activities or ideologies. However, this is also the pool from which individuals may begin a journey toward radicalization. Interventions at this level typically involve outreach programs aimed at educating the public about the dangers of extremism and promoting social cohesion.
b) *Radicalized (Yellow Layer):* The middle layer indicates individuals who have been radicalized. These people have adopted extremist views but have not yet resorted to violence. Preventive measures here are crucial and often revolve around deradicalization efforts. Such efforts can include counter-narrative strategies, engagement with community leaders, and offering support for those who may be susceptible to radical messages.
c) *Violent Extremists (Red Layer):* At the peak of the pyramid are those who have taken the step beyond radical beliefs into violent action. These are individuals or groups who are actively planning or carrying out extremist activities. Interventions at this stage are much more severe, often involving law enforcement and security services to prevent acts of terrorism and other forms of violent extremism.

The boxes around the pyramid denote the process and potential exit pathways from radicalization:

a) *Exit:* This box, connected to the top of the pyramid, signifies the aim of completely removing someone from the cycle of extremism, effectively ending their engagement with radical ideologies or groups. This can involve various methods, including exit programs specifically designed to help individuals leave extremist groups.
b) *Disengagement:* This refers to the process where individuals still hold radical beliefs but have decided to refrain from violence or have withdrawn from participating in violent activities. Disengagement strategies may focus on individual psychological support, vocational training, and creating alternative social networks.
c) *Deradicalization:* Positioned toward the lower half of the pyramid, this process involves changing an individual's beliefs, moving them away from radical ideologies. Deradicalization programs often target the underlying causes of radicalization, such as addressing grievances, correcting misbeliefs, and reintegrating individuals into mainstream society.
d) *Re-Integration:* This box is linked to the base of the pyramid, indicating the end goal of bringing a previously radicalized individual back into the fold of society as a non-radicalized member. This is a long-term process that involves social

support systems, continuous monitoring, and assistance in finding a place in the community.

e) *Capacity Building:* This area emphasizes strengthening the ability of communities and institutions to prevent radicalization and deal with its consequences. It can include training for law enforcement, development of community programs, and enhancing the resilience of communities to extremist messaging.

- *Digital Propagation of Extremist Content and Challenges:* The characterization of extremist content in the digital space encompasses various forms of communication, including text, images, videos, and even memes, that advocate for, glorify, or incite radical ideologies and actions. This content often targets susceptible individuals, capitalizing on feelings of disenfranchisement, injustice, and identity crises. It can range from overt calls for violence to more subtle messages intended to sow division, propagate hate, and normalize extremist views. The character of such content is multifaceted, often tailored to resonate with specific audiences, bypass censorship, and evade detection by digital platforms' moderation systems.

  The challenges in characterizing extremist content lie in its diversity and adaptability. Extremists have become increasingly sophisticated in their communication strategies, employing coded language, symbolism, and strategic ambiguity. This evolving landscape makes it difficult to create a one-size-fits-all definition or criteria for what constitutes extremist content, further complicating the tasks of identification, monitoring, and moderation.

  Digital platforms have inadvertently become accelerators of radicalization. The very features that make social media platforms engaging and user-friendly also contribute to the rapid spread of extremist content. Algorithms designed to increase user engagement can create echo chambers and filter bubbles that reinforce extremist beliefs. Through mechanisms like suggested groups, friend recommendations, and targeted advertising, individuals may be exposed to progressively more radical content. These platforms also offer tools that extremist groups exploit to build communities, spread propaganda, and recruit members. For instance, live-streaming features have been misused to broadcast acts of terrorism in real-time, while encrypted messaging apps provide a secure space for radical groups to communicate and plan out of sight of law enforcement. Moreover, the international and borderless nature of the internet allows extremist content to reach a global audience instantly. Content moderation challenges are exacerbated by the need to consider different cultural contexts, languages, and legal frameworks, which may affect what is considered extremist in one locale but not in another.

  Combatting the spread of extremist content online requires a nuanced understanding of the technological and human factors at play. It necessitates a multi-stakeholder approach involving platform providers, regulators, civil society, and users themselves. Digital literacy, robust content moderation policies, and the development of counter-narratives are essential components in addressing the digital propagation of extremist content. Furthermore, there is an increasing role for advanced technologies, such as NLP, machine learning, and artificial intelligence, to assist in the rapid identification and removal of such content while respecting users' rights to free expression and privacy.

In the battle against digital extremism, content moderators and algorithms alike must tackle subtle nuances and clever veiling tactics employed by those with radical agendas. Table 7.9 describes the key challenges faced in identifying extremist content, outlining the intricate play between linguistic subtlety, coded communications, and the overwhelming deluge of information circulating online.

- *Multilayered NLP Strategies in the Combat Against Online Extremism:* NLP emerges as a critical tool in both safeguarding online spaces and unearthing problematic content related to extremism and radicalization. In its gatekeeping role, NLP systems are instrumental in pre-emptively moderating content, filtering out material that may promote or incite extremist ideologies before it can reach a broader audience. In its investigative capacity, NLP digs deep into the digital terrain, identifying and flagging content that may endorse or lean toward radical views, even when such messages are subtly embedded in seemingly innocuous communications. By leveraging advanced linguistic and computational techniques, NLP facilitates a more secure digital ecosystem, actively working to deter the spread of radical and extremist narratives online.
  a) **NLP at the Frontlines of Moderation**
     In the continuous effort to monitor and moderate online content, NLP stands as a critical technological ally. The complexity of human language, with its nuances, idioms, and cultural specificities, poses significant challenges in identifying harmful extremist content. Here, we inspect the sophisticated realm of NLP and its tools that, while not infallible, provide substantial support in this ongoing battle.
     - **Text Analysis and Interpretation:** At the core of NLP's capabilities is text analysis and interpretation. This process involves breaking down content into understandable segments for machines. Techniques like tokenization, stemming, and lemmatization are employed to normalize the text. Further, parsing and syntactic analysis help in understanding grammatical structures, while pragmatic analysis aims to comprehend the intended message beyond the literal words.
     - **Sentiment Analysis and Intent Detection:** Sentiment analysis and intent detection are pivotal in distinguishing between general content and that which harbours extremist sentiments. By evaluating the tone

Table 7.9 Challenges in Identifying Extremist Content Online.

Challenge	Description	Examples
Ambiguity and Context in Language	Differentiating extremist content from benign material can be difficult due to the nuanced use of language and the requirement of contextual understanding.	A phrase like "great replacement" might appear innocuous but is often linked with white supremacist narratives. Satirical content or dark humor can sometimes be misinterpreted as extremist.
Evolving Language and Code Words	Extremists frequently change their lexicon and use coded language to evade detection, which necessitates constant updates to moderation systems.	The use of seemingly non-threatening symbols or numbers that have extremist significance, such as "1488", where 14 stands for a white supremacist slogan and 88 for "Heil Hitler". The term "boogaloo" has evolved to reference a coming civil war and is used among certain militia groups.
Scale and Volume of Online Content	The sheer amount of data generated online makes it a gargantuan task to monitor and identify extremist content efficiently.	Billions of posts are shared across social media platforms daily, making manual monitoring unfeasible. During the Russia-Ukraine war, social media platforms were inundated with millions of posts, narratives that dehumanize opponents or call for violence against specific groups. Additionally, state-sponsored troll farms produced content at a massive scale, aiming to shift public opinion or sow discord.

and emotion behind words, NLP can gauge whether a text leans toward hate speech or incitement to violence. However, this is not straightforward. Sarcasm, satire, and coded language can mask true sentiments, requiring advanced models that can interpret such complexities.

- **Machine Learning Models in NLP for Content Flagging:** Machine learning models, particularly those using deep learning, have transformed the ability of NLP to flag problematic content. These models, trained on large datasets, can recognize patterns and learn from new data, becoming more adept over time. They can classify texts, detect anomalies, and even predict which content is likely to be extremist, thus flagging it for human review.

b) **NLP Techniques Against Extremism**
The battle against online extremism leverages various NLP techniques to detect and neutralize harmful content. These techniques range from basic to highly sophisticated, reflecting the arms race between content moderators and those attempting to evade detection.

- **Keyword and Phrase Detection:** The most fundamental method is keyword and phrase detection. This involves creating lists of words and phrases commonly used by extremists. However, this method has limitations due to the dynamic nature of language and the context-dependent meaning of words.
- **Semantic Analysis and Thematic Extraction:** Semantic analysis takes keyword detection further by understanding the meaning of words in context. NLP tools can extract themes and topics from large volumes of text, which helps in identifying content with extremist undertones even if they don't use specific flagged keywords.
- **Relationship and Network Analysis:** Beyond individual posts, NLP can analyze relationships and networks within textual data. This includes detecting communication patterns between users, identifying influential nodes in social networks, and uncovering hidden structures within the data that might signal coordinated extremist campaigns.

Combining all these techniques, NLP tools provide a multi-faceted approach to detecting and mitigating the spread of extremist content online. Yet, they require continuous refinement and human oversight to adapt to the ever-evolving landscape of online communication and ensure the protection of free speech while combating digital extremism.

Knowledge Checkpoint 9

Mixed Worksheet

Multiple Choice Questions (MCQs)

1. **Sentiment Analysis:** What does advanced sentiment analysis extend to beyond identifying basic emotions?
   A Predicting future emotions
   B Translating emotions across languages
   C Identifying complex emotional states
   D Calculating the speed of emotional changes

2. **Emotion Recognition:** Which aspect is specifically analyzed in emotion recognition compared to sentiment analysis?

A Polarity of the text
B Specific emotions conveyed
C Overall content length
D Keyword frequency

3 **Irony and Sarcasm Detection:** What linguistic tool is crucial for detecting irony and sarcasm in text?
A Semantic congruency
B Pragmatic analysis
C Syntactic simplicity
D Lexical density

4 **Humor Identification:** What is a key linguistic feature often involved in humor?
A Jargon usage
B Puns and wordplay
C Passive voice
D Technical terms

5 **Psychometric NLP for Personality Trait Estimation:** Which personality framework is commonly associated with psychometric analysis in NLP?
A OCEAN Model (Big Five)
B Rorschach Test
C Freudian Theory
D Pavlovian Response Patterns

True/False Statements

6 Sentiment analysis can only classify texts as positive, negative, or neutral. (True/False)

7 Emotion recognition in text can detect nuanced states like excitement, disappointment, or relief. (True/False)

8 Sarcasm is always easy to detect in text due to its distinct linguistic structure. (True/False)

9 One application of humor identification in NLP is to enhance engagement in educational platforms. (True/False)

10 Psychometric NLP cannot be used to analyze and predict behavior based on text analysis. (True/False)

Scenario-Based Questions

11 If a machine learning model is analyzing a product review that says, "Rarely have I been this thrilled with a purchase," and identifies it as a positive sentiment, what aspect of sentiment analysis is being demonstrated?
A Polarity shift recognition
B Literal analysis
C Contextual misunderstanding
D Irony detection

12 A researcher is using NLP to determine the most prevalent emotions in a series of therapy session transcripts. Which type of NLP application is being used?
A Sentiment tracking
B Emotion recognition
C Psychometric evaluation
D Content filtering

13 An online forum uses NLP to automatically flag posts with potential mental distress signals for immediate review. This is an application of:
A Sentiment analysis
B Emotion recognition
C Psychometric NLP
D Content moderation

14 A virtual assistant that can engage in banter and tell jokes is likely utilizing:
A Irony detection algorithms
B Humor identification models
C Sentiment analysis
D Psychometric profiling

15 In an educational app, NLP is used to adapt learning content based on the student's language use, indicating their learning preferences and challenges. This application of NLP is part of:
A Learning disabilities detection
B Personality trait estimation
C Sentiment analysis in education
D Content personalization

8

Multilingual Natural Language Processing

Natural Language Processing (NLP) has come a long way, evolving from basic rule-based models to advanced deep learning systems capable of nuanced understanding and generation of human language. The advent of multilingual NLP is a testament to the field's growth, addressing the need for cross-language communication and making technology accessible in myriad languages. This branch of NLP not only facilitates global connectivity but also enhances inclusivity, allowing people to interact with machines in their native languages. Critical processes like machine translation and transliteration have matured significantly, with neural network-based models like Google's NMT delivering near-human accuracy. However, these advancements are not uniformly distributed, with low-resource languages often left behind due to a lack of data, prompting the development of innovative solutions like transfer learning and multilingual training.

8.1 Translation and Transliteration

Translation and transliteration serve as the foundational pillars of multilingual NLP. Machine translation, once a speculative vision, now underpins the operations of global businesses, breaks down communication barriers in social services, and even facilitates diplomatic interactions. It has been a field of study since the 1950s, beginning with rule-based systems and evolving through statistical meth ods to today's neural networks. Modern translation systems leverage the latest advancements in neural networks to deliver translations with remarkable accuracy and fluency, a far cry from the literal and often error-ridden outputs of their rule-based ancestors. The pursuit of translation fidelity and fluency has led to several approaches:

- *Rule-Based Machine Translation (RBMT):* These systems rely on a comprehensive set of linguistic rules and dictionaries. An example is SYSTRAN, which was used for translating between English and Russian as early as the 1960s.

Language Intelligence: Expanding Frontiers in Natural Language Processing, First Edition. Akshi Kumar.
© 2025 The Institute of Electrical and Electronics Engineers, Inc. Published 2025 by John Wiley & Sons, Inc.

- *Statistical Machine Translation (SMT):* This technique involves algorithms that learn from bilingual text corpora. Phrase-based SMT was popularized by Moses, an open-source translation system.
- *Neural Machine Translation (NMT):* Google's NMT system exemplifies this approach, utilizing a sequence-to-sequence architecture that significantly improves translation quality over SMT.

Table 8.1 presents a systematic comparison of various foundational translation techniques that have shaped the field of Natural Language Processing over the years. Each technique is evaluated based on its underlying methodology, exemplar systems, and intrinsic strengths and weaknesses, providing a snapshot of its role and performance in the context of language translation tasks.

Beyond the foundational approaches, newer models have pushed the boundaries of translation quality and efficiency:

- *Transformer Models:* These models use self-attention mechanisms to weigh the importance of each word in a sentence, regardless of its position, enabling parallel processing and capturing richer contextual information. Example: Google's BERT and OpenAI's GPT series have set new standards in translation quality.
- *Zero-Shot and Few-Shot Learning:* These techniques allow models to translate between language pairs they have never seen together during training, facilitating translation for low-resource languages. Example: Facebook's M2M-100 is designed to directly translate between any pair of 100 languages without translating to English first.

Transliteration, though less discussed, is equally crucial. It is not about translating the meaning but rather converting the script, ensuring that names, places, and other proper nouns are recognizable and pronounceable across different languages. This subtle yet vital process ensures that individuals and entities are

Table 8.1 Comparison of Foundational Translation Techniques.

Technique	Methodology	Example	Strengths	Weaknesses
RBMT	Linguistic rules and dictionaries	SYSTRAN	Good for consistent grammar	Inflexible to new phrases
SMT	Statistical analysis of text corpora	Moses	Adapts with more data	Less fluent than NMT
NMT	Deep neural networks	Google NMT	High fluency and context awareness	Requires substantial computational resources

accurately referenced in diverse linguistic contexts. Transliteration approaches include:

- *Statistical Transliteration:* Similar to SMT, it uses statistical models, often building a phonetic model of the source and target languages.
- *Neural Transliteration:* Google's NMT also extends to transliteration, showing remarkable accuracy in converting words into scripts of different languages.

Translation and transliteration serve as pivotal tools in the ever-expanding landscape of global communication, each with its distinct applications across various domains. Translation, the more complex of the two, has become indispensable in international diplomacy and business, enabling stakeholders from different linguistic backgrounds to negotiate, collaborate, and exchange information. It's critical in the global marketplace, allowing companies to localize their products, marketing materials, and services to suit diverse cultural contexts, thereby reaching a wider customer base. In the literary world, translation brings the richness of world literature to a global audience, allowing people to enjoy works beyond the language in which they were originally written. Furthermore, in the digital domain, translation powers search engines and social media platforms, making information and communication accessible to users worldwide, regardless of language barriers.

Transliteration, while it does not involve converting meaning, plays a crucial role in rendering scripts from one writing system into another, thus enabling readers unfamiliar with the source script to phonetically interpret the text. This is essential in academics, particularly in fields that require cross-referencing materials in different languages, such as linguistics, history, and religious studies. It's also significant in technology, for instance, in the creation of internationalized domain names that allow web addresses to be represented in local scripts, thus democratizing Internet access. Transliteration is invaluable in everyday life as well, from mapping systems that need to display place names understandably to diverse users, to personal name transliteration in passports for international travel. It also plays a role in education, assisting language learners to bridge the gap between familiar and unfamiliar alphabets, which is particularly beneficial in the initial stages of learning a new language. Together, translation and transliteration not only facilitate communication and commerce but also foster cultural exchange and understanding by transcending the barriers posed by different languages and scripts. Fig. 8.1 presents a clear distinction between translation and transliteration using the English word "Hello" as an example. Two arrows stem from the word, pointing to its different forms in another language, which appears to be Hindi.

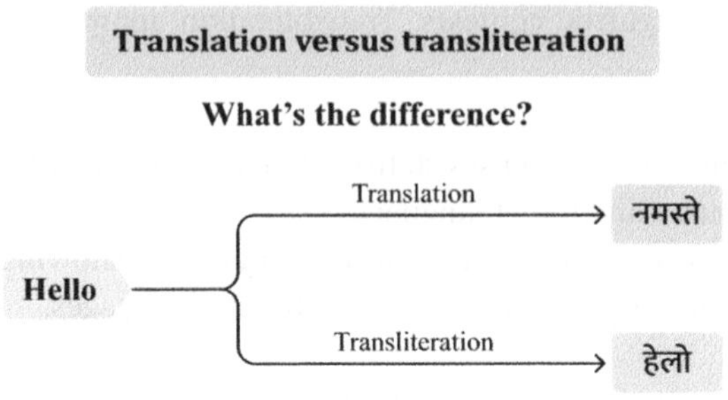

Figure 8.1 Translation versus Transliteration: What's the Difference?

- The first arrow points to "नमस्ते" which is the translation of "Hello" in Hindi, conveying the same greeting.
- The second arrow points to "हेलो" which is the transliteration of "Hello" into Hindi, representing an approximate pronunciation of the word using Hindi script.

Fig. 8.1 demonstrates the fundamental difference between translation, which is about converting the meaning of a word or text into another language, and transliteration, which is about converting the sounds of words from one language's script into another.

8.1.1 Challenges with Translation and Transliteration

Both translation and transliteration are complicated by the sheer diversity of languages and the complexity of human communication.

The realm of translating text from one language to another is fraught with intricate challenges. One of the most significant is grappling with contextual nuances, where words or phrases in the source language carry implicit meanings that are not easily transferred into the target language. This issue is compounded by the structural and grammatical chasms that often exist between languages from different families, such as the dissimilarity between English and Japanese. Polysemy presents its own set of hurdles, with words bearing multiple meanings that require careful contextual consideration to translate correctly. Equally problematic is the conveyance of sarcasm and humor, which is often deeply entrenched in the source culture and can be incredibly elusive for translation algorithms to detect and render effectively.

Transliteration, while seemingly more straightforward, introduces its own set of complexities. Each script has unique phonetic elements that may not find direct counterparts in another script, leading to a variety of possible transliterations for the same word or sound. This is especially evident in languages with a wide array of vocal sounds, such as Arabic, when mapped to the Latin alphabet. The absence of standardized transliteration schemes further muddies the waters, allowing for multiple interpretations and representations of the same words. Homographs add an additional layer of complexity, demanding a contextual understanding to discern correct pronunciation before transliteration. Furthermore, regional dialects and accents within the same language can alter pronunciation, affecting the transliteration output. Languages with deep orthographies, where the relationship between spelling and pronunciation is non-linear, such as English, pose further challenges for consistent and accurate phonetic transliteration.

Both translation and transliteration not only test the limits of computational techniques but also demand a nuanced understanding of linguistic and cultural idiosyncrasies. As vital components of NLP, they continue to spur research aimed at bridging linguistic divides and enhancing communication across the globe.

8.1.2 Evaluation of Translation and Transliteration Quality

Evaluating the quality of translation and transliteration is a multifaceted process that incorporates both automated metrics and human judgment to ensure accuracy, fluency, and cultural appropriateness.

- *Evaluation of Translation Quality:*
  a) **Automated Metrics:** Tools such as BLEU (Bilingual Evaluation Understudy), METEOR (Metric for Evaluation of Translation with Explicit Ordering), and TER (Translation Edit Rate) are commonly used to evaluate machine translation output. They compare the machine-generated text to one or more human-translated reference texts, calculating scores based on the correspondence.
     - **BLEU** assesses the closeness of a machine translation to human translations by counting matching n-grams in the candidate translation to the n-grams in the reference text and then computing the precision score, with a penalty for too-short translations.
     - **METEOR** goes a step further by incorporating synonyms and stemming and aligning for semantic and syntactic congruity with the reference.
     - **TER** calculates the number of edits required to change a translation into a reference translation, providing a more direct measure of how much work is needed to correct a translation.

  b) **Human Evaluation:** Despite the convenience of automated metrics, human evaluation remains the gold standard. This involves bilingual experts or target audience members assessing translations for not only accuracy but also for fluency, idiomatic correctness, and cultural relevance. Parameters often include adequacy (how much information is preserved), fluency (how natural the translation reads), and comprehension (whether the translation is understandable and conveys the original meaning).

- *Evaluation of Transliteration Quality:*

a) **Direct Comparison:** For transliteration, quality is often evaluated by comparing the transliterated text to a standard or commonly accepted version of the text in the target script. The evaluation considers the phonetic accuracy and consistency of the transliterated text.
b) **Phonetic Accuracy:** This involves checking if the transliteration correctly represents the source text's pronunciation. It may require a phonetic expert or native speakers to judge whether the transliteration is phonetically faithful to the source language.
c) **Dictionary or Database Lookup:** In some cases, transliterated words can be checked against a pre-compiled dictionary or database that contains accepted transliterations. This is especially useful for names of people and places.
d) **User Testing:** Similar to translation, human judgment is crucial. Native speakers can evaluate whether the transliterated text is understandable and if it accurately conveys the sound of the original script. User testing can also involve pronunciation tests to ensure that the transliterated words guide correct pronunciation.
e) **Standards Compliance:** Adherence to established transliteration standards (like ISO or the Library of Congress standards) is a measure of quality, particularly in academic and official contexts.

Both translation and transliteration evaluations should account for the intended use of the text, as different applications may require different levels of precision and localization. For instance, a literary translation might prioritize capturing stylistic nuances over strict literal accuracy, whereas a legal translation would necessitate exact correspondence. Similarly, transliteration for a linguistic study may need to strictly follow phonological representation, while for everyday use, a more accessible version that approximates pronunciation for non-speakers might be preferred.

8.2 Cross-Lingual Models and Embeddings

In a world where information transcends language barriers, the ability to process and understand multiple languages through a single computational model has become a critical asset in the field of NLP. Cross-lingual models are designed to understand and process multiple languages using a single model. These models leverage shared representations across languages to enable language-agnostic processing.

8.2.1 Cross-Lingual Models

The inception of cross-lingual models marks a significant milestone in NLP. These models are not only multilingual but are also capable of transferring knowledge from one language to another. We begin by examining the architecture and functionality of such models, particularly focusing on transformer-based models like mBERT and XLM-RoBERTa.

- *Transformer Architecture:*
  At the heart of these models lies the transformer architecture, renowned for its self-attention mechanism that allows models to weigh the importance of different words in a sentence, irrespective of their position. This flexibility is crucial for understanding the syntax and semantics of languages, which often have varying structures. The transformative impact of the transformer architecture on NLP stems largely from its self-attention mechanism. Self-attention allows each token (word or sub-word) in the input sequence to interact with all other tokens in a parallel fashion. This interaction is quantified as a set of attention scores, which determine how much focus should be placed on other parts of the input when encoding a particular token. These attention scores are calculated using a scaled dot-product attention mechanism, which computes the relevance of all tokens to a given token. To account for the order of words, which is lost during the self-attention process, transformers introduce positional encoding. This encoding adds information about the position of each token in the sequence to its vector representation, ensuring that the model can recognize patterns related to the order of words.
  The full transformer model comprises stacks of encoders and decoders. Each encoder contains a self-attention layer followed by a feedforward neural network, with normalization layers inserted in between. Similarly, each decoder contains a self-attention layer, a cross-attention layer that attends to the encoder's output, and a feedforward neural network, also separated by normalization layers. These stacks allow transformers to process a vast amount of information simultaneously and to capture complex linguistic patterns.
- *Multilingual BERT (mBERT):*
  mBERT takes the transformer architecture and extends it to multiple languages. It is pre-trained on a masked language model (MLM) task, where random tokens in the input text are masked, and the model learns to predict them. The pre-training corpus is a concatenated set of Wikipedia articles from over 100 languages, which imbues the model with knowledge across a wide linguistic spectrum. mBERT's innovation lies in generating deep contextualized word representations. Unlike earlier models that generate static embeddings for words, mBERT's embeddings are dynamic, varying based on the surrounding

context. This property is particularly useful in capturing the meaning of polysemous words—those that have multiple meanings based on context.

After pre-training, mBERT can be fine-tuned on specific tasks with additional training data. Its robust pre-trained multilingual representations allow it to transfer the knowledge learned from one language to another, even with little to no task-specific data in the target language. This capability is vital for performance on NLP tasks in low-resource languages.

- *XLM-RoBERTa (XLM-R):*
  Building upon mBERT's success, XLM-RoBERTa (XLM-R) expands the volume and diversity of training data and modifies the training methodology. It utilizes a more extensive corpus sourced from CommonCrawl, which provides a richer and more varied linguistic dataset. Furthermore, XLM-R employs a longer training procedure with more optimization steps, enhancing the model's linguistic understanding. The extensive pre-training allows XLM-R to develop a more nuanced comprehension of language intricacies and context, which translates to enhanced performance on a variety of benchmarks. It shows particular advancements in tasks that require deep understanding of context, such as natural language inference and commonsense reasoning. XLM-R's performance is not only notable in high-resource languages but also in how it generalizes across languages it was not directly trained on. This cross-lingual generalization is a significant step toward creating truly language-agnostic NLP models capable of understanding and operating across the full spectrum of human languages.

In summary, both mBERT and XLM-R represent pivotal developments in the field of NLP, leveraging the transformer architecture to create models with unprecedented multilingual capabilities. They lay the groundwork for future models that could potentially learn from an even broader range of languages and dialects, moving closer to the goal of universal language understanding.

8.2.2 Cross-Lingual Embeddings: A Shared Semantic Space

Cross-lingual embeddings are a pivotal development in the field of NLP, serving as the cornerstone for constructing a unified semantic space shared by multiple languages. The evolution from monolingual to cross-lingual embeddings signifies a shift toward a more interconnected and language-agnostic perspective in NLP. These embeddings are engineered to encapsulate the semantics of words from different languages into a single, coherent vector space.

At the core of cross-lingual embeddings is the concept of semantic alignment. The goal is to map words from various languages into a high-dimensional space where semantically similar words are proximal, regardless of their language. This spatial arrangement enables models to detect semantic similarities across languages, facilitating cross-lingual transfer learning and multilingual processing. Table 8.2 represents a high-level overview of the methods used for creating

Table 8.2 Methods Used for Creating Cross-Lingual Embeddings.

Technique	Description	Methodology	Advantages	Limitations
Canonical Correlation Analysis (CCA)	A statistical tool to align word embeddings from two languages in a shared space.	Identifies transformation matrices that maximize correlation between two sets of language embeddings.	• Effective in finding linear relationships • Does not require parallel corpora	• Assumes linear relationship • May not capture complex, non-linear nuances
Adversarial Training	Inspired by GANs, it creates language-agnostic embeddings.	A generator creates embeddings, while a discriminator attempts to identify their language; the generator learns to make language-indistinguishable embeddings.	• Can handle non-linearities • Does not require parallel corpora • Encourages robust, language-neutral embeddings	• Can be computationally intensive • May require careful tuning to avoid mode collapse
Bilingual Dictionary Induction	Utilizes a bilingual dictionary to align the embeddings from two languages.	Starts with seed word translations and learns a mapping of embeddings from one language to another.	• Straightforward implementation • Utilizes existing bilingual resources	• Dependent on the quality of the bilingual dictionary • Limited to language pairs with sufficient dictionaries
Joint Multilingual Training	Trains embeddings on multiple languages simultaneously.	Embeddings for different languages are learned at the same time, using a shared vocabulary and structure.	• Naturally aligns embeddings through joint learning • Can leverage context from multilingual data	• Requires large multilingual corpora • Potential for language interference

(continued)

Table 8.2 (Continued)

Technique	Description	Methodology	Advantages	Limitations
Sub-Word Tokenization	Breaks down words into smaller, shareable sub-word units across languages.	Uses common sub-word units (like BPE) to represent similar morphemes across languages, aiding in alignment.	• Handles morphological richness • Good for languages with shared roots or structures	• May struggle with entirely distinct language families • Can lead to fragmentation of meaning
Unsupervised Methods	Align embeddings without parallel corpora or bilingual dictionaries.	Uses structures within the monolingual corpora to align the embeddings based on their geometric arrangements.	• Scalable and less resource-dependent • Opens possibilities for low-resource languages	• May be less accurate than supervised methods • Requires sophisticated algorithms to discover alignment

cross-lingual embeddings, which enable transfer learning and various NLP tasks across different languages. The effectiveness of each technique may depend on the specific languages being aligned, the size and quality of the available corpora, and the particular NLP tasks they are intended to support.

Creating a shared semantic space for cross-lingual embeddings is an ambitious endeavor in NLP that aims to build a unified representational framework for multiple languages. However, this process is riddled with linguistic, cultural, and technical challenges:

- *Linguistic Diversity and Complexity:*
  a) **Syntactic Structures:** Languages exhibit a vast array of syntactic diversity. For example, the subject-verb-object (SVO) order is common in English, while the subject-object-verb (SOV) order is prevalent in Japanese. Aligning such syntactically diverse languages in a shared semantic space requires the model to abstract away from word order and focus on deeper syntactic functions, which is non-trivial.
  b) **Cultural Nuances:** Words and phrases are imbued with cultural significance that can vary dramatically from one language to another. These subtleties influence the use and meaning of language in context, which can be challenging for a model to learn, especially if it has been trained primarily on data from a different cultural context.
  c) **Idiomatic Expressions:** Idioms and figurative language are highly language-specific and often lack direct translations. This makes it difficult for cross-lingual embeddings to capture and align the nuanced meanings of such expressions across languages.
- *Script and Typology Differences:*
  a) **Different Writing Systems:** Cross-lingual embeddings must bridge the gap between languages with different scripts (e.g., Latin alphabet versus Chinese characters). This difference extends beyond mere visual representation; it affects the fundamental structure of language processing models.
  b) **Typological Distance:** Languages can be typologically distant, meaning they have different origins and language families (e.g., English versus Finnish). This distance can manifest in vastly different vocabularies, grammatical structures, and usage patterns, complicating the creation of a coherent shared semantic space.
- *Technical and Resource Constraints:*
  a) **Resource Scarcity for Low-Resource Languages:** While high-resource languages like English or Chinese have vast amounts of data to train on, low-resource languages may have very little, leading to less robust embeddings for these languages when placed in a shared space.

b) **Alignment Quality:** The quality of alignment is pivotal. Poorly aligned spaces can lead to significant performance drops, especially when transferring knowledge from one language to another. This is a particular concern in unsupervised methods, where there's no clear signal to guide the alignment.

Addressing the challenges of creating shared semantic spaces in cross-lingual embeddings requires innovative solutions and methodologies that cater to the inherent diversity of languages. One such approach is sub-word tokenization, exemplified by Byte Pair Encoding (BPE). BPE addresses the challenges posed by different vocabularies and scripts, dissecting words into smaller, common subunits, and facilitating the creation of a more universal embedding space where languages with disparate scripts can be connected through shared sub-word units. Complementing this, bilingual dictionary induction serves as a bridge between languages, using existing bilingual lexicons to provide a supervised element to the alignment of embeddings. This is particularly valuable for languages that lack large parallel corpora, offering an anchor for translation and semantic similarity that is grounded in human-curated language pairs.

Moreover, the advent of enhanced contextualization through models like BERT has revolutionized the landscape of cross-lingual embeddings. These models understand words in context, providing nuanced, dynamic representations that are better suited to capturing idiomatic and culturally specific expressions. They adapt to the syntactic and semantic variances of language as influenced by surrounding words, which is critical for maintaining meaning across different languages. The architecture of cross-lingual models also plays a pivotal role. By designing architectures that are inherently adaptable to various scripts and linguistic typologies, researchers can build more robust models capable of dealing with the complexities of global languages. Such architectures might integrate mechanisms specifically aimed at handling the idiosyncrasies of language families and scripts, making them more universally applicable.

Last, the scarcity of labelled datasets for many languages necessitates a reliance on unsupervised and semi-supervised learning approaches. These methods capitalize on the wealth of unlabelled monolingual data, enabling the discovery of linguistic patterns and alignments without the need for direct translation. By doing so, they open up possibilities for language pairs that have been historically underrepresented in NLP research, democratizing language technology.

Together, these strategies represent a multifaceted effort to tackle the daunting task of building embeddings that not only translate words but also convey the rich tapestry of human language and culture.

8.3 Low-Resource Language Processing

In the expansive realm of NLP, low-resource language processing stands as a distinct challenge and a focal point for linguistic inclusivity. Low-resource languages are those for which digital tools, corpora, and datasets are limited or non-existent. A language may be spoken by millions yet remain digitally underrepresented. Factors contributing to a language's low resource status include limited written material, socio-economic barriers, digital divide, and a lack of governmental or institutional support. Consequently, this affects the development of NLP tools like speech recognizers, machine translators, and text-to-speech systems.

8.3.1 Challenges in Low-Resource Language Processing

The processing of low-resource languages presents several challenges. The paucity of annotated corpora and language data significantly impedes the application of data-driven approaches, such as deep learning, which require large amounts of data to achieve high performance. Furthermore, the absence of benchmark datasets makes it difficult to evaluate and compare models reliably. Some specific challenges in low-resource language processing are listed next:

- *Scarce Data Availability:* The most significant challenge in processing low-resource languages is the scarcity of digital text and speech data. For high-resource languages like English or Mandarin, there are countless datasets available for tasks such as machine translation, speech recognition, and sentiment analysis. For low-resource languages, such datasets might be minimal or entirely non-existent. Take, for instance, the Ainu language of Japan, which UNESCO classifies as critically endangered. Computational resources for Ainu are scarce. There is a lack of digitized texts, and as a result, it is challenging to build statistical models that can predict or generate Ainu text.
- *Limited Annotated Corpora:* Even when raw data is available, it often lacks annotations necessary for supervised machine learning approaches. Annotations might include part-of-speech tags, syntactic trees, or named entity labels. Creating these annotations requires linguistic expertise and resources that are not always available for low-resource languages. For example, in the case of Kinyarwanda, a Bantu language spoken in Rwanda, while there is a substantial amount of spoken and written material, there is a deficit of annotated corpora. Without this, creating an NLP model to perform even basic tasks is greatly hindered.

- *Lack of Pre-Trained Models:* Many modern NLP techniques rely on pre-trained models that have been exposed to vast amounts of data. However, these models are predominantly available only for high-resource languages. For example, in languages like English, pre-trained models such as BERT or GPT-3 are readily available, whereas for a language like Tigrinya, spoken in Eritrea and Ethiopia, such resources are rare. NLP practitioners wishing to work with Tigrinya have to start from scratch, which is a time-consuming and costly process.
- *Difficulty in Evaluation and Benchmarking:* The absence of standardized evaluation benchmarks for low-resource languages means that assessing the performance of NLP models can be challenging. Without benchmarks, it's difficult to measure progress or compare different approaches effectively. For example, if one were to develop a sentiment analysis tool for Lao, the lack of a standardized and publicly available dataset for evaluation would make it hard to gauge the tool's effectiveness or compare it against any future tools developed for the same purpose.
- *Technological Infrastructure:* Low-resource languages often coincide with regions that have limited technological infrastructure. This lack of infrastructure can restrict the data collection process and the deployment of NLP applications. For example, building a voice recognition system for Pashto, predominantly spoken in Afghanistan and Pakistan, encounters infrastructural challenges such as limited Internet access and fewer digital devices, which restricts the collection of voice data and the deployment of voice-based applications.
- *Orthographic Variation:* Many low-resource languages suffer from a lack of standardization in their writing systems. This orthographic variation introduces additional complexity in processing the language data. For example, Somali, which was primarily oral until the 1970s, exhibits significant orthographic variation. Different texts may spell the same word in different ways, complicating text analysis and requiring pre-processing to normalize these variations.
- *Morphological Complexity:* Low-resource languages often have rich and complex morphologies. This makes the processing of such languages particularly challenging because the language models need to handle a large number of word forms and grammatical structures. For example, the Greenlandic language (Kalaallisut) has a polysynthetic structure where words are composed of multiple morphemes, and a single word can represent a complete sentence. NLP models trained on languages with simpler morphologies struggle to parse and generate text in Greenlandic accurately.
- *Cultural Nuances and Context:* Capturing the cultural context and nuances in low-resource languages is critical. Without a deep understanding of the culture and usage context, NLP models might misinterpret the meaning of the text or speech. For example, in many indigenous languages, such as Guarani in South

America, context plays a significant role in understanding the meaning of words and phrases. Translating phrases without cultural context can lead to significant inaccuracies and loss of meaning.

8.3.2 Techniques for Low-Resource Language Processing

Techniques for low-resource language processing are centered around making the most efficient use of the data and resources that are available. They often involve innovative applications of machine learning that require less data, adaptations of models developed for other languages, and leveraging the knowledge and efforts of the community of speakers. These methods demonstrate the flexibility and creativity necessary to advance NLP for all languages, not just those with extensive resources. Table 8.3 provides an overview of the diverse strategies adopted in the field to address the scarcity of resources for certain languages and to build robust NLP systems.

8.3.3 Case Study: Natural Language Processing for Hindi

Hindi, an Indo-Aryan language, is one of the official languages of India. Despite its large number of speakers, Hindi can be considered a low-resource language in the NLP domain when compared to languages like English or Mandarin. This case study will explore the development of NLP tools for Hindi, highlighting the challenges faced and the innovative solutions implemented. The challenges in Hindi language processing include:

- *Data Scarcity:* Although Hindi is spoken by a large population, the digital presence of large-scale, annotated datasets necessary for training robust NLP models was limited. This scarcity is a significant hurdle because modern machine learning techniques, particularly deep learning, are data hungry. They require vast amounts of varied and high-quality data to learn from. In the case of Hindi, the existing corpora were either too small, not diverse, or lacked the annotations needed for tasks like sentiment analysis, named entity recognition, or syntactic parsing. For example, a team working on sentiment analysis for Hindi might find plenty of raw text data from news websites, but this data might not be labelled with sentiment annotations (positive, negative, neutral). Creating a large, annotated corpus manually is time-consuming and expensive, and without it, training accurate models is challenging.
- *Orthographic Variation:* Hindi uses the Devanagari script, which is relatively standard but includes inherent challenges due to orthographic variations. These variations occur because the script must accommodate words from regional languages and the way it represents sounds can vary. For example, the use of

Table 8.3 Summary of Techniques for Low-Resource Language Processing.

Technique	Description	Example Application
Cross-Lingual Transfer Learning	Leverages models trained on high-resource languages to benefit a related low-resource language.	Using a model pre-trained on English to bootstrap one for Afrikaans.
Semi-Supervised Learning	Combines small amounts of labelled data with larger amounts of unlabelled data to train models.	Training a Kazakh text classifier using a small hand-annotated corpus and large raw text.
Unsupervised Learning	Utilizes algorithms that do not require labelled data to discover patterns in data.	Developing a Belarusian machine translation system by finding latent structures in text.
Synthetic Data Generation	Artificial creation of annotated data using various methods, such as rule-based systems or translation for parallel corpora creation.	Creating a Guarani parallel corpus by translating a Spanish text and refining it.
Few-Shot Learning	Trains models on very small datasets to perform NLP tasks with minimal examples.	Training a model to recognize named entities in Chichewa with limited examples.
Zero-Shot Learning	Extends few-shot learning to enable models to perform tasks without any task-specific data.	Using knowledge from other languages to apply to Chukchi without direct examples.
Meta-Learning	"Learning to learn"—trains models on a variety of tasks to generalize to new tasks with little data.	Developing a model using several similar languages that can adapt to Chukchi language tasks.
Multilingual Models	Models trained on multiple languages at once to improve performance on all languages, especially low-resource ones.	Using mBERT for sentence classification in Swahili after training on related languages.
Use of Linguistic Resources	Informs model development using existing linguistic resources like typological databases and grammatical descriptions.	Creating models for Quechua that understand morphological structures using linguistic databases.
Crowdsourcing and Community Engagement	Engages community members in creating, annotating, or validating data to build a corpus for NLP tasks.	Involving Inuktitut speakers in contributing translations and transcriptions.

'half letters' in the script to denote conjunct consonants can lead to different orthographic representations for the same phonetic sound. Additionally, the transcription of proper nouns, particularly names and technical terms, can vary widely, making it difficult to ensure consistency across datasets. Consider the Hindi word for 'school', which can be written as "स्कूल" or "शाला." An NLP model trained on a dataset where "स्कूल" is the prevalent term might struggle to recognize "शाला" as the same entity, leading to inconsistencies in understanding or translation.

- *Morphological Complexity:* Hindi is a morphologically rich language, with words often composed of several morphemes that can modify their meaning and grammatical function. This complexity presents challenges for NLP tasks that require understanding the structure of words, such as tokenization, part-of-speech tagging, and syntactic parsing. Tokenization, which involves breaking down text into meaningful units, is not straightforward because Hindi does not use spaces to separate words as consistently as space-delimited languages like English. Moreover, a single word in Hindi can have many suffixes that change its meaning, number, tense, mood, or gender. For example, the verb "खेल" (play) in Hindi can be conjugated in many ways based on tense, aspect, mood, and politeness. For instance:
  - "खेलता हूँ" (I play) for a male speaker in the present tense.
  - "खेलती हूँ" (I play) for a female speaker in the present tense.
  - "खेल चुका हूँ" (I have played) to indicate completion.

A model that cannot accurately parse these variations may misinterpret the tense or the gender of the subject, leading to errors in tasks like translation or information extraction.

To address these challenges, researchers and developers working on Hindi NLP have had to be innovative. They have leveraged machine translation to create parallel corpora, developed sophisticated tokenization and morphological analysis tools tailored to Hindi's unique characteristics, and employed semi-supervised techniques to make the best use of the limited annotated data available. Fig. 8.2 shows a typical classification model that is trained on a resource rich language, typically English, using a cross-lingual transformer model and zero-shot transfer learning (while training, the model is not seeing even a single example of test language, but it can still make predictions in test language) is performed on a resource-poor language, i.e., Hindi.

The development of a more robust Hindi NLP ecosystem is a testament to the perseverance and ingenuity of the NLP community in the face of such challenges.

While significant progress has been made, challenges in Hindi NLP remain. Variations in dialects, code-switching (mixing Hindi with English or other regional languages), and the continuous evolution of language in digital media

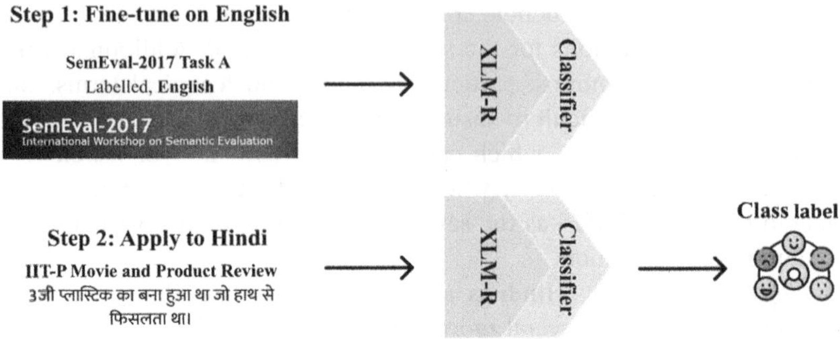

Figure 8.2 Cross-Lingual XLM-R Transformer Model.

present ongoing hurdles. Future directions may involve more sophisticated models that can handle code-switching, greater emphasis on speech and video data processing, and improved models for understanding context and sarcasm in text, which are particularly nuanced in Hindi.

8.4 Cultural Nuance and Idiom Recognition in Natural Language Processing

The complex tapestry of language is often woven with threads of cultural nuance and colorful idioms, which present both a challenge and an opportunity in the field of NLP. To effectively interpret and engage with human communication, NLP systems must navigate the mesh of contextual nuances and figurative speech that characterizes natural language.

Understanding cultural nuance in language involves recognizing that words and expressions often carry specific meanings and connotations that are deeply rooted in a particular cultural context. NLP applications must, therefore, be culturally aware, adapting to the variability in language use across different communities. For instance, the phrase "breaking the ice," while commonly understood in English-speaking cultures as initiating conversation in a social setting, may not have a direct or meaningful translation in other languages or cultures. Thus, an effective NLP system must either find the culturally equivalent phrase or appropriately interpret the sentiment behind the idiom for non-English speakers.

Techniques for tackling this cultural diversity include the development of large, annotated datasets that are culturally inclusive and representative of diverse linguistic backgrounds. Machine learning models, particularly those employing deep learning, can be trained on such datasets to detect and understand idioms and cultural references. The utilization of transformer-based models like BERT (Bidirectional Encoder Representations from Transformers) has been revolutionary, allowing for context-dependent representations of words and phrases.

Transfer learning is another critical technique in this context. It allows an NLP model trained on data from one language or culture to adapt to another. By fine-tuning pre-trained models with specific idiomatic and cultural data, the model can better handle the nuances of a new language or cultural setting. Cross-lingual transfer learning is especially valuable for languages with limited NLP resources. To illustrate, consider the idiom "to kick the bucket," which signifies 'to die' in English. An NLP system can recognize this as an idiomatic expression rather than a literal action involving a bucket by using a technique called idiom tokenization. By tokenizing the phrase as a single unit and linking it to its idiomatic meaning in a lexicon, the system can process the expression accurately. Furthermore, semantic role labelling can discern the subject and the action, indicating that the phrase is figurative. Another example of idiom recognition involves sentiment analysis, where idioms pose a particular challenge due to their non-literal nature. Idioms like "a piece of cake," meaning something is very easy, can lead to incorrect sentiment analysis if taken literally. Techniques such as context embedding, and sentiment lexicons tailored to idiomatic expressions can help NLP systems correctly interpret these phrases.

Moreover, cultural nuances also extend to non-verbal communication cues, which can greatly influence the meaning of verbal communication. Multimodal NLP systems, which incorporate visual and acoustic data along with text, are beginning to address this aspect. For example, a phrase accompanied by a smile might be friendly, while the same phrase with a frown could be sarcastic. Multimodal systems can integrate these cues to better understand the intended meaning.

In the realm of NLP applications, chatbots and virtual assistants are prominent examples where idiom recognition and cultural nuance are paramount. To be effective, these systems must not only grasp the literal meaning of user input but also the cultural context that shapes the conversation. This means not only understanding when a user is using an idiom but also responding in a culturally appropriate manner, which often involves using idioms or culturally nuanced language in return. As the field progresses, the goal is for NLP systems to become as adept at navigating the subtleties of human language as the most culturally savvy human speakers.

Knowledge Checkpoint Worksheet 10

Multilingual Natural Language Processing

1 Fill in the Blanks:

A Translation and transliteration are the foundational pillars of ________ NLP.

B Modern translation systems leverage ________ to deliver translations with remarkable accuracy and fluency.

C ________ is a translation technique that involves algorithms learning from bilingual text corpora.

D The main goal of multilingual NLP is to facilitate ________ communication and enhance inclusivity.

E Transformer models like Google's BERT and OpenAI's GPT series use ________ mechanisms to process language.

2 True/False:

A Neural Machine Translation uses a rule-based approach to translate between languages. (True/False)

B Cross-lingual models are designed to process multiple languages using a single model. (True/False)

C Transliteration is about converting the meaning of words from one language to another. (True/False)

D Low-resource languages often have a wealth of digital tools and corpora available. (True/False)

E Phonological complexity and orthographic variation pose significant challenges in processing low-resource languages. (True/False)

3 Match the Following Techniques with Their Descriptions:

A. Rule-Based Machine Translation (RBMT)	1. Relies on a comprehensive set of linguistic rules and dictionaries.
B. Statistical Machine Translation (SMT)	2. Utilizes deep neural networks and sequence-to-sequence architecture.
C. Neural Machine Translation (NMT)	3. Involves algorithms that learn from bilingual text corpora.

9

Domain-Specific Natural Language Processing

Domain-specific NLP further pushes the boundaries of the field by delving into industry-specific terminologies and requirements. Different sectors such as healthcare, law, education, automobile, customer service, and finance have unique linguistic contexts that general NLP tools cannot adequately handle. This chapter sets out to methodically deconstruct the unique challenges inherent in domain-specific NLP, investigate the advanced technical models crafted to surmount these issues, and offer a detailed analysis of the nuances associated with customizing NLP to suit the varied terrains of different industry sectors.

9.1 Healthcare Natural Language Processing

Healthcare NLP stands as a transformative force in the realm of medicine, wielding the potential to revolutionize how clinical data is interpreted, how patients' needs are understood, and how care is delivered. At its core, healthcare NLP is about extracting meaningful information from unstructured text—the rich, narrative language of clinicians' notes, patient records, academic research, and more. The application of NLP in healthcare serves a multitude of purposes, from clinical decision support to the management of health records, predictive analytics, and even in direct patient care through the development of more sophisticated chatbots and virtual health assistants. NLP can take the subtleties of human language with its ambiguities, variations, and complexity and make sense of it at scale, something that traditional data processing methods cannot do. For example, clinicians' notes, which are a gold mine of nuanced patient information, have traditionally been underutilized due to their unstructured nature; with NLP, this information can be analyzed rapidly, unlocking insights into patient conditions, treatment outcomes, and more. Moreover, NLP systems can help to aggregate and synthesize information from a plethora of sources such as electronic health records (EHRs), published research papers, and clinical trial reports, making it accessible and actionable.

Language Intelligence: Expanding Frontiers in Natural Language Processing, First Edition. Akshi Kumar.
© 2025 The Institute of Electrical and Electronics Engineers, Inc. Published 2025 by John Wiley & Sons, Inc.

In essence, NLP serves as a bridge between the human language of healthcare and the binary precision of computational systems.

The deployment of NLP in healthcare also addresses the significant challenge of interoperability. The healthcare industry is notorious for its siloed data systems and inconsistent use of medical terminologies. NLP can harmonize these disparate data sources, enabling systems to communicate with each other and facilitating a more cohesive view of a patient's health history. For instance, a doctor in one hospital can understand the medical history of a patient treated in another facility, even if the two institutions use different systems for recording and storing patient data. Furthermore, NLP aids in the classification and organization of medical literature. With an ever-increasing volume of research publications, staying abreast of the latest findings is a herculean task for any medical professional. NLP algorithms can rapidly sift through the literature, summarize findings, and even highlight the most pertinent information for clinicians and researchers. This capability not only saves time but also ensures that decision-making can be based on the latest evidence. Fig. 9.1 presents a graphical representation of the six key factors that are driving the integration of NLP in the healthcare sector.

Domain-specific healthcare NLP refers to NLP systems and applications that are tailored to understand, interpret, and process language as it is used in the healthcare sector. In healthcare, language comes with its own set of terminologies, abbreviations, and idiosyncrasies that are not commonly found in other types of everyday language processing. Here's how domain-specific NLP is shaping healthcare:

- *Clinical Decision Support:* NLP systems analyze unstructured clinical notes to extract critical data that support clinical decision-making. By identifying trends and patterns in symptoms, diagnoses, and treatment outcomes, these systems provide clinicians with insights that can inform patient care.
- *Electronic Health Records (EHRs):* Domain-specific NLP aids in the structuring of data from EHRs. It extracts pertinent information from free-text notes,

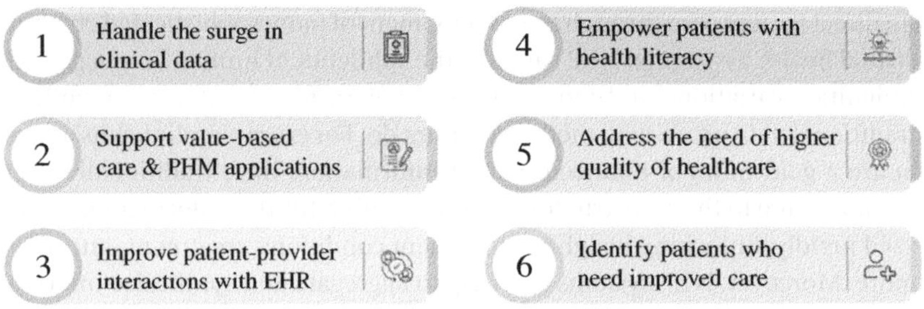

Figure 9.1 Driving Factors Behind NLP in Healthcare.

making it searchable and actionable, and inputs this data into standardized forms for better interoperability.

- *Medical Coding and Billing:* NLP assists in translating clinical documentation into appropriate medical codes used for billing and insurance purposes. This helps in reducing errors and improving the efficiency of the billing process.
- *Pharmacovigilance:* By monitoring drug efficacy and adverse drug reactions from various data sources such as social media, forums, and medical literature, NLP systems contribute to drug safety surveillance and reporting.
- *Patient Engagement:* NLP facilitates the creation of chatbots and virtual health assistants that can communicate with patients using natural language, providing them with information on medication, treatment plans, and appointment scheduling.
- *Literature Review and Research:* NLP is employed to sift through large volumes of medical research papers and clinical trials to find relevant studies, synthesize findings, and support evidence-based medicine.
- *Predictive Analytics:* NLP, combined with machine learning algorithms, is used to predict patient outcomes, readmissions, and potential diagnoses by analyzing patterns in historical patient data.
- *Information Retrieval:* Healthcare professionals use NLP-powered search engines to find relevant information quickly from medical databases and libraries, saving time and improving the quality of care.
- *Speech Recognition:* In busy healthcare settings, voice-to-text systems allow for hands-free documentation and data entry, increasing productivity and allowing providers to focus more on patient care.
- *Sentiment Analysis:* NLP helps in gauging patient satisfaction and experiences by analyzing feedback from surveys, social media, and other communication channels.

To effectively serve these functions, domain-specific NLP systems must be trained on specialized healthcare datasets and incorporate medical ontologies such as the Unified Medical Language System (UMLS). They must also comply with healthcare regulations concerning data privacy and security, such as HIPAA in the United States.

9.1.1 Predictive Analytics in Healthcare NLP

Predictive analytics represents one of the most potent and transformative applications of NLP in healthcare. It exemplifies the convergence of big data with advanced analytics, leveraging the ability to read and understand vast amounts of unstructured data that healthcare systems generate. The practical outcomes of this fusion are profoundly impactful, leading to proactive healthcare management and enhanced patient care.

- *Early Detection and Intervention:* The earlier a health condition is detected, the better the chances are for a successful intervention. Predictive analytics powered by NLP can process extensive datasets from EHRs, clinical notes, patient-reported outcomes, and more, to identify patterns and signals that might be indicative of a developing condition. For chronic diseases, such as diabetes or heart disease, this can mean the difference between managing a condition at home or facing a life-threatening emergency. For instance, by analyzing a patient's historical health data alongside real-time inputs, such as notes from recent doctor's visits or updates in their health records, NLP systems can flag early signs of deterioration. This might involve recognizing subtle changes in language that suggest a patient is experiencing new or worsening symptoms, or identifying trends in biometric data that indicate risk of an acute event. As these systems evolve, they will become even more adept at understanding the context of a patient's health, providing clinicians with actionable insights long before traditional methods would have raised the alarm.
- *Resource Allocation:* In a sector where resources are often stretched thin, the ability to predict which patients will require additional care, and when, is invaluable. By forecasting patient trajectories, healthcare providers can better allocate resources such as staff, beds, and medications. During events like flu seasons or pandemics, this capability can facilitate more efficient responses, ensuring that resources are directed where they are most needed. For health systems, the financial implications are substantial. Predictive analytics via NLP can help reduce unnecessary hospital admissions, target interventions to avoid costly complications, and improve overall care quality. By predicting which patients are at risk of readmission, providers can tailor discharge planning and follow-up care to reduce the likelihood of a return visit.
- *Chronic Disease Management:* Chronic disease management is an area that stands to gain immensely from predictive analytics in NLP. The chronic nature of diseases like hypertension, diabetes, and COPD necessitates a continuous monitoring approach, which can be both resource-intensive and challenging to maintain. NLP can sift through mountains of patient data to help healthcare providers identify which patients are managing their conditions well and which ones are showing signs of instability. Predictive models can alert clinicians and patients to the risks of potential exacerbations. For example, an NLP system might analyze data from a patient's glucometer readings, food intake logs, and physical activity records to predict glycemic control issues, enabling timely adjustments to treatment plans. In another scenario, NLP could evaluate patients' speech or written communication for signs of mental health distress, potentially averting crises by triggering early intervention.
- *Intelligent Virtual Health Assistants:* NLP-driven virtual health assistants are emerging as a pivotal tool in patient engagement and self-management.

These assistants are designed to provide a user-friendly interface for patients to interact with their health data and care teams. They can decode patient input, whether it's typed text or spoken word, and provide personalized feedback and support. For instance, a virtual health assistant could remind a patient to take their medication, answer questions about their health condition, or provide encouragement and education on managing their disease. Beyond just reminders, these systems can offer tailored advice based on the patient's history and current condition. A diabetes patient, for instance, could receive diet and exercise recommendations based on their latest blood sugar readings and historical trends. Such systems could also serve as a first point of contact, triaging patient queries and determining whether they need to see a healthcare provider. By using NLP to understand and respond to patient needs, virtual health assistants can offload routine tasks from human staff, allowing them to focus on more complex care needs.

Predictive analytics through healthcare NLP is an area rich with possibilities, addressing some of the most pressing challenges in healthcare today. From enabling early disease detection to optimizing resource allocation, and empowering patients in their self-care, the potential benefits are as broad as they are significant. As NLP technologies continue to mature and integrate deeper into clinical workflows, the promise of a more predictive, preventive, and personalized healthcare system becomes increasingly tangible. This innovative synergy of data analytics and NLP stands not only to improve health outcomes but also to reshape the healthcare landscape into one that is more efficient, responsive, and patient-centred.

9.1.2 Domain-Specific Models in Healthcare

In healthcare, domain-specific NLP models are designed to understand and process the specialized language and unique context found in medical records, scientific literature, and other healthcare-related texts. These models differ from general-purpose NLP models in that they are trained on domain-specific datasets and are tailored to address the intricacies and nuances of medical language. Here are some examples of domain-specific models and applications in healthcare:

- *Clinical BERT:* Building upon the original BERT architecture, Clinical BERT is fine-tuned on clinical notes and medical records to capture the context of medical dialogue and terminology more effectively than its general-purpose counterpart.
- *BioBERT:* A variant of BERT that has been pre-trained on large-scale biomedical corpora. It is designed to perform various biomedical text mining tasks,

including named entity recognition (NER), relation extraction, and question answering in the biomedical domain.
- *Clinical Text Analysis and Knowledge Extraction System (cTAKES):* An open-source NLP system for extracting information from EHRs, developed by the Mayo Clinic. It's specialized in identifying clinical terms and mapping them to standardized code systems such as SNOMED CT and RxNorm.
- *UMLS Metathesaurus:* While not a model in itself, the UMLS provides a rich source of medical terminologies that can be used to enhance domain-specific NLP models.
- *Med7:* A pre-trained model specifically developed for the recognition of seven different entities in prescription text: drug names, dosages, durations, frequencies, forms, routes, and strengths.
- *GPT-3 for Healthcare:* Customized versions of GPT-3 are being trained with medical datasets to improve performance on healthcare-related tasks. This includes answering medical questions, summarizing patient records, and even generating medical coding from clinical text.
- *DeepPhe:* A deep phenotyping framework that uses NLP to extract cancer phenotypes from EHRs. It is capable of recognizing detailed clinical information about tumors, treatments, and outcomes, which can be crucial for research and treatment planning.
- *MT-DNN for Biomedical:* A multitask deep neural network model that can handle multiple NLP tasks simultaneously. When fine-tuned on biomedical datasets, it shows enhanced performance on a range of bioinformatics tasks.
- *HealthBERT:* Fine-tuned specifically on health-related data, HealthBERT demonstrates improved performance over BERT for tasks like medical coding, clinical event detection, and patient risk prediction.

These models are typically fine-tuned on specific tasks within the healthcare domain, such as:

- *Named Entity Recognition (NER):* Identifying medical terms, medications, diseases, and other relevant entities from clinical text.
- *Relation Extraction:* Identifying relationships between entities in medical literature, such as drug-disease interactions or symptom-disease associations.
- *Sentiment Analysis:* Analyzing patient feedback, physician notes, or social media to gauge sentiments about treatments, medications, or healthcare experiences.

The development of domain-specific models requires substantial amounts of annotated medical data and expertise in both machine learning and the medical domain. As such, these models often result from collaborative efforts between AI researchers, medical professionals, and bioinformaticians.

9.1.3 Challenges in Implementing Healthcare NLP

The implementation of Natural Language Processing (NLP) in healthcare is a task replete with technical, regulatory, and ethical complexities. These challenges shape the landscape within which healthcare NLP must operate, influencing both the efficacy of NLP solutions and the pace at which they can be adopted in clinical settings.

- *Data Annotation and Quality Challenges:* The foundation of effective NLP lies in the quality of data used to train the algorithms. In healthcare, the data must be annotated meticulously, which means labelling the data to indicate the presence of certain features or information that the algorithms should learn to recognize. For instance, a dataset might be annotated to highlight symptoms, diagnoses, medication names, dosages, and patient outcomes. The annotation process is painstaking, often requiring medical experts who can interpret clinical notes and identify relevant information. Such a process is not only labour-intensive but also requires significant expertise, which can be a bottleneck in developing robust NLP systems.

  Moreover, the nature of healthcare data exacerbates these challenges. Privacy concerns are paramount, as patient data is highly sensitive. Ensuring that data is de-identified correctly without losing critical information for NLP tasks is a delicate balance. The data must be handled in such a way that it preserves patient confidentiality while remaining useful for algorithm training.
- *Complexity of Medical Language:* Medical language is a complex domain with its jargon, abbreviations, and diverse ways of documenting the same concepts. Clinicians may use different terms to describe the same condition, and personal notes may include shorthand or idiosyncratic expressions that are clear to the individual clinician but obscure to outsiders. Furthermore, medical documents can contain a mix of structured data (like checkboxes and predefined fields) and unstructured data (like free-text notes), each presenting its own challenges for NLP systems.

  To navigate this complexity, advanced machine learning techniques, especially deep learning, are utilized. Models based on transformer architecture, like BERT (Bidirectional Encoder Representations from Transformers), have shown remarkable results in grasping the nuances of language, making them highly suitable for interpreting the intricacies of medical documentation. However, training these sophisticated models requires large volumes of high-quality data, and they must be fine-tuned to grasp the specificities of medical terminology.
- *Ethical Considerations and Bias:* Ethical concerns are at the forefront when discussing healthcare NLP. The utmost concern is the protection of patient privacy. Ensuring that NLP systems comply with strict regulations like HIPAA and GDPR is essential to maintaining trust and safeguarding against breaches of

confidentiality. Each step, from data collection to model deployment, must be scrutinized to ensure compliance and protect sensitive health information.

A further ethical challenge arises in the form of bias. If the data used to train NLP systems is not representative of the diverse patient populations, the resulting algorithms could exhibit biases. For instance, if an NLP system is trained predominantly on data from a particular demographic, it may not perform as well for individuals outside that demographic. Such biases can lead to disparities in care recommendations, risk assessments, and patient outcomes.

Bias in NLP is not just a data problem; it can also be a design problem. If the developers of NLP systems do not consider diversity in their design processes or fail to test their systems across diverse populations, they risk perpetuating and even amplifying existing biases. This can have dire consequences in healthcare, where decisions based on biased algorithms could lead to misdiagnoses, inappropriate treatments, and unequal access to care.

Overcoming these challenges requires a concerted effort from multiple stakeholders in healthcare, including data scientists, healthcare providers, regulatory bodies, and patients themselves. Innovative approaches to data annotation, like crowd-sourcing and semi-supervised learning, can help build comprehensive datasets while reducing the time and expertise required. To address the complexity of medical language, continued research and development in domain-specific models are essential. These models must be trained and validated on data that encompasses the breadth of medical communication. For ethical concerns, ongoing vigilance and an emphasis on fairness and transparency are crucial. This includes conducting regular audits for bias, involving diverse groups in the development and validation of algorithms, and implementing robust data governance frameworks that prioritize patient privacy. In sum, while the road to fully realizing healthcare NLP's potential is fraught with challenges, these obstacles are not insurmountable. The promise of NLP in transforming healthcare is a worthy impetus to drive innovation, forge collaborations, and establish new standards that safeguard both efficacy and ethics in this vital application of artificial intelligence.

9.2 Legal Natural Language Processing

The promising field of Legal NLP represents a significant stride toward the digitization and automation of the legal industry. It is a specialized branch of NLP that focuses on the understanding and manipulation of legal texts. Legal texts, whether they be laws, contracts, court decisions, or patents, are notorious for their complexity, dense structure, and specialized vocabulary. Thus, Legal NLP has evolved as a bespoke field to handle such characteristics.

9.2.1 Applications of Legal NLP: Automation and Predictive Analytics

The suite of applications derived from Legal NLP has catalyzed a revolutionary shift in legal operations, enabling a degree of efficiency and predictive power that was once the stuff of fiction. Two primary applications—automated document analysis and predictive analytics—stand out for their profound impact on the legal profession.

- *Automated Document Analysis:* At the forefront of Legal NLP's applications is automated document analysis. This technology harnesses the power of AI to sift through thousands of pages of legal documentation in search of pertinent information—tasks that would traditionally require extensive manual labour. The precision of Legal NLP algorithms allows for the rapid extraction of key elements such as names, dates, contractual obligations, and legal references with remarkable accuracy.
  The significance of automated document analysis cannot be overstated. It extends beyond mere convenience, touching upon the essential cost and time efficiencies that could redefine legal practice. For instance, during the discovery phase of a lawsuit, legal teams must review large volumes of documentation to identify relevant evidence. Legal NLP can expedite this process, highlighting material information and flagging inconsistencies or key terms that might otherwise be missed. Moreover, contract review and management benefit immensely from NLP. The automation of clause extraction, risk assessment, and compliance checks fundamentally changes the contract lifecycle, allowing lawyers to concentrate on strategic aspects rather than routine scrutiny.
- *Predictive Analytics:* Predictive analytics represents another groundbreaking application of Legal NLP. By analyzing historical legal decisions, NLP models can predict outcomes of current cases with a notable degree of confidence. This predictive capability supports lawyers in assessing the merits of a case before proceeding, potentially saving time and resources on untenable legal battles. The potential of predictive analytics in legal applications is as immense as it is complex. Law firms can use these insights to strategize on cases, while clients benefit from a more transparent view of their legal standing. In-house legal departments of corporations can forecast the risks of litigation or compliance issues, informing better business decisions.

Fig. 9.2 gives an overview of Legal NLP tasks, illustrating how different NLP techniques can be applied within the legal domain.

9.2.2 Domain-Specific Models in Legal

The development of domain-specific models within Legal NLP represents a concerted effort to address the nuanced complexities of legal language and the

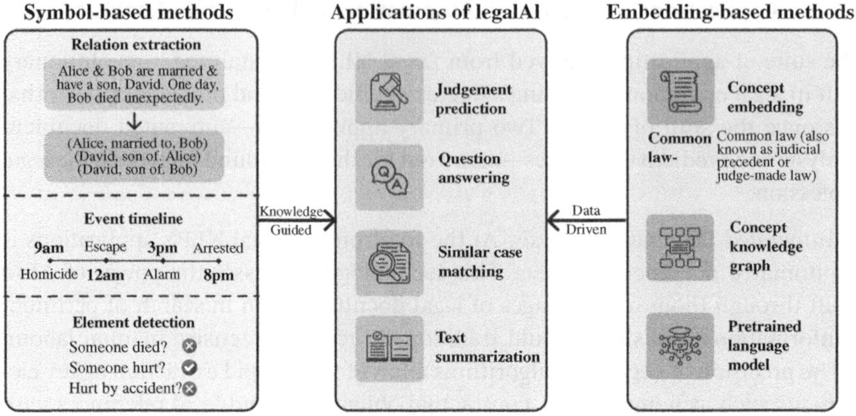

Figure 9.2 Overview of Legal NLP.

particularities of legal reasoning. These models are tailored to comprehend the jargon, concepts, and structure inherent to legal texts, enabling a more accurate and contextually relevant analysis than general-purpose NLP models could achieve.

- *Bespoke Legal Language Models:* Unlike generic NLP models, domain-specific Legal NLP models are often pre-trained on extensive legal corpora. These corpora contain statutes, case law, contracts, and other legal documents that provide the model with the vocabulary and syntactic understanding necessary for legal text interpretation. The success of these models hinges on their ability to grasp not just the language, but the underlying legal principles and logic that guide the construction of legal documents.
  Models like BERT and its adaptations (e.g., Legal-BERT) have been further trained or fine-tuned on legal data, enhancing their ability to handle legal-specific entities and relationships. This specialization allows them to perform better on tasks such as entity recognition, where the model must identify and classify legal references, terms of art, and even the parties involved in legal proceedings.
- *Application-Specific Legal Models:* Further refinement leads to application-specific legal models, which are not only trained on legal texts but also on particular tasks within the legal domain. For example, a model might be fine-tuned to predict the outcomes of contract litigation or to assess the enforceability of certain contractual clauses. This fine-tuning process involves training the model on annotated datasets that are labelled with outcomes, clause types, or other task-specific annotations. These models are highly valuable in tasks like e-discovery, where the identification of relevant documents can save significant time and resources in litigation. Additionally, they assist in due diligence

processes by scanning large volumes of documents to identify potential legal issues, such as compliance risks or intellectual property infringements.

- *Ethical and Fair Machine Learning in Legal NLP:* While domain-specific models offer substantial benefits in legal tasks, there is an acute need for these models to incorporate ethical and fair machine learning practices. This is particularly challenging in the legal domain, where data may reflect historical biases in sentencing, judicial decisions, or law enforcement. Developers of Legal NLP models must therefore be vigilant in dataset curation and model training, actively seeking to identify and mitigate biases. Ethical model development in Legal NLP also encompasses explainability. The legal field demands a high degree of transparency and the ability to understand and explain decisions made by AI systems. Models that provide interpretable outputs and rationales for their predictions are essential, as they align with the legal industry's standards for evidence and justification.
- *Interoperability and Standardization:* Another key aspect of domain-specific models in Legal NLP is the push toward interoperability and standardization. Legal systems differ significantly across jurisdictions, and thus, models must be adaptable to various legal frameworks and languages. Efforts in creating standardized annotation schemes and sharing pre-trained models across the legal community are steps toward a more unified approach in Legal NLP.

In conclusion, domain-specific models in Legal NLP are integral to the ongoing digital transformation of the legal industry. By infusing AI models with deep legal knowledge, these tools are becoming indispensable for legal professionals. However, this progress must be tempered with a steadfast commitment to ethical practices, ensuring that Legal NLP tools uphold the principles of justice and fairness that are core to the legal system.

9.2.3 Challenges in Legal Natural Language Processing

Legal NLP is an area rife with technical and ethical challenges unique to its domain. The high stakes associated with legal proceedings necessitate that NLP systems used in this context operate with the utmost accuracy and reliability. This section explores the complexities and hurdles that define Legal NLP, offering a nuanced understanding of the field's distinctive challenges.

- *Demand for High Accuracy:* In legal contexts, the margin for error is exceedingly small. Incorrect or imprecise processing of legal texts by NLP applications can lead to severe consequences, including miscarriages of justice or substantial financial losses. Legal decisions often have profound impacts on an individual's rights, finances, and freedoms. Hence, the demand for high accuracy is not just a preference but a stringent requirement. Legal NLP systems must, therefore, operate within tight error margins, far stricter than those acceptable in other domains.

- *Ambiguity of Legal Language:* Legal language is characterized by a high degree of ambiguity. Legal texts often contain complex sentences with multiple clauses and nuanced vocabulary that can be open to interpretation. This inherent ambiguity poses a significant challenge for NLP technologies, which must be capable of deciphering the intended meaning with precision. The interpretative nature of law, with concepts such as "reasonable doubt" or "fair use," adds another layer of complexity, as these terms do not have universally agreed-upon definitions and often require contextual understanding.
- *Variability in Document Structures:* The legal domain contains a wide array of document types, each with its own structural conventions. From statutes and contracts to case law and legal commentary, the variability in format and organization presents a daunting challenge for NLP systems. Extracting information from such a heterogeneous set of documents requires models to be highly adaptable and sensitive to the context and format of each document type.
- *Precise Contextual Interpretation:* Context is king in legal interpretation. The meaning of terms can change significantly based on context, precedent, and jurisdiction. Legal NLP systems must not only understand the language used in documents but also the broader legal context in which terms and phrases are used. This requirement for precise contextual interpretation extends beyond linguistic capability, necessitating an understanding of legal reasoning and principles that can be incredibly complex and abstract.
- *Ethical Considerations:* The ethical dimension of Legal NLP is profound. The potential for bias in AI systems is a concern across all domains, but in the legal domain, such bias can perpetuate systemic injustices. Ensuring that Legal NLP systems are free from both overt and subtle biases is a monumental challenge that requires constant vigilance. Privacy is another significant concern, as legal documents often contain sensitive personal information. Legal NLP systems must be designed with robust privacy protections to ensure that confidential information is not inadvertently disclosed.
- *Accountability and Transparency:* Given the potential impacts of their use, Legal NLP systems must be developed with accountability and transparency at their core. Stakeholders in legal outcomes—be they individuals or organizations—must be able to understand how NLP-driven decisions are made. This transparency is not only important for building trust in NLP systems but is often a legal requirement. The "black box" nature of many AI systems clashes with this need, making the development of interpretable and explainable NLP models a priority in the legal field.

Undoubtedly, the challenges in Legal NLP are as multifaceted as they are critical. They demand a level of sophistication and sensitivity from NLP technologies that is unmatched in other domains. Addressing these challenges is not an insurmountable task, but it requires a concerted effort from technologists, legal professionals, and ethicists to create NLP systems that are accurate, context-aware, and ethically sound. As the field of Legal NLP matures, tackling these challenges head-on will be essential for realizing the full potential of AI in legal applications.

9.3 Finance Natural Language Processing

NLP, a pivotal technology in the realm of AI, has steadily carved out a significant niche in the financial sector. At its core, NLP involves the application of computational techniques to the analysis and synthesis of natural language and speech. This technology's infiltration into finance marks a revolutionary shift in how financial data, traditionally quantified and structured, is processed and analyzed. The integration of NLP into finance is not just an addition to the toolkit; it represents a paradigm shift, opening new avenues for data interpretation and decision-making.

In the financial context, NLP serves a multitude of purposes, ranging from sentiment analysis to automated report generation, risk management, and fraud detection. One of the most impactful applications of NLP in finance is sentiment analysis, where it is used to scour vast expanses of unstructured data—including news articles, social media posts, financial reports, and more—to gauge public sentiment toward market developments, individual stocks, or the financial market as a whole. This analysis can provide a more nuanced understanding of market dynamics, going beyond what traditional numerical data can offer. Another significant application of NLP in finance is in risk management. Financial institutions can leverage NLP to analyze news, reports, and other textual information to identify potential risks that might not be evident through traditional data analysis methods. For instance, NLP can help in detecting shifts in political or economic policies that might affect investments or market stability. Automated reporting is another area where NLP shows its prowess. By automating the extraction of relevant information from financial documents and generating summaries, NLP can significantly enhance efficiency and accuracy. This automation extends to the generation of financial news summaries, earnings reports, and even personalized investment advice, saving time and reducing the margin for human error.

Furthermore, NLP plays a crucial role in fraud detection and regulatory compliance. By analyzing communication patterns and financial transactions, NLP systems can identify anomalies that may indicate fraudulent activities. They also help in ensuring compliance with ever-evolving regulatory requirements by monitoring communications and flagging potential non-compliant behavior. Integrating NLP into existing financial models and systems has been a journey of transformation. Traditional financial models are predominantly numerical and based on structured data. The integration of NLP allows these models to incorporate unstructured data, providing a more comprehensive view of the financial landscape. This integration has led to the development of more robust predictive models, which are essential for tasks like market trend analysis and algorithmic trading.

In conclusion, the role of NLP in finance is multifaceted and transformative. Its ability to process and analyze vast amounts of unstructured data provides insights that were previously inaccessible to financial analysts. From enhancing market understanding through sentiment analysis to improving risk management and compliance, NLP is reshaping the financial landscape. As it continues to integrate with traditional financial models and systems, its potential to revolutionize the sector only grows, promising a future where financial decisions are more informed, efficient, and accurate.

9.3.1 Core Applications of NLP in Finance

The application of NLP in market sentiment analysis, risk management, automated reporting, fraud detection, and compliance highlights its versatility and efficacy in the financial sector. NLP not only enhances the efficiency and accuracy of financial processes but also plays a crucial role in safeguarding against risks and ensuring adherence to regulatory standards. These applications underscore the growing importance of NLP in modern financial operations.

- *Sentiment Analysis in Finance:* Sentiment Analysis, a critical component of NLP, has become an indispensable tool in the financial sector. It involves the computational interpretation and classification of sentiments (positive, negative, neutral) expressed in textual data. In finance, this technique is primarily used to analyze market sentiment by scrutinizing various sources such as news articles, social media content, and financial reports. The goal is to assess the collective mood or opinion of investors and the public toward specific financial markets, assets, or even broader economic conditions.

  The sources for sentiment analysis in finance are diverse. News articles from financial news agencies provide insights into market trends and investor reactions to economic events. Social media platforms, especially Twitter and financial forums, are rich in real-time investor opinions and discussions. Financial reports and earnings call transcripts offer a more formal view of a company's performance and future outlook. Techniques in sentiment analysis range from simple keyword-based methods to complex machine learning algorithms. These methods involve identifying specific words or phrases that convey sentiment and then quantifying them to gauge overall sentiment. Advanced techniques use machine learning models to understand context, sarcasm, and subtle nuances in language, providing a more accurate sentiment analysis.

a. **Case Study—Social Media Sentiment and Stock Prices:**
   A notable example is the correlation between social media sentiment and stock prices. Research has shown that a significant change in sentiment on social media platforms can precede a corresponding movement in stock prices. For instance, a study analyzing Twitter sentiment found that an increase in positive tweets about a company often led to a short-term increase in its stock price.
b. **Case Study—News Sentiment and Market Movements:**
   Another case study involves analyzing sentiment in financial news. A significant shift in the tone of news articles, either positive or negative, about specific sectors or markets can be a precursor to market movements. For example, negative news sentiment about the technology sector might indicate an impending downturn in tech stocks.
c. **Case Study—Earnings Reports and Investor Sentiment:**
   Sentiment analysis of earnings reports and conference calls can also provide valuable insights. Positive sentiment in a company's earnings report, like optimistic future projections or strong past performance, can lead to an increase in investor confidence and, consequently, the stock price. Conversely, negative sentiment can lead to a decrease in stock value.
   Undoubtedly, sentiment analysis in finance is a powerful tool for gauging market mood and investor sentiment. By analyzing diverse data sources through sophisticated NLP techniques, financial professionals can gain insights into potential market movements. These case studies demonstrate the tangible impact sentiment analysis can have on understanding and predicting market trends, making it an invaluable asset in financial decision-making.

- *NLP in Assessing and Monitoring Risks*
  In the financial industry, risk management is a critical process, and NLP has become a vital tool in enhancing this process. NLP technologies allow for the effective monitoring and assessment of risks by analyzing unstructured data sources, which are often overlooked by traditional risk management models. These sources include news articles, social media posts, financial blogs, and other textual data that can provide early indicators of market changes, credit risk, operational risk, or compliance risk. Examples of Risk Assessment Models Using NLP include:

a. **Credit Risk Assessment:** NLP models are utilized to analyze news and social media sentiments about a company to assess its credit risk. By evaluating the public perception and sentiment trends, these models can predict the likelihood of default or financial distress before it is reflected in the company's financial statements.
b. **Market Risk Analysis:** In market risk analysis, NLP is used to process global news and economic reports to predict market volatility. For instance, models that analyze geopolitical news and international relations can provide early warnings about potential market disruptions.

- *Enhancing Financial Reporting with NLP*
  Automated reporting, powered by NLP, is transforming how financial data is compiled, analyzed, and presented. NLP systems can automatically extract relevant financial information from various data sources, such as earnings reports, SEC filings, and market news, to generate comprehensive financial reports and analytics. It impacts the efficiency and accuracy.

a. The use of NLP in automated reporting significantly increases efficiency by reducing the time and labour required to compile and analyze financial data.
b. It also enhances the accuracy of reports by minimizing human errors and providing a more consistent analysis of data.
c. Furthermore, NLP-enabled reporting tools can provide real-time updates and insights, which are crucial for timely financial decision-making.

- *Fraud Detection and Compliance: Leveraging NLP*
  NLP plays a pivotal role in identifying fraudulent activities and ensuring regulatory compliance within the financial sector. By analyzing patterns in communication and transactional data, NLP models can detect anomalies that may indicate fraud or non-compliant behavior. The following case studies on Fraud Detection exemplify the use of Language Pattern Recognition:

a. **Detecting Fraudulent Transactions:**
   A case study involves the use of NLP to identify irregularities in transaction data. By analyzing the language and patterns in transaction descriptions, NLP models can flag transactions that deviate from normal patterns, indicating potential fraud.
b. **Compliance Monitoring in Communications:**
   Another application is in monitoring communications for regulatory compliance. For example, banks use NLP to scan emails and messages for language that may suggest insider trading or other non-compliant activities.

9.3.2 NLP in Financial Analysis

NLP has become a cornerstone in the field of financial analysis, offering advanced techniques to mine, analyze, and interpret vast amounts of textual data. In this complex domain, three key NLP techniques stand out for their significant impact: Text Mining and Information Extraction, Topic Modelling and Classification, and NER. Each of these techniques plays a vital role in transforming unstructured text into actionable financial insights.

- *Text Mining and Information Extraction*
  Text Mining in the context of financial analysis involves the extraction of meaningful information from large volumes of unstructured text data, such as financial reports, news articles, and corporate filings. This process is crucial for analysts who need to sift through immense data sets to find relevant information quickly. Key techniques and applications include:
  a. **Keyword Search and Frequency Analysis:** This basic technique involves identifying specific keywords or phrases and quantifying their frequency to extract insights. For example, the frequent occurrence of terms like "merger" or "acquisition" in company filings might indicate significant corporate actions
  b. **Contextual Analysis and Relevance Scoring:** More advanced text mining involves understanding the context around keywords, and using NLP algorithms to determine the relevance of a document or a section within it. This is particularly useful in processing earnings call transcripts where the context around financial performance is key.
  c. **Summarization:** Automated summarization tools use NLP to distil lengthy financial documents into concise summaries, highlighting the most critical points, which aids in rapid decision-making.
- *Topic Modelling and Classification*
  Topic Modelling and Classification involve identifying underlying themes or topics within large sets of text data and classifying texts based on these themes. This technique is particularly useful for gaining an overview of the main topics being discussed in financial texts. Key techniques and applications include:
  a. **Latent Dirichlet Allocation (LDA):** LDA is a popular method for identifying topics in a corpus of text. In finance, LDA can reveal the prevalent themes in a set of financial news articles or investor reports, such as "market volatility," "regulatory changes," or "emerging markets."
  b. **Sentiment Classification:** This involves classifying text based on the sentiment conveyed—positive, negative, or neutral. For instance, sentiment classification can be used to gauge investor sentiment on a particular stock or the financial market as a whole.
  c. **Document Clustering:** Clustering algorithms group similar documents together. In financial analysis, this helps in categorizing documents into groups such as market reports, regulatory updates, or company-specific news.

- *Named Entity Recognition (NER)*
  NER in financial analysis involves identifying and classifying key entities mentioned in text, such as company names, stock tickers, financial metrics, and currencies. This technique is critical for structuring data extracted from financial texts. Key techniques and applications include:
  a. **Entity Identification:** Using NLP models to identify entities in text. For instance, in an analyst report, NER systems can highlight company names, stock symbols, and financial metrics.
  b. **Entity Linking:** Linking identified entities to external databases or knowledge bases. For example, linking a company name to its stock symbol or financial profile.
  c. **Entity Relationship Analysis:** Analyzing the relationships between different entities. In financial news, this might involve understanding how a news event about a company (entity) affects its stock price (another entity).

9.3.3 Domain-Specific NLP Models

In the financial sector, domain-specific NLP models have been developed to address unique challenges and requirements. These models are tailored to comprehend and analyze financial language, which often includes industry-specific jargon, complex concepts, and unique data structures. Table 9.1 summarizes the domain-specific NLP models in finance outlining their primary purpose, core functionalities, and examples of each model type.

9.3.4 Challenges Within Financial NLP and Future Scope

Implementing NLP in finance brings unique challenges. Firstly, the financial sector is laden with specialized jargon, acronyms, and terms that can vary in meaning based on context. NLP systems must continuously adapt and learn to accurately interpret this evolving language. Additionally, financial texts often contain subtleties and nuances, such as sarcasm or implied meanings, which are difficult for NLP algorithms to decipher accurately. Another significant challenge is data quality and availability. Financial NLP systems rely heavily on large datasets, which must be clean, well-structured, and representative. However, obtaining such datasets can be difficult due to privacy concerns, data rights, and the sheer variety of data sources.

Moreover, ensuring regulatory compliance and data security is paramount in finance. NLP applications must adhere to stringent financial regulations and data privacy laws, complicating their design and implementation. There's also the challenge of bias in AI models. If the training data is biased or not sufficiently

Table 9.1 Overview of Domain-Specific NLP Models in Finance.

Model Type	Purpose	Functionality	Examples
Financial Sentiment Analysis Models	Gauge sentiment of market-related news, social media, earnings calls, and financial reports	Trained on financial lexicon to accurately interpret sentiments unique to the financial domain	Bloomberg's sentiment analysis tools, Refinitiv's MarketPsych Indices
Regulatory Compliance and Risk Management Models	Monitor compliance with regulations and identify potential risks in communication/documentation	Scan through communications for detecting non-compliant language or risky propositions	Digital Reasoning's Conduct Surveillance system, IBM's Watson Compliance solutions
Fraud Detection Models	Identify patterns and anomalies in financial data indicating fraudulent activity	Analyze transactional data, communication patterns, and financial reports to detect irregularities	SAS's Fraud Management, Oracle Financial Services Analytical Applications
Algorithmic Trading Models	Inform and automate trading decisions by analyzing market sentiment and financial news	Process real-time data to make predictions about market movements and facilitate automated trading	Quantopian's trading algorithms, Alpaca's commission-free algorithmic trading platform
Financial Forecasting and Predictive Analytics Models	Forecast market trends, stock movements, and economic changes	Analyze historical data and current market indicators to predict future trends	Moody's Analytics, FactSet's financial data and analytics software
Credit Scoring and Underwriting Models	Assess creditworthiness and risk in lending	Analyze a range of unstructured data to assess credit risk	ZestFinance, Upstart's underwriting model
Customer Service and Chatbots	Provide automated customer support and financial advice	Use NLP to understand and respond to customer queries effectively	Bank of America's chatbot Erica, Capital One's Eno
Market Research and Analysis Models	Deep analysis of market reports, research papers, and financial news	Extract insights, trends, and key information from vast amounts of text data	AlphaSense, Sentieo's market intelligence platform

diverse, the NLP models may produce skewed or unfair results, leading to inaccurate analyses or decisions.

Despite these challenges, the future of NLP in finance is promising and ripe with potential. One area of growth is the enhancement of AI algorithms for better context understanding and sentiment analysis, allowing for more accurate predictions and insights. Additionally, the integration of NLP with other AI technologies, like machine learning and deep learning, is expected to further refine data processing and analysis capabilities. Another emerging trend is the use of NLP in personal financial management and customer service, with more advanced and interactive chatbots and virtual assistants. These tools can offer personalized financial advice and customer support, enhancing the overall customer experience. Furthermore, advancements in NLP are likely to lead to more sophisticated risk management and fraud detection tools. By analyzing patterns and anomalies in financial texts and transactions, these tools can provide early warnings of potential risks and fraudulent activities. Lastly, there's a growing interest in using NLP for ESG (Environmental, Social, and Governance) investing. NLP can process vast amounts of unstructured data to extract insights related to ESG criteria, aiding investment decisions that align with ethical and sustainable values.

While there are challenges in implementing NLP in finance, the ongoing advancements in AI and machine learning, coupled with a growing emphasis on personalized financial services and sustainable investing, point toward a dynamic and impactful future for NLP in the financial sector.

9.4 NLP in Education

NLP in education refers to the application of computational techniques to understand, interpret, and generate human language in a way that supports educational objectives. This includes facilitating learning, automating administrative tasks, and providing personalized educational experiences. NLP technologies can interpret student input, assess written assignments, power intelligent tutoring systems, and provide insights into learning patterns.

9.4.1 Facilitating Learning Through NLP

The utilization of NLP within educational environments is vast, encompassing the interpretation of student input during interactive learning activities. For example, when students engage with intelligent tutoring systems, NLP algorithms are at work behind the scenes, parsing student responses, evaluating their correctness, and providing tailored feedback. These systems can interpret natural language answers, allowing for a more conversational and engaging learning experience.

They can understand a student's explanation in a science lesson or a reasoning process in a math problem, providing educators with insights into a student's thought process beyond right or wrong answers.

In language learning, NLP is the powerhouse behind applications that support speech recognition and machine translation. These applications help students practice pronunciation, listening skills, and conversational fluency. Speech recognition technology can provide immediate feedback on language pronunciation, cadence, and intonation, which are crucial for mastering a new language. Furthermore, machine translation tools break down language barriers, allowing students to access educational material in various languages and providing multilingual support in increasingly diverse educational settings.

NLP's impact extends to adaptive learning technologies, which are reshaping the educational landscape. These technologies leverage NLP to analyze texts students interact with, determining their reading level, subject comprehension, and learning styles. Based on this analysis, adaptive learning platforms can present content that is paced and styled to fit each learner's needs. For instance, if a student excels in a particular subject area, the system can introduce more challenging material, or conversely, offer remediation if a student struggles. This level of personalization ensures that each student can learn at an appropriate pace, with content that is neither too difficult nor too easy, thereby maximizing the learning potential.

Moreover, NLP facilitates the creation of dynamic educational content. It can automatically generate quizzes, flashcards, and summaries from textbooks or lecture notes, providing students with additional resources to aid their studies. These resources can be customized to focus on areas where the student has shown the need for further practice, reinforcing learning objectives in a targeted manner.

Incorporating NLP into educational software allows for the creation of a more interactive and responsive learning environment. By analyzing and responding to student inputs, NLP-driven applications can simulate one-on-one interactions with a tutor, providing explanations, guiding problem-solving, and engaging in dialogue. This level of interaction encourages active learning and critical thinking, as students are not merely passive recipients of information but active participants in a conversational learning process. NLP's role in education is multifaceted and increasingly integral. By interpreting student input during learning activities, supporting language acquisition through speech recognition and translation, and enabling adaptive learning technologies, NLP is paving the way for a future where education is more personalized, accessible, and aligned with individual learning trajectories. As this technology continues to evolve, its potential to support and enhance educational outcomes becomes ever more promising. Fig. 9.3 showcases the benefits of using NLP in education.

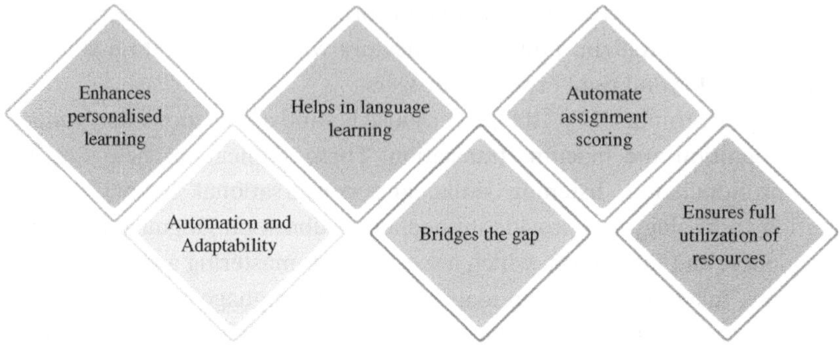

Figure 9.3 Benefits of Using Natural Language Processing in Education.

9.4.2 NLP Techniques and Their Application in Education

NLP has a suite of techniques that, when applied to education, can significantly enhance both the delivery and the individual experience of learning. Among these, text classification, sentiment analysis, and topic modelling stand out for their direct applications in educational settings.

- *Text Classification* is an NLP technique used to automatically sort text into predefined categories. In education, this can be utilized for organizing and recommending relevant academic content. For instance, an NLP system could classify library resources for students researching a specific topic, or it can sort through student forum posts to identify the most frequently discussed subjects or questions that need academic support.
- *Sentiment Analysis* involves assessing the emotional tone behind a body of text. This is particularly useful in education for evaluating student feedback on courses and instructors. By analyzing the sentiment of student evaluations, educational institutions can glean insights into the overall student satisfaction and the emotional impact of their teaching methods and course materials. This feedback can then inform improvements and adaptations in teaching strategies and curriculum design.
- **Topic Modelling** is an NLP technique used to uncover abstract topics within a large volume of text. In an educational context, topic modelling can be applied to large sets of academic papers or course evaluations to identify common themes and trends. This can help in curriculum development by highlighting subjects that are emerging as areas of interest or concern among students. Moreover, it can assist in content recommendation systems by mapping student interests to available educational materials.

These NLP techniques not only aid in the operational aspects of education but are also crucial in measuring and enhancing student engagement. By providing educators with the tools to analyze content and student feedback at scale, NLP techniques help create a more responsive and student-centered educational environment. As these technologies continue to mature, they promise to play an even larger role in the personalization and effectiveness of educational experiences.

9.4.3 Domain-Specific Models in Education

In the realm of education, the application of NLP has given rise to sophisticated domain-specific models that significantly bolster learning and teaching methodologies. These models range from language proficiency applications to complex learning analytics platforms.

- *State-of-the-Art Language Proficiency Models:* Modern NLP has been pivotal in developing state-of-the-art language proficiency tools. Such models include those like Duolingo's AI-driven language lessons, which personalize vocabulary and grammar exercises, or tools like Grammarly, which provide real-time corrective feedback to enhance writing skills. These platforms leverage advanced NLP techniques to evaluate a student's language use, offering targeted feedback on aspects like semantic errors, contextual appropriateness, and idiomatic expressions. They facilitate continuous language practice, serving not just learners in academic settings but also professionals seeking to refine their communication skills.
- *Learning Analytics and Performance Prediction Models:* In learning analytics, NLP models like Turnitin leverage linguistic databases to assist educators in plagiarism detection and writing pedagogy. Other platforms use NLP-driven analytics to sift through discussion forums and student essays, enabling the prediction of student success and identification of those who might require additional support. For example, the Canvas Learning Management System incorporates NLP to analyze discussion threads, providing teachers with insights into student engagement and comprehension levels.
- *Engagement and Personalization through Adaptive Learning Models:* The impact of these NLP models is profound in terms of personalized education. They create a dynamic learning environment by adapting to individual student needs. Tools like Carnegie Learning's MATHia and Pearson's MyLab use NLP to adapt math and science problems to the learner's skill level, offering hints and tailored instruction that mimic a human tutor's guidance. This personalization leads to increased student engagement, as each learner receives attention akin to one-on-one tutoring, enhancing both motivation and the effectiveness of learning.
- *Tracking Mastery and Progress:* Moreover, these models equip educators with the ability to monitor progress over time. Through dashboards that display analytics

on student performance, educators can adjust teaching strategies to fit the class's evolving needs. The real-time data provided by NLP models also means that intervention strategies can be implemented promptly, often preventing minor issues from becoming significant roadblocks to student achievement.

9.4.4 Challenges and Considerations in Educational NLP

Implementing NLP in education is not without challenges. Contextual understanding is a significant hurdle, as educational content often contains complex concepts, abstract ideas, and domain-specific language that NLP algorithms can struggle to interpret. Data privacy is another concern, especially when dealing with minors or sensitive information. Ensuring that NLP applications comply with legal frameworks such as FERPA and GDPR is crucial. Bias and fairness in NLP models are also pressing issues. If the training data for these models contain biases, the models may perpetuate or even amplify these biases, leading to unfair or discriminatory outcomes. This is particularly problematic in assessment tools that might influence a student's academic trajectory.

Moreover, educational NLP requires interdisciplinary knowledge. Developers of NLP applications must understand pedagogical principles and the specific educational contexts to create effective learning tools. Lastly, language diversity presents a challenge. Educational content and student populations are incredibly diverse, and NLP tools must accommodate a multitude of languages and dialects, as well as varying levels of language proficiency, to be truly inclusive and effective. Addressing these challenges is essential for the responsible and equitable use of NLP in education.

Knowledge Checkpoint 11

Fill in the Blanks

1. Healthcare NLP is essential for extracting meaningful information from unstructured text such as ____________ and patient records.

2. NLP in healthcare aids in clinical decision support by extracting critical data to inform ____________.

3. One of the main challenges of NLP in healthcare is data ____________, which involves making different systems work together seamlessly.

4. Legal NLP focuses on the understanding and manipulation of ____________ texts.

5 Automated document analysis in Legal NLP is used for extracting key information from ____________ during the discovery phase of a lawsuit.

6 Predictive analytics in Legal NLP can help in predicting the ____________ of current cases.

7 In the financial sector, NLP is used for sentiment analysis to gauge public sentiment toward ____________ or individual stocks.

8 NLP in finance also plays a crucial role in ____________ detection by analyzing communication patterns and transactional data.

9 In education, NLP can facilitate learning by interpreting student input during ____________ activities.

10 One application of NLP in education is to provide feedback on language pronunciation, cadence, and intonation in ____________ learning.

11 Domain-specific NLP models in healthcare, like Clinical BERT, are fine-tuned on clinical notes to better capture the context of ____________ dialogue and terminology.

12 The integration of NLP in finance has led to the development of more robust predictive models for tasks like ____________ trend analysis.

13 Legal NLP is crucial for ____________ management by scanning large volumes of documents to identify potential legal issues.

14 Educational NLP uses text classification to organize and recommend ____________ content.

15 NLP in healthcare helps synthesize information from sources like EHRs, research papers, and ____________, making it actionable and accessible.

10

Measuring Success in Natural Language Processing Evaluation and Metrics

In Natural Language Processing (NLP), the measure of success is not just about building models but about how effectively these models perform in real-world applications. Evaluating NLP systems is complex, given the diversity of tasks they undertake, from text classification and sentiment analysis to machine translation (MT), summarization, and beyond. Each of these tasks requires tailored evaluation metrics to accurately assess the system's performance.

10.1 Intrinsic versus Extrinsic Evaluation Techniques

Evaluation in NLP is crucial for determining the effectiveness of models and ensuring they meet the specific needs of real-world applications. The complexity of human language, coupled with the broad spectrum of NLP tasks, necessitates diverse evaluation strategies. Intrinsic and extrinsic evaluations serve as the cornerstone for assessing these systems, each addressing different aspects of performance and utility.

10.1.1 Intrinsic Evaluation Techniques

Intrinsic evaluation focuses directly on the task-specific performance of an NLP system. It assesses the accuracy and quality of the output in a controlled environment, usually independent of any larger system or application.

- *Definition:* This method measures how well an NLP model performs a particular linguistic task, ignoring the potential end-use of the model.
- *Why it's important:* Intrinsic evaluation provides a detailed understanding of the model's capabilities and limitations in processing and understanding language. It helps in fine-tuning model parameters and diagnosing specific issues within the NLP system.

Language Intelligence: Expanding Frontiers in Natural Language Processing, First Edition. Akshi Kumar.
© 2025 The Institute of Electrical and Electronics Engineers, Inc. Published 2025 by John Wiley & Sons, Inc.

- *Examples:*
  a) **Sentiment Analysis:** Evaluating how accurately the model identifies and categorizes sentiments in texts, typically through metrics like precision, recall, and F1 score.
  b) **Syntax Parsing:** Assessing the accuracy of a model in generating the correct parse trees for sentences, often measured by parse success rate or comparison against a gold standard treebank.

10.2 Extrinsic Evaluation Techniques

Extrinsic evaluation measures the performance of an NLP system based on its impact on an external task or its contribution to the overall objectives of a larger system.

- *Definition:* This approach assesses the utility and effectiveness of an NLP model in the context of a real-world application or workflow, evaluating how the integration of the NLP system improves or impacts the end-task performance.
- *Why it's important:* Extrinsic evaluation is crucial for understanding how well an NLP component functions within a larger system and how it contributes to the ultimate goals of the application, providing insight into the practical value and impact of the model.
- *Examples:*
  a) **Information Retrieval**: Measuring the improvement in search relevance and user satisfaction when NLP is used to enhance search algorithms.
  b) **Machine Translation in E-commerce**: Evaluating the effect of MT on international customers' purchasing behavior, assessing not just the translation quality but also its impact on sales and customer engagement.

10.2.1 Combining Intrinsic and Extrinsic Evaluations

While intrinsic evaluation is essential for technical refinement and understanding of an NLP system, extrinsic evaluation bridges the gap between technical performance and real-world utility. A comprehensive evaluation strategy often involves both intrinsic and extrinsic methods to provide a holistic view of an NLP system's capabilities and its effectiveness in practical applications. For instance, a machine learning model for language translation might be intrinsically evaluated for grammatical accuracy and lexicon coverage, while its extrinsic evaluation could involve assessing user satisfaction in a live translation application.

Intrinsic and extrinsic evaluation techniques in NLP serve complementary roles. Intrinsic evaluation helps in optimizing the core functionalities of NLP systems, while extrinsic evaluation demonstrates their practical value in real-world scenarios. Together, they provide a comprehensive framework for measuring the success and impact of NLP technologies, ensuring they are not only technically proficient but also effective and beneficial in their applied contexts.

Deciding between intrinsic and extrinsic evaluation methods for NLP systems depends on the objectives of the evaluation, the development stage of the system, and the context in which the system will be used. Here's when to use each method:

- *When to Use Intrinsic Evaluation*
  a) **During Early Development Stages:** Intrinsic evaluation is particularly useful in the initial phases of NLP system development. It helps in fine-tuning the algorithms and models by closely examining their linguistic capabilities and performance on specific tasks.
  b) **For Technical Assessment:** When the goal is to understand the technical performance of a system, such as its ability to parse syntax, recognize entities, or detect sentiment accurately, intrinsic evaluation is appropriate. It allows for a detailed analysis of how well the system processes and understands language data.
  c) **To Identify and Diagnose Issues:** Intrinsic evaluation helps in pinpointing specific areas of weakness or failure within the NLP system. This can guide developers in making targeted improvements and optimizations.
- *When to Use Extrinsic Evaluation*
  a) **Assessing Real-World Utility:** Extrinsic evaluation is crucial when you need to understand how the NLP system performs in a real-world context, contributing to the end goals of a larger application or service.
  b) **Post-Development and Deployment:** Once the system has been developed and is ready for deployment, extrinsic evaluation can assess its impact and effectiveness within its operational environment, determining how well it meets the users' needs.
  c) **For Cross-System Comparisons:** When comparing different NLP systems to determine which one best supports the objectives of a larger application or task, extrinsic evaluation can provide insights into their relative effectiveness and utility in a practical context.
- *Examples of When to Use Each Method*
  a) **Intrinsic Evaluation:** If developing a new text classification model to distinguish between positive and negative product reviews, intrinsic evaluation methods would be used to measure the model's accuracy, precision, and recall directly on a labelled dataset of reviews.
  b) **Extrinsic Evaluation:** If integrating this text classification model into a customer feedback analysis system, extrinsic evaluation would measure the impact of the model on the business's ability to effectively respond to customer feedback and improve product quality.

Hence, intrinsic evaluation is best applied during the technical refinement of NLP models to ensure their linguistic accuracy and efficiency. Extrinsic evaluation, however, is critical for understanding the real-world value and effectiveness of these models within larger applications or systems. Selecting the appropriate evaluation method involves considering the current stage of the NLP system's development and the ultimate goals of its deployment.

10.3 Metrics for Text Classification

Text classification is a fundamental task in NLP where text data is categorized into predefined classes or categories. The performance of text classification models is typically assessed using several key metrics, each offering unique insights into the model's effectiveness.

10.3.1 Confusion Matrix

A confusion matrix is a tabular summary of the number of correct and incorrect predictions made by a classifier. It shows the actual versus predicted classifications, where each cell in the matrix represents a different type of outcome (true positive, true negative, false positive, false negative). This matrix helps in understanding the complete performance of the model, including its errors. Fig. 10.1 illustrates a confusion matrix for a binary classification problem.

Following are the basic terminology, which will help us in determining the metrics we are looking for:

- *True Positives (TP):* when the actual value is Positive and predicted is also Positive.
- *True negatives (TN):* when the actual value is Negative, and prediction is also Negative.

	Predicted +ve	**Predicted −ve**
Actual −ve	True negatives (TN)	False positives (FP) Type I error
Actual +ve	False negatives (FN) Type II error	True positives (TP)

Figure 10.1 Binary Classification Problem (2 × 2 matrix).

- *False positives (FP):* When the actual is Negative, but prediction is Positive. Also known as the Type 1 error
- *False negatives (FN):* When the actual is Positive, but the prediction is Negative. Also known as the Type 2 error

10.3.2 Accuracy

Accuracy is the most straightforward metric, representing the proportion of correctly classified instances out of the total instances. It is calculated by dividing the number of correct predictions by the total number of predictions made. While accuracy is intuitive and easy to understand, it can be misleading in imbalanced datasets where one class dominates the others. It provides a quick snapshot of the overall effectiveness of a model in correctly classifying text.

- *Formula:* $\text{Accuracy} = \dfrac{\text{Number of Correct Predictions}}{\text{Total Number of Predictions}}$
- *Example:* If a sentiment analysis tool processes 100 reviews and correctly classifies 90 of them, the accuracy is 90 100 = 0.9010090 = 0.90 or 90%.

Accuracy is most appropriate as an evaluation metric when dealing with datasets where the classes are evenly distributed, meaning each class has approximately the same number of instances. This balance ensures that the metric provides a fair representation of the model's overall performance, without being skewed towards the more prevalent class. It's particularly useful in scenarios where the consequences of false positives and false negatives are relatively equal, so neither type of error is disproportionately more harmful than the other. In practical terms, accuracy is best suited for general assessment tasks across various domains, such as when evaluating a model's capability to correctly classify news articles into categories like sports, politics, or entertainment. In these situations, the goal is to gain a quick and clear understanding of how well the model is performing across all categories, without needing to search the specifics of each type of error. Hence, in environments where the primary concern is the overall effectiveness of the model and each class holds similar significance to the outcome, accuracy serves as a reliable and straightforward metric.

10.3.3 Precision

Precision (also known as positive predictive value) measures the proportion of true positive predictions in the positive class. It is crucial in situations where the cost of false positives is high. Precision is calculated by dividing the number of true positive predictions by the total number of positive predictions (true positives plus false positives). It gauges the accuracy of the positive predictions made by the model, ensuring that when the model predicts a positive result, it is likely correct. This characteristic makes precision invaluable in fields like spam detection, where erroneously filtering legitimate emails as spam can be disruptive, or in fraud detection, where false positives can lead to unwarranted investigations and reputational damage. Similarly, in medical testing, high precision is essential because a false positive diagnosis can lead to unnecessary anxiety, invasive testing, and treatment.

- *Formula:* $\text{Precision} = \dfrac{TP}{TP + FP}$
- *Example:* In spam filtering, if 40 out of 50 emails labelled as spam are actually spam, precision is $4050 = 0.805040 = 0.80$ or 80%.

10.3.4 Recall

Recall (or sensitivity) indicates the proportion of actual positives that are correctly identified. It is important in scenarios where missing a positive instance is costly, like in disease screening. High recall means most of the positive instances are correctly captured by the model. Recall is calculated by dividing the number of true positives by the sum of true positives and false negatives. Recall is a critical metric when the cost of overlooking true positives is substantial. It measures the model's ability to identify and capture all actual positive instances, which is vital in areas such as disease screening where missing a positive case (a true patient) can have life-threatening consequences, or in legal discovery, where failing to identify all relevant documents could affect the outcome of a case. Therefore, recall is prioritized in environments where capturing every potential positive instance is paramount to the task's success.

- *Formula:* $\text{Recall} = \dfrac{TP}{TP + FN}$
- *Example:* In disease screening, if 90 out of 100 actual cases are identified by the model, recall is $90\,100 = 0.9010090 = 0.90$ or 90%.

10.3.5 F1 Score

The F1 score is the harmonic mean of precision and recall, providing a single metric that balances the two. It is particularly useful when you need to consider both false positives and false negatives. The F1 score reaches its best value at 1 (perfect precision and recall) and worst at 0. It is a better measure than accuracy for imbalanced datasets. The F1 score balances precision and recall, providing a more comprehensive measure of a model's accuracy.

- *Formula:* $\text{F1 Score} = \dfrac{2 \times \text{Precision} \times \text{Recall}}{\text{Precision} + \text{Recall}}$
- *Example:* With precision at 80% and recall at 90%, the F1 score would be $\dfrac{2 \times 0.80 \times 0.90}{0.80 + 0.90} \approx 0.85$ or 85%.

10.3.6 ROC Curve and AUC

The Receiver Operating Characteristic (ROC) curve is a graphical plot that illustrates the diagnostic ability of a binary classifier system. The AUC represents a measure of separability or how much the model is capable of distinguishing between classes. The ROC curve plots the true positive rate (recall) against the false positive rate at various threshold settings, while the AUC summarizes the performance across all possible thresholds. Higher AUC values indicate better model performance. The ROC Curve and its associated metric, the AUC, are especially relevant in binary classification tasks, such as credit scoring or assessing the likelihood of diseases, where understanding the trade-offs between true positive rates and false positive rates at various thresholds can inform better decision-making and model tuning.

- *ROC Curve Explanation:* The curve plots TPR against FPR, showing the trade-off between true positive and false positive rates.
- *AUC Explanation:* A measure of the model's ability to discriminate between classes, with a higher AUC indicating better performance.
- *Example:* If a binary classifier has an AUC of 0.95 as shown in Fig. 10.2, it means there's a 95% chance it will correctly distinguish between positive and negative instances.

Each metric offers a unique perspective on the model's performance in text classification tasks. Accuracy gives a general idea of performance, while precision, recall, and the F1 score provide more detail on its ability to handle positive and negative classes. The confusion matrix breaks down the performance into the most fundamental components, offering a clear view of the model's predictive capabilities. ROC and AUC together assess how well the model can differentiate between classes across different thresholds. Understanding and applying these

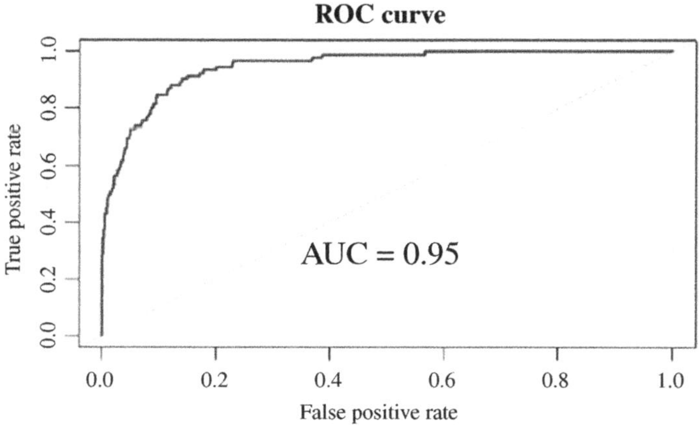

Figure 10.2 ROC Curve.

metrics appropriately is key to developing, tuning, and deploying effective NLP models in various text classification applications.

10.4 Evaluating Machine Translation and Text Summarization

Evaluating the performance of MT and text summarization systems is essential to ensure the quality and usefulness of their output. Different metrics have been developed to assess various aspects of these systems, from the accuracy of translation to the coherence and conciseness of summaries.

10.4.1 Machine Translation Evaluation

MT systems are evaluated based on their ability to produce accurate, natural, and coherent translations. Key metrics include:

- *BLEU (Bilingual Evaluation Understudy):* BLEU score calculates the average n-gram precision of the machine-translated text against one or more reference translations, with a penalty for too-short translations. It is widely used because it correlates well with human judgment, providing a quick and easy way to gauge translation quality. If a translated sentence matches the reference translation perfectly, it will score a BLEU of 1 (or 100%). However, if only half of the n-grams match, the score would be lower, factoring in the brevity penalty for unnatural conciseness. Suppose we have a source sentence in English: "*The quick brown fox jumps over the lazy dog.*" And we have two reference translations in another language (let's say French):
  a) Reference 1: "Le renard brun rapide saute par-dessus le chien paresseux"
  b) Reference 2: "Le rapide renard brun saute au-dessus du chien paresseux"
  Now, consider a machine-translated sentence: *"Le renard rapide brun saute dessus le chien paresseux."*
  To calculate the BLEU score, we compare the machine-translated sentence with the reference sentences. We check for n-gram overlap, starting with 1-grams (individual words), then 2-grams (word pairs), and so forth.

a) For 1-grams: The MT has 7 out of 8 words that appear in either reference translation.
b) For 2-grams (like "le renard", "renard rapide", etc.): Let's say 5 out of 7 two-word sequences match with the references.

If we just look at 1-grams and 2-grams for simplicity, the BLEU score would involve calculating these overlaps, and then applying a brevity penalty if the MT is shorter than the references.

- *METEOR (Metric for Evaluation of Translation with Explicit Ordering):* METEOR considers exact word matches, synonymy, and stemming while aligning the translated text with reference translations, and then calculates a harmonic mean of precision and recall. For example, if a translated text uses synonyms of the words in the reference and maintains the meaning, METEOR will give a higher score than BLEU, which only considers exact matches (EMs). METEOR is appreciated for its balance of precision and recall, offering a nuanced evaluation of translation quality, especially in handling synonyms and paraphrases.

10.4.2 Text Summarization Evaluation

Text Summarization systems are evaluated based on how effectively they condense the source material while retaining key information and readability.

- *ROUGE (Recall-Oriented Understudy for Gisting Evaluation):* ROUGE measures the overlap between the content of the system-generated summary and a set of reference summaries, typically counting matches of n-grams, word sequences, and word pairs. For example, a summary that captures all the key points of a reference summary will have a high ROUGE score, indicating effective information coverage. ROUGE is crucial for understanding how well a summarization model captures the essence of the source material, often used to evaluate recall.
  Consider a source document: *"The quick brown fox jumps over the lazy dog. It is a famous sentence that contains every letter of the alphabet."*
  And a reference summary: *"A sentence with every alphabet letter involves the quick brown fox and lazy dog."*
  Now, a system-generated summary: *"The quick brown fox and the lazy dog are in a famous sentence."*
  To calculate the ROUGE score, specifically ROUGE-N (let's use ROUGE-1 for single words)
  a) We find all the 1-grams in the system-generated summary and reference summary.
  b) Count how many 1-grams in the generated summary appear in the reference summary.
  In our example:

a) Total 1-grams in the generated summary: 12
b) Total 1-grams in the reference summary: 12
c) Overlapping 1-grams: 10 (like "the", "quick", "brown", "fox", "lazy", "dog", "sentence")

So, the ROUGE-1 recall score = 10 (overlaps)/12 (reference total) = approximately 0.83 or 83%

- *Length-adjusted Precision:* This involves evaluating the precision of the summary by considering the length of the generated text relative to the source or reference summaries. For example, a summary that is concise and includes most of the key points from the source content will score well in length-adjusted precision metrics. This metric is important for ensuring that summaries are not just accurate but also appropriately concise, avoiding verbosity or unnecessary detail.

Evaluating MT and text summarization systems requires a careful balance of quantitative metrics and qualitative judgments. BLEU and METEOR are critical for translation, offering insights into the accuracy and naturalness of the translated text. ROUGE and length-adjusted precision are key for summarization, assessing how well the summary captures the source content's essential information and whether it does so concisely. These metrics, while not perfect, provide valuable tools for developers and researchers to measure and enhance the performance of NLP systems in these complex tasks.

10.5 Metrics for Question-Answering and Conversational AI

Evaluating question-answering (QA) and conversational AI systems requires metrics that can accurately reflect the systems' ability to provide relevant, correct, and contextually appropriate responses. These metrics help assess not only the factual accuracy but also the user experience and engagement quality.

EM is one such metric that provides a binary indication of performance, assessing whether the system's response exactly matches the correct answer. It's particularly stringent, reflecting the system's precision in delivering precise answers, such as in machine reading comprehension tasks. For example, if a QA system correctly identifies "Paris" as the capital of France, it achieves a perfect EM score for that query. However, this metric's strictness means it doesn't account for near-correct responses, where the essence of the correct answer is present but not worded exactly. EM is best used when you need to measure the accuracy of responses in a QA system where answers are either completely right or wrong. It's suitable for tasks with definitive, clear-cut answers, such as fact-based queries or when evaluating systems like trivia games or compliance checks, where precision in answers is paramount.

The F1 score, another crucial metric, considers both precision and recall, offering a more nuanced view of a system's performance, especially in open-ended QA settings. It calculates the overlap between the predicted and correct answers, capturing how much essential information the response contains and how much excess or irrelevant information it omits. For instance, if the system responds "Paris is the capital" when the answer "Paris" is expected, the F1 score will evaluate this partial correctness, balancing the comprehensive and accurate representation of the answer. F1 Score should be employed when partial correctness of an answer carries value and when both the presence of relevant information (recall) and the absence of irrelevant information (precision) are important. It's ideal for open-ended QA scenarios, such as in customer service bots or any system where answers can be correct to varying degrees and contain multiple important elements.

In the field of conversational AI, **BLEU (Bilingual Evaluation Understudy)** has been adapted from its origins in MT to evaluate the linguistic quality of dialogue responses. This metric assesses how well the n-gram sequences of the generated response match with those of a set of reference responses, indicating the syntactical and grammatical alignment with expected dialogue patterns. BLUE is particularly useful in conversational AI when assessing the linguistic quality of generated text or spoken responses. It's applicable in scenarios where the flow and structure of dialogue are important, like in chatbots or virtual assistants, ensuring that the system's responses are not only accurate but also grammatically and syntactically coherent.

Perplexity is another key metric used predominantly in language modelling, which serves to evaluate the fluency and predictability of responses in conversational systems. A model with lower perplexity is deemed better, as it suggests that the system can predict the next word in a sequence more accurately, leading to more coherent and contextually appropriate dialogue. Perplexity is utilized primarily in the development and tuning of language models within conversational AI systems. It helps gauge how well a model can predict dialogue or text sequences, indicating fluency and coherence. This metric is most relevant in scenarios where the natural flow of conversation is critical, such as in storytelling bots, advanced customer support systems, or any platform where engaging and contextually appropriate dialogue is key.

Together, these metrics form a comprehensive toolkit for evaluating QA and conversational AI systems, addressing aspects from factual accuracy and information relevance to linguistic fluency and interaction quality. By leveraging these metrics, developers and researchers can finely tune their systems, ensuring they meet both the technical and experiential standards required for effective and engaging human-computer interaction.

10.5.1 Evaluation in Ranking and Information Retrieval

Evaluating ranking and information retrieval in NLP involves nuanced metrics that assess how well these systems manage and prioritize textual information in response to user queries. These evaluations are crucial for optimizing the retrieval of relevant, accurate content in a vast sea of data, ensuring users efficiently find what they need.

In NLP tasks, **Precision at k (P@k)** is a key metric for determining the exactness of a system in retrieving relevant documents within the top "k" results. For instance, in a semantic search task within a legal document database, if a user retrieves 10 documents and 7 are relevant, the P@10 is 70%. This metric is vital for measuring the system's ability to deliver pertinent results at the forefront, which is especially important in applications where users are likely to consider only the first few results. **Recall at k (R@k)**, meanwhile, measures the system's capacity to capture all pertinent documents within the top "k" results compared to the total available relevant documents. This metric is crucial in comprehensive research tasks, like conducting a literature review in scientific databases, where capturing a broad spectrum of relevant documents is more critical than the precision of individual documents. The **Mean Average Precision (MAP)** offers an aggregated measure of the system's performance across multiple queries, calculating the average precision at each rank where a relevant document is found. In NLP, MAP can be particularly insightful in evaluating multi-faceted queries in large corpora, like assessing the retrieval quality across different topics in a news article database, providing a holistic view of system performance.

Normalized Discounted Cumulative Gain (nDCG) addresses both the quality and rank of the retrieved information, emphasizing the importance of higher-ranked documents. In NLP applications such as QA systems or personalized content recommendation, nDCG assesses how well the system ranks highly relevant documents higher than less relevant ones, crucial for user satisfaction and system effectiveness. For example, in a QA NLP task querying a knowledge base for specific information, if the most relevant answers consistently appear at the top of the result set, the system would achieve a high nDCG score, indicating effective prioritization and relevance of the provided information.

These metrics collectively provide a comprehensive framework for evaluating ranking and information retrieval in NLP tasks. By precisely measuring the relevance and ranking quality of textual information retrieved in response to user queries, NLP professionals can refine their systems, enhancing the accuracy, relevance, and user trust in the retrieved information.

10.6 Metrics for Text-Based Forecasting and Prediction

In the domain of NLP, text-based forecasting and prediction involve analyzing textual data to forecast future events or trends. These tasks often merge traditional NLP techniques with time series analysis and predictive modelling, necessitating specific metrics to evaluate their accuracy and effectiveness.

For text-based forecasting and prediction, metrics traditionally used in predictive analytics, like Root Mean Square Error (RMSE) and Mean Absolute Percentage Error (MAPE), become relevant. These metrics help quantify the accuracy of predictions in continuous numerical terms, essential for tasks where NLP outputs are used to forecast quantitative variables.

10.6.1 Root Mean Square Error (RMSE)

RMSE is a standard way to measure the error of a model in predicting quantitative data. It represents the square root of the average squared differences between the predicted and actual values, offering a clear measure of the model's prediction error.

$$\mathrm{RMSE} = \sqrt{\frac{1}{n}\sum_{i=1}^{n}(y_i - \hat{y}_i)^2}$$

where y_i is the actual value, $\hat{y}_i$ is the predicted value, and n is the number of predictions.

For example, in a stock market prediction model using NLP analysis of financial news, if the actual stock prices versus the predicted prices are [100, 104, 102] and [102, 103, 101], respectively, the RMSE would provide a numerical value reflecting the average prediction error across these three predictions. RMSE is particularly useful in NLP tasks like financial forecasting or demand prediction where the predictions are continuous, and the magnitude of the error is crucial. It gives more weight to larger errors, making it sensitive to outliers and significant prediction deviations.

10.6.2 Mean Absolute Percentage Error (MAPE)

MAPE measures the size of the error in percentage terms, providing a normalized, intuitive understanding of the average prediction error's proportion to actual values.

$$\mathrm{MAPE} = \left(\frac{1}{n}\sum_{i=1}^{n}\left|\frac{y_i - \hat{y}_i}{y_i}\right|\right) \times 100\%$$

where y_i is the actual value, $\hat{y}_i$ is the predicted value, and n is the number of observations.

For example, in sentiment trend prediction where actual sentiment scores on a scale of 0 to 100 are compared with predicted scores, if the actual scores are [90, 80, 85] and predicted scores are [85, 78, 88], MAPE would calculate the average percentage difference between these sets of scores. MAPE is valuable in scenarios where understanding the prediction error relative to the actual value size is important. It's commonly used in economic forecasting, inventory demand, and other NLP applications where predictions relate to scalable metrics or indices.

In text-based forecasting and prediction within NLP, RMSE and MAPE serve as critical evaluative tools, providing insights into the accuracy and reliability of predictive models. RMSE offers a measure of the prediction error magnitude, ideal for models where large errors are particularly detrimental, while MAPE gives a percentage-based error measure, useful for understanding the prediction error in relation to the scale of the data. Together, these metrics facilitate a comprehensive evaluation of NLP-driven predictive models, ensuring their efficacy and reliability in practical applications.

Knowledge Checkpoint 12

Scenario-Based Worksheet: Choosing the Right Evaluation Metric in NLP

This worksheet is designed to help understand the context in which different evaluation metrics are most appropriately used within the field of NLP.

Scenario 1: Sentiment Analysis on Social Media Posts

You are developing a sentiment analysis model to classify social media posts into positive, negative, or neutral categories. The dataset is imbalanced, with a majority of the posts being neutral.

Which metric(s) would be most appropriate to evaluate your model and why?

Scenario 2: Machine Translation System

You've created a MT system to translate sentences from English to French. The quality of translation varies, and you need to evaluate the system's performance comprehensively.

Identify which metric(s) you would use to evaluate the translation quality. Explain your choice.

Scenario 3: Email Spam Detection

Your model is designed to filter out spam emails from users' inboxes. It is crucial that legitimate emails are not incorrectly classified as spam (false positives).

Which evaluation metric would you prioritize to minimize false positives and why?

Scenario 4: Customer Support Chatbot

A company uses a chatbot to answer customer queries. The chatbot's effectiveness is measured by its ability to provide the correct answer on the first attempt.

What metric would best evaluate the chatbot's first-attempt success rate?

Scenario 5: Stock Market Prediction

An NLP model predicts the next day's stock prices based on news articles. Accuracy in prediction is crucial to avoid significant financial losses.

Which metric(s) would most accurately measure the model's prediction performance?

Scenario 6: Named Entity Recognition (NER) System

Your NER system identifies and classifies names of persons, organizations, locations, expressions of times, quantities, monetary values, percentages, etc., in unstructured text.

What metric(s) would be most suitable for evaluating the precision and recall of your NER system?

Scenario 7: Fake News Detection

An NLP system is tasked with identifying and flagging fake news articles.

What metric(s) would you use to evaluate the system's ability to accurately distinguish between fake and real news?

Scenario 8: Predictive Text Modelling for Email Composition

A model suggests the next word or phrase as the user composes an email to improve efficiency and reduce typing effort.

Which evaluation metric(s) would best assess the model's performance in accurately predicting the next word or phrase?

Knowledge Checkpoint Answers

Knowledge Checkpoint 1-Chapter 1:

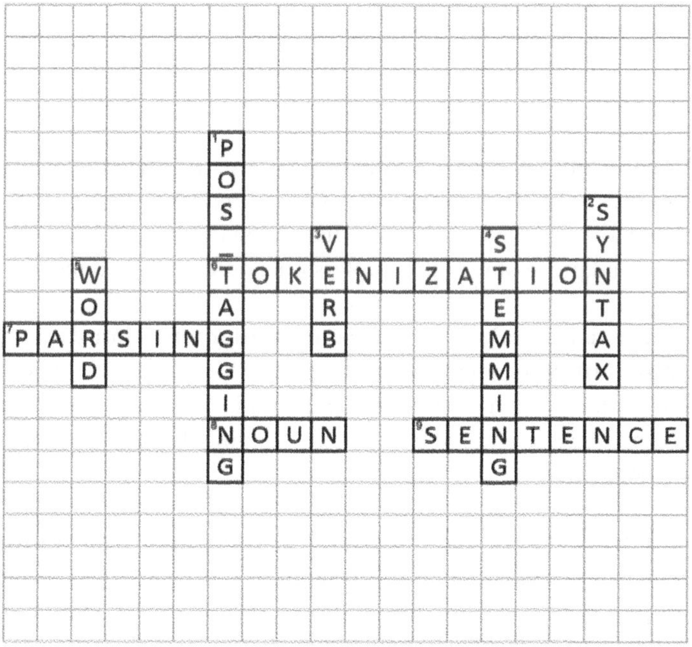

Language Intelligence: Expanding Frontiers in Natural Language Processing, First Edition. Akshi Kumar.
© 2025 The Institute of Electrical and Electronics Engineers, Inc. Published 2025 by John Wiley & Sons, Inc.

Knowledge Checkpoint 2-Chapter 2:

1. **c. Social media posts** Social media posts are a common source of textual data for NLP tasks because they provide a large volume of real-time, varied, and often informal language data.

2. **b. It helps in building models that can understand and process multiple languages.** Multilingual data is crucial for developing NLP systems that can operate across different linguistic boundaries, enhancing their versatility and global applicability.

3. **c. Data that is tagged with specific information like sentiment or entities.** Annotated or labelled data refers to text that has been marked with specific information, such as sentiment labels or named entities, which is essential for training supervised machine learning models in NLP.

4. **b. Data augmentation** Data augmentation is a technique used to artificially expand the dataset, often through methods like synonym replacement or back translation, to improve the robustness of NLP models.

5. **b. It contains specialized vocabulary and knowledge pertinent to a specific field.** Domain-specific data is important because it includes the unique vocabulary and contextual knowledge necessary for accurate analysis and processing within professional or technical domains.

6. **c. Care must be taken to ensure that augmentation does not skew the distribution or meaning of the data.** This statement implies that data augmentation, if not properly managed, can introduce biases that affect the representativeness and reliability of the training dataset, leading to skewed model outcomes.

7. **b. A dataset where each sentence is translated into multiple languages.** A parallel corpus is a collection of text data where each sentence or document is translated into multiple languages, facilitating tasks like machine translation and cross-linguistic studies.

8. **c. Presence of slang, abbreviations, and non-standard language.** The primary challenge with informal text data from social media is managing the variability and idiosyncrasies of language use, including slang, abbreviations, and informal expressions.

9 **b. Consistency.** Consistency in data quality refers to the uniformity of formats and conventions throughout the dataset. This is essential for algorithms to process data correctly, ensuring that all data is interpreted in the same way by the NLP model.

10 **b. Resampling or synthetic data generation.** Resampling or creating synthetic data can help address class imbalances by either oversampling the minority class, undersampling the majority class, or generating new synthetic examples of the underrepresented class. This helps ensure that each class is adequately represented, preventing the model from favoring the majority class excessively.

11 **c. Decreasing the size of the dataset randomly.** Decreasing the dataset size randomly is not a method of data augmentation; augmentation aims to increase or diversify the dataset, not reduce it.

12 **b. It makes the model outdated due to changes in language use and semantics.** Data drift refers to the phenomenon where the statistical properties of the target variable, which the model is predicting, change over time, making the model less accurate or relevant as language evolves.

Knowledge Checkpoint 3-Chapter 3:

1

Text Cleaning in Social Media Posts:

- Handle slang by creating a dictionary of common slang terms and their standard equivalents.
- Use spelling correction libraries like TextBlob or PySpellChecker to correct misspellings.
- For emoticons, either translate them into text that conveys the same emotion or remove them if they do not add value to the sentiment analysis.

2

Chatbot Sentence Splitting and Tokenization:

- Sentence splitting is crucial for understanding where one query ends and another begins, impacting the chatbot's response accuracy.
- Tokenization breaks down each sentence into words or phrases, helping the chatbot to process and understand user queries.
- Tools like NLTK and spaCy in Python are effective for implementing these processes.

3

Lemmatization in Machine Translation:
- Lemmatization is preferred as it considers the word's context, part of speech, and correct base form, ensuring a more accurate translation.
- For example, translating "running" to other languages requires knowing whether it's used as a verb or a noun, which lemmatization can identify.

4

Stop Word Removal in Ancient Text Analysis:
- Contextual relevance is key; aggressive filtering might remove words that, while common today, had significant meanings in ancient texts.
- A customized stop word list should be developed, considering the historical and linguistic context of the texts.

5

Parsing and Syntactic Analysis in Document Summarization:
- These processes identify the grammatical structure and relationships between words, helping extract key sentences and phrases that represent the document's main ideas accurately.

6

Tokenization in Multilingual Feedback Analysis:
- Employ multilingual tokenization tools like spaCy, which can handle various languages and scripts, to accurately process and analyze customer feedback.

7

Text Cleaning and Stop Word Removal in SEO:
- Proper text cleaning improves the search engine's ability to index and understand content, while customized stop word removal ensures that only meaningful keywords are emphasized for SEO.

8

Sentence Splitting in Voice Recognition:
- Accurate sentence splitting helps in transcribing natural speech pauses and endings, improving the transcription's readability and accuracy.
- Machine learning models can be trained on large datasets to better predict sentence boundaries in speech.

9

Stemming vs. Lemmatization in Sentiment Analysis:

- Choose lemmatization for deeper analysis where understanding the exact word form and meaning is crucial, especially in nuanced sentiment detection.

10

Sub-Word Tokenization in News Language Processing:

- Sub-word tokenization helps manage the vast vocabulary and evolving terms in news language, ensuring that even new or uncommon words can be processed effectively.

11

Parsing and Syntactic Analysis in Legal Document Analysis:

- Use advanced syntactic analysis tools to maintain the legal text's structural and semantic integrity, ensuring that the legal meaning and nuances are preserved.

12

Syntactic Analysis Methods in Language Learning Apps:

- Constituency and dependency parsing methods can be used to teach sentence structure, helping users understand how different parts of a sentence interact and depend on each other.

Knowledge Checkpoint 4-Chapter 3:

1. **Unicode Normalization:** b. To standardize characters into a consistent form

2. **Sentence Splitting:** b. Because punctuation marks like periods can serve multiple functions

3. **Tokenization:** b. To convert text into a series of tokens or meaningful pieces

4. **Lemmatization vs. Stemming:** b. Lemmatization reduces words to their root form based on actual language usage, whereas stemming cuts off the ends of words heuristically

5. **Stop Word Removal:** b. When doing sentiment analysis and context is important
6. **Part-of-Speech Tagging:** b. It assigns grammatical labels to words, aiding in understanding sentence structure
7. **Parsing and Syntactic Analysis:** c. To analyze the grammatical structure of the text
8. **Text Processing Libraries in Python:** b. spaCy
9. **Unicode Normalization Description:** c. Standardizing text to a uniform encoding standard
10. **Regular Expressions in Text Cleaning:** b. To search and manipulate strings based on patterns
11. **Sentence Boundary Disambiguation Technique:** c. Dictionary lookups
12. **Sub-Word Tokenization Advantage:** b. It helps in handling out-of-vocabulary words.
13. **Part-of-Speech Tagging in NLP Tasks:** b. Sentiment analysis
14. **Text Cleaning Challenge:** c. Maintaining the meaning and context of the text
15. **Stemming in Information Retrieval:** b. It groups different forms of a word together.
16. **Retaining Stop Words in Language Modelling:** b. They contribute to understanding the grammatical structure.
17. **Focus of Dependency Parsing:** c. The relationships between words in a sentence
18. **Lemmatization Importance in Machine Translation:** b. It helps in maintaining the meaning of words across languages.
19. **Benefit of Tokenization in Machine Translation:** b. It separates text into tokens, making it easier to translate individual elements.
20. **Non-Text Processing Python Library:** a. Matplotlib

Knowledge Checkpoint 5-Chapter 4:

Part 1: Word Frequency Analysis

1

Count the Words:

- A simplified example (not exhaustive):
  - University: 5 times
  - Goldsmiths: 3 times
  - Education: 2 times
  - London: 2 times
  - Creative: 1 time
  - Innovation: 1 time

2

Reflection:

- Most frequent words are often common nouns or verbs related to the university (e.g., "university," "education").
- Surprising to see some specific words like "creative" and "innovation" not as frequent, considering the university's focus.

Part 2: Word Relationships

1

Identify Word Pairs:

- Goldsmiths — University
- Creative — Innovative
- Arts — Design

2

Reflection:

- These word pairs often appear together due to their direct association in the context of the university (e.g., "Goldsmiths" is often followed by "University").
- Identifying word pairs helps in understanding how certain concepts are interconnected in the text.

Part 3: Word Prediction Game

1

Guess the Word:

- The missing word in the sentence "The United Kingdom is known for its diverse landscapes, from the rolling hills of the English countryside to the rugged Scottish Highlands and the picturesque Welsh _______." could be "beaches" or "coastline" or "landscape."

Part 4: Categorizing Words

1

Categorize the Words:

- Nouns: University, Goldsmiths, London, education, arts, design
- Adjectives: Creative, innovative, diverse, vibrant
- Verbs: Established, include, blends, engaging

2

Reflection:

- The text uses a variety of nouns to describe specific aspects (e.g., "university," "arts") and adjectives for qualitative description (e.g., "creative," "vibrant").
- Categorizing words helps in understanding the focus of the text and how different types of words contribute to the overall message.

Part 5: Creating Word Representations

1

Represent Words Visually:

- University: A mortarboard (graduation cap).
- Innovation: A lightbulb.
- Creative: A paintbrush.
- Arts: A palette.
- London: An outline of the London skyline or Big Ben.

2

Reflection:

- Chose representations that are widely recognized symbols for each concept.
- Challenge was to simplify complex ideas like "innovation" into a universally understood symbol like a lightbulb.

Concept Mapping

After you have studied linguistic feature engineering concepts in this chapter, this will help you connect these concepts learned to the exercises you have done in the above activity.

Part 1: Word Frequency Analysis

Concepts: Bag of Words, TF-IDF

- **Mapping:** In this activity, you counted how often each word appeared in a text, which directly relates to the Bag of Words model where the presence and frequency of words are used to represent text data. The reflection on the importance of word frequency ties into the TF-IDF (Term Frequency-Inverse Document Frequency) concept, which weights words based on their frequency across documents, highlighting the importance of certain terms over others.

Part 2: Word Relationships

- **Concepts:** Co-occurrence Matrix, N-gram Model
- **Mapping:** Identifying pairs of words that often appear together introduces you to the idea of word relationships and context, foundational for understanding Co-occurrence Matrices (which track how often pairs of words occur together) and N-gram Models (which predict the next item in a sequence). This exercise lays the groundwork for understanding how words' relationships can provide context and meaning in text analysis.

Part 3: Word Prediction Game

- **Concepts:** N-gram Model, Contextual Embeddings
- **Mapping:** Guessing a missing word based on its surrounding words is a practical application of the N-gram model, where the probability of a word occurring is based on the occurrence of its preceding words. It also introduces the concept of contextual embeddings, where the meaning of a word is influenced by its context, as seen in advanced models like BERT and GPT.

Part 4: Categorizing Words

- **Concepts:** One-hot Encoding, Non-contextual Embeddings
- **Mapping:** Categorizing words into nouns, verbs, and adjectives gets you thinking about differentiating features of words, similar to how one-hot encoding assigns a unique identifier to each word. This exercise also touches on the idea of non-contextual embeddings, where words are represented in vector space without considering the context, focusing instead on their categorical characteristics.

Part 5: Creating Word Representations

- **Concepts:** Embeddings (Non-contextual and Contextual)
- **Mapping:** Representing words visually encourages you to think about abstract representation forms, akin to how embeddings work in NLP. This activity can be linked to both non-contextual embeddings, where a word has a fixed representation regardless of its use case, and contextual embeddings, where the representation might change based on the word's meaning in different contexts.

Knowledge Checkpoint 6-Chapter 4:

Part 1: Sentence Analysis
Answers:

1

Subject, Verb, and Objects:

- **Sentence 1:** Subject: "He," Verb: "heated," Object: "the soup," Instrument: "in the microwave."
- **Sentence 2:** Subject: "He," Verb: "heated," Object: "the soup," Instrument: "in the microwave."

2

Pronoun Reference:

- **Sentence 1:** "It" refers to "the soup." The context indicates that "it was hot" describes the soup's temperature after being heated.
- **Sentence 2:** "It" also refers to "the soup." Here, "it was boiling" specifically describes the soup reaching a boiling state due to heating.

Part 2: Linguistic Differences
Answers:

1

Change of Meaning:

- Changing "hot" to "boiling" alters the intensity or degree of heat applied to the soup. "Hot" suggests a comfortably warm state, while "boiling" implies reaching the boiling point, which is a specific temperature where bubbles form.

2

Grammatical/Syntactic Features:

- The use of the adjective "hot" versus "boiling" impacts the interpretation of the end state of the heating process. Both adjectives modify the soup but suggest different levels of heat. The context provided by "until" leads to understanding that the heating process continued until reaching these states.

Part 3: NLP Approaches
Answers:

1

Dependency Parsing:

- **What is it?** Dependency parsing is the process of analyzing the grammatical structure of a sentence by identifying relationships between "head" words and words which modify those heads.
- **Application:** For both sentences, dependency parsing can help identify that "it" is dependent on "soup," helping link the action and

its effect directly to the soup rather than any other element like the microwave.

2

Coreference Resolution:

- **What is it?** Coreference resolution is the task of finding all expressions that refer to the same entity in a text. It links pronouns with their specific antecedents.
- **Application:** A coreference resolution algorithm would determine that "it" in both scenarios refers to "the soup." By understanding this linkage, the system can accurately interpret the result of the action described in each sentence.

Part 4: Practical Application
Answers:

1

Consequences of Misinterpretation:

- Misinterpreting these sentences could lead to incorrect heating settings in the microwave, potentially underheating (if "hot" is misinterpreted as less warm than intended) or overheating the soup (if "boiling" is not recognized as a cue to reach a boiling state).

2

Verification Methods:

- The system could ask for confirmation or clarification if the end-state temperature is critical: "Would you like the soup just warm, or should it start boiling?" This approach helps confirm the user's intent and ensures safety and satisfaction.

Part 5: Reflective Questions
Answers:

1

Importance of Context:

- Context is crucial as it helps determine the specific meaning of terms within the interaction. In NLP, context helps distinguish between different uses of words, such as "hot" and "boiling," which both describe temperature but have distinct meanings.

2

Future Handling of Ambiguities:

- Advanced NLP systems may use more sophisticated context-aware algorithms that incorporate a broader range of linguistic features and real-world knowledge to handle ambiguities. Techniques like deep learning and more dynamic models can predict and interpret nuances based on extensive training data and improved algorithms.

Knowledge Checkpoint 7-Chapter 5:

MCQs

1. b. Ability to handle long-term dependencies
2. d. Transformer
3. b. Learn from a small amount of data by applying knowledge from a related task

Match the Following

1. c. Neurosymbolic models
2. b. Attention mechanism
3. a. LSTM
4. d. Transfer learning

True/False Statements

1. False
2. False
3. True
4. False
5. False

Knowledge Checkpoint 8-Chapter 6:

1. **What is the main objective of topic modelling in NLP?**
   - Correct Answer: b. To uncover abstract topics within a collection of documents

2

Which technique is often used for Semantic Role Labelling (SRL)?
- Correct Answer: b. Conditional Random Field

3

_____________ is the process of identifying the main subject or theme from a piece of text.
- Correct Answer: Subject identification

4

In Named Entity Recognition (NER), "Apple" identified as an organization is an example of a(n) _____________ entity.
- Correct Answer: Named

5

Latent Semantic Analysis (LSA) is used for correcting spelling errors in text.
- Correct Answer: False

6

Guided LDA allows users to define seed words for topics, guiding the topic modelling process.
- Correct Answer: True

7

Cohesion analysis in NLP involves examining how grammatical and lexical ties create unity in a text.
- Correct Answer: True

8

If an NLP model needs to identify specific financial terms within market analysis reports, it is likely using:
- Correct Answer: b. Named Entity Recognition

9

In analyzing a large collection of historical documents to uncover common themes over centuries, the best NLP technique would be:
- Correct Answer: c. Topic Modelling

10

A system designed to assess the sentiment expressed in customer reviews about a new product uses:
- Correct Answer: d. Sentiment Analysis

11

An NLP tool that breaks down a legal document into who (agent), what (action), and whom (beneficiary) is primarily performing:

- Correct Answer: c. Semantic Role Labelling

12

A chatbot that can understand and manage user inquiries by identifying keywords and their purpose is employing:

- Correct Answer: c. Subject Identification

Knowledge Checkpoint 9-Chapter 7:

Multiple Choice Questions (MCQs)

1. **c. Identifying complex emotional states:** Advanced sentiment analysis extends to identifying complex emotional states beyond just positive, negative, or neutral sentiments.

2. **b. Specific emotions conveyed:** Emotion recognition specifically analyzes the particular emotions conveyed in the text, different from sentiment analysis which often focuses on overall polarity.

3. **b. Pragmatic analysis:** Pragmatic analysis is crucial for detecting irony and sarcasm, as it involves understanding the context and the speaker's intent.

4. **b. Puns and wordplay:** Humor often involves puns and wordplay, exploiting the linguistic features for comedic effect.

5. **a. OCEAN Model (Big Five)** The OCEAN model, also known as the Big Five personality traits, is commonly associated with psychometric analysis in NLP.

True/False Statements

6. False—Sentiment analysis can go beyond these basic classifications to detect a range of emotions and sentiments.

7. True—Emotion recognition can indeed detect nuanced emotional states like excitement, disappointment, or relief.

8. False—Sarcasm detection in text can be challenging due to subtleties in language and context.

9 True—Humor identification can be used to enhance engagement, including in educational platforms.

10 False—Psychometric NLP can analyze and predict behaviors based on textual analysis.

Scenario-Based Questions

11 **a. Polarity shift recognition:** The phrase “Rarely have I been this thrilled with a purchase” shows a positive sentiment despite the initially negative construction (“Rarely”), demonstrating polarity shift recognition.

12 **b. Emotion recognition:** Analyzing therapy session transcripts to determine prevalent emotions is an application of emotion recognition.

13 **c. Psychometric NLP:** Using NLP to flag potential mental distress signals in an online forum shows the application of psychometric NLP.

14 **d. Humor identification models:** A virtual assistant engaging in banter and telling jokes would utilize humor identification models.

15 **b. Personality trait estimation:** Adapting learning content based on students’ language use in an educational app is an application of personality trait estimation, showing how NLP can understand and adapt to individual learning preferences.

Knowledge Checkpoint 10-Chapter 8

Fill in the Blanks:

1 Translation and transliteration are the foundational pillars of **multilingual** NLP.

2 Modern translation systems leverage **neural networks** to deliver translations with remarkable accuracy and fluency.

3 **Statistical Machine Translation (SMT)** is a translation technique that involves algorithms learning from bilingual text corpora.

4 The main goal of multilingual NLP is to facilitate **global** communication and enhance inclusivity.

5 Transformer models like Google’s BERT and OpenAI’s GPT series use **self-attention** mechanisms to process language.

True/False:

1 Neural Machine Translation uses a rule-based approach to translate between languages. (False)

2 Cross-lingual models are designed to process multiple languages using a single model. (True)

3 Transliteration is about converting the meaning of words from one language to another. (False)

4 Low-resource languages often have a wealth of digital tools and corpora available. (False)

5 Phonological complexity and orthographic variation pose significant challenges in processing low-resource languages. (True)

Match the Following Techniques with Their Descriptions:

- A. Rule-Based Machine Translation (RBMT)
  - Relies on a comprehensive set of linguistic rules and dictionaries.
- B. Statistical Machine Translation (SMT)
  - Involves algorithms that learn from bilingual text corpora.
- C. Neural Machine Translation (NMT)
  - Utilizes deep neural networks and sequence-to-sequence architecture.

Knowledge Checkpoint 11-Chapter 9

1

Healthcare NLP is essential for extracting meaningful information from unstructured text such as ____________ and patient records.

- **Answer:** Clinicians' notes

2

NLP in healthcare aids in clinical decision support by extracting critical data to inform ____________.

- **Answer:** patient care

3

One of the main challenges of NLP in healthcare is data ____________, which involves making different systems work together seamlessly.

- **Answer:** interoperability

4

Legal NLP focuses on the understanding and manipulation of ____________ texts.

- **Answer:** legal

5

Automated document analysis in Legal NLP is used for extracting key information from ____________ during the discovery phase of a lawsuit.

- **Answer:** legal documents

6

Predictive analytics in Legal NLP can help in predicting the ____________ of current cases.

- **Answer:** outcomes

7

In the financial sector, NLP is used for sentiment analysis to gauge public sentiment toward ____________ or individual stocks.

- **Answer:** market developments

8

NLP in finance also plays a crucial role in ____________ detection by analyzing communication patterns and transactional data.

- **Answer:** fraud

9

In education, NLP can facilitate learning by interpreting student input during ____________ activities.

- **Answer:** interactive learning

10

One application of NLP in education is to provide feedback on language pronunciation, cadence, and intonation in ____________ learning.

- **Answer:** language

11

Domain-specific NLP models in healthcare, like Clinical BERT, are fine-tuned on clinical notes to better capture the context of ____________ dialogue and terminology.

- **Answer:** medical

12

The integration of NLP in finance has led to the development of more robust predictive models for tasks like ____________ trend analysis.

- **Answer:** market

13

Legal NLP is crucial for ____________ management by scanning large volumes of documents to identify potential legal issues.

- **Answer:** due diligence

14

Educational NLP uses text classification to organize and recommend ____________ content.

- **Answer:** academic

15

NLP in healthcare helps to synthesize information from sources like EHRs, research papers, and ____________, making it actionable and accessible.

- **Answer:** clinical trial reports

Knowledge Checkpoint 12-Chapter 10

Scenario 1: Sentiment Analysis on Social Media Posts
Answer: Given the imbalanced dataset, the F1 Score or a weighted average F1 Score would be most appropriate. These metrics balance precision and recall, crucial for datasets where one class dominates. Additionally, considering macro or micro averages can help address the imbalance by treating all classes equally or weighting them by their prevalence, respectively.

Scenario 2: Machine Translation System
Answer: BLEU (Bilingual Evaluation Understudy) and METEOR scores would be ideal for evaluating translation quality. BLEU measures the correspondence between a machine's output and that of a human, focusing on the precision of n-grams, while METEOR considers synonymy, stemming, and word order, providing a more nuanced assessment.

Scenario 3: Email Spam Detection
Answer: Precision should be prioritized to minimize false positives, ensuring legitimate emails are not incorrectly classified as spam. A high precision rate means fewer non-spam emails are marked as spam, which is crucial for user trust and utility.

Scenario 4: Customer Support Chatbot
Answer: Accuracy or the Top-1 accuracy metric would best evaluate the chatbot's first-attempt success rate. It directly measures the proportion of queries correctly answered on the first attempt.

Scenario 5: Stock Market Prediction
Answer: RMSE (Root Mean Square Error) and MAPE (Mean Absolute Percentage Error) would most accurately measure the model's prediction performance. RMSE provides a measure of the magnitude of error, while MAPE gives an understanding of the error in percentage terms, which is intuitive for financial predictions.

Scenario 6: Named Entity Recognition (NER) System
Answer: Precision, Recall, and the F1 Score are most suitable. These metrics assess the accuracy of the identified entities (precision), the model's ability to identify all relevant entities (recall), and a balanced measure of both (F1 Score), crucial for NER systems.

Scenario 7: Fake News Detection
Answer: Precision, Recall, F1 Score, and AUC (Area Under the ROC Curve) are crucial metrics. They help understand the system's ability to accurately identify fake news (precision and recall) and evaluate its performance across various threshold settings (AUC), considering the balance between true positive rate and false positive rate.

Scenario 8: Predictive Text Modelling for Email Composition
Answer: Perplexity would be the best metric to assess the model's performance in accurately predicting the next word or phrase. It measures how well a probability model predicts a sample and is particularly useful in language modelling, where lower perplexity indicates a model is better at predicting the next word.

A

Text Representation Techniques: A Unified Overview

Understanding various text representation techniques is essential for mastering NLP. Let's use the sentence *Light can behave as both a particle and a wave.* to demonstrate how different NLP models process and analyze this text, including Bag of Words (BoW), TF-IDF, n-gram, One-Hot Encoding, Word2Vec, GloVe, BERT, and GPT (a type of Large Language Model). By illustrating these techniques with a single sentence, we capture a snapshot of how each model processes text, offering insights into their applications and effectiveness for different NLP tasks.

1. **Bag of Words (BoW)** creates a simple vector representing the frequency of words regardless of order or context. For our sentence:
   Light: 1 can: 1 behave: 1 as: 1 both: 1 a: 2 particle: 1 and: 1 wave: 1
2. **TF-IDF (Term Frequency-Inverse Document Frequency)** enhances BoW by considering not only the frequency of words in a single document but also how rare they are in all documents (corpus). For example, "particle" and "wave" might score higher than "a" due to their specificity in the context of physics across a larger corpus.
3. **N-gram** captures contiguous sequences of words, providing insights into the flow of language. For a bigram (2-gram) model:
   <Light can> <can behave> <behave as> <as both> <both a> <a particle> <particle and> <and a> <a wave>
4. **One-Hot Encoding** assigns a unique binary vector to each word. The vector length equals the number of distinct words, with '1' at the index of the word and '0's elsewhere. For instance:
   Light: [1, 0, 0, 0, 0, 0, 0, 0, 0] can: [0, 1, 0, 0, 0, 0, 0, 0, 0]
5. **Word2Vec** maps words into a continuous vector space where semantically similar words are embedded closer together. "Particle" and "wave" would be closely positioned in this space, reflecting their related meanings in physics.
6. **GloVe (Global Vectors for Word Representation)** also provides word embeddings but is constructed based on the aggregation of global word-word

Language Intelligence: Expanding Frontiers in Natural Language Processing, First Edition. Akshi Kumar.
© 2025 The Institute of Electrical and Electronics Engineers, Inc. Published 2025 by John Wiley & Sons, Inc.

co-occurrence statistics from a corpus, aiming to preserve both local context and global word statistics.

7. **BERT (Bidirectional Encoder Representations from Transformers)** understands words based on all other words in a sentence (contextually), rather than one-directional or isolated interpretations. It would interpret "light" within the context of its dual properties as described in the sentence, recognizing the complex physical concept being discussed.
8. **GPT (Generative Pre-trained Transformer)**, as an LLM, goes beyond understanding to generating text. Given the sentence "Light can behave as both a particle and a wave," GPT could continue explaining or contextualizing this concept in quantum mechanics, potentially elaborating on how these properties are demonstrated in scientific experiments.

B

Step-by-Step Guide to NLP Processing on E-Commerce Customer Feedback

This detailed guide provides a systematic approach to processing and analyzing customer feedback using Natural Language Processing (NLP) techniques. We'll use a hypothetical e-commerce customer review as a running example to demonstrate each step.

Example Text

"Absolutely loved the smartwatch I bought last month! 😍 The battery lasts forever, and the interface is super user-friendly. However, the strap broke after just two weeks, which was disappointing😞. Customer service handled my complaint promptly though, and a replacement was sent out quickly. Five stars for service! ★★★★★ Will shop here again. #Happy Customer #Smartwatch Love"

Step-by-Step NLP Analysis

1. **Text Cleaning**
   - **Process:** Remove any irrelevant characters, correct misspellings, and standardize text format, while carefully handling emojis and hashtags which may be relevant for sentiment analysis.
   - **Application:** Ensure terms like "smartwatch" are consistently used and not misspelled. Keep emojis and hashtags intact as they provide emotional and contextual cues.
2. **Sentence Splitting**
   - **Process:** Divide the text into individual sentences using punctuation as a guide, taking care not to split hashtags or emoticons.

Language Intelligence: Expanding Frontiers in Natural Language Processing, First Edition. Akshi Kumar.
© 2025 The Institute of Electrical and Electronics Engineers, Inc. Published 2025 by John Wiley & Sons, Inc.

- **Application:** Split the review into distinct thoughts, e.g., one sentence about the product's features, another about the issue with the strap, etc., while preserving entities like "#Happy Customer".

3. **Tokenization**
   - **Process:** Break sentences into words or tokens, including emojis and hashtags.
   - **Application:** Identify individual words and symbols such as "loved", "battery", "interface", "disappointing", "😍", "#Smartwatch Love".
4. **Lemmatization and Stemming**
   - **Process:** Reduce words to their base or root form while ignoring emojis and hashtags.
   - **Application:** Convert words like "bought" to "buy" and "was" to "be", without altering non-text tokens.
5. **Stop-Word Removal**
   - **Process:** Eliminate common words that may not contribute significant meaning, avoiding the removal of hashtags and emojis as they carry meaning.
   - **Application**: Remove words like "the", "and", "is", which do not offer much value in understanding sentiment, while keeping "#Happy Customer" and emoticons.
6. **Part-of-Speech Tagging**
   - **Process:** Assign tags to each word as noun, verb, adjective, etc., excluding non-textual elements like emojis.
   - **Application:** "Absolutely" as an adverb, "loved" as a verb, "smartwatch" as a noun, "disappointing" as an adjective, and treat hashtags and emojis separately.
7. **Named Entity Recognition (NER)**
   - **Process:** Identify and classify key entities mentioned like names, products, and companies, including the detection of hashtags as entities.
   - **Application:** Recognize "last month" as a time expression, "smartwatch" as a product, and "#Happy Customer" as a sentiment-related tag.
8. **Sentiment Analysis**
   - **Process:** Determine the sentiment expressed in the text, considering the emotional impact of emojis and the contextual relevance of hashtags.
   - **Application:** Identify positive sentiments about the battery and interface, and a negative sentiment about the strap, with additional sentiment insight from emojis like 😍 and 😞.
9. **Dependency Parsing**
   - **Process:** Analyze the grammatical structure of a sentence to establish relationships between "head" words and words which modify them,

excluding emojis and hashtags from the syntactic structure but recognizing their positioning.
- **Application:** Parse the sentence to understand that "smartwatch" is the subject liked by the customer, with "😍" following as an emotional enhancer.

10. **Topic Modelling**
    - **Process:** Determine the underlying topics or themes within the text, including analyzing hashtags as part of topic identification.
    - **Application**: Extract topics like "product quality", "customer service", and "product durability", along with tagged topics "#Happy Customer" and "#Smartwatch Love".
11. **Text Coherence and Cohesion Analysis**
    - **Process:** Assess how well the parts of the text fit together logically and stylistically, considering the role of emojis and hashtags in linking ideas or expressing tone.
    - **Application:** Evaluate transitions between positive and negative aspects in the review to maintain a logical flow, noting how emojis and hashtags contribute to the overall coherence.

C

Harnessing Python Libraries for NLP

Python enthusiasts, explore the rich assortment of libraries designed to make NLP tasks more effective and innovative. Whether you're parsing text, engaging in deep learning for language understanding, or analyzing linguistic data, Python's breadth of libraries is unparalleled in its capability to tackle these challenges.
Core Libraries for NLP

- **NLTK (Natural Language Toolkit):** A foundational library for processing text with facilities for tokenization, parsing, classification, and more, making it ideal for basic NLP tasks.
- **spaCy:** Offers robust features for large-scale information extraction and natural language understanding with an emphasis on speed and efficiency.

Deep Learning in NLP

- **BERT (Bidirectional Encoder Representations from Transformers):** A transformative model that uses deep learning to understand the context of words in text by considering the entire sequence of words for optimal comprehension and performance.
- **TensorFlow, Keras and Hugging Face Transformers:** These libraries provide comprehensive tools for building complex machine learning models, including deep neural networks that are fundamental for advanced NLP applications. Hugging Face Transformers, in particular, is a widely adopted library for accessing and fine-tuning pretrained transformer models, enabling rapid development of high-performance NLP applications.

Supporting Libraries for Data Manipulation and Visualization

- **Pandas:** Essential for handling structured data, particularly useful in pre-processing stages of NLP for organizing and formatting textual data.
- **NumPy:** Plays a critical role in numerical operations which are often necessary for feature extraction in NLP tasks.

Language Intelligence: Expanding Frontiers in Natural Language Processing, First Edition. Akshi Kumar.
© 2025 The Institute of Electrical and Electronics Engineers, Inc. Published 2025 by John Wiley & Sons, Inc.

- **Matplotlib and Plotly:** Useful for visualizing data and the results of linguistic analyses, helping interpret patterns and insights from text data.

Extended Applications

- **Scikit-Learn:** Integrates with NLP workflows for applying machine learning algorithms, including text classification and clustering.
- **Gensim:** Specializes in unsupervised topic modelling and similarity detection within large text corpora, which is invaluable in NLP for identifying themes and patterns in text.

These libraries represent just a fraction of what Python has to offer for NLP. They facilitate a wide range of operations from data handling and preprocessing to complex model training and analysis, ensuring that developers can both experiment with innovative solutions and deploy efficient, scalable applications. Python's ecosystem encourages continual exploration and optimization, making it a cornerstone for modern NLP developers.

Through the lens of Python, every word holds the potential to unlock new insights—harness its libraries and decode the language of tomorrow.

Further Reading

Bird, S., Klein, E., and Loper, E. (2009). *Natural Language Processing with Python*. Sebastopol, CA: O'Reilly Media, Inc.

Ingersoll, G.S., Morton, T.S., and Farris, A.L. (2013). *Taming Text: How to Find, Organize, and Manipulate It*. Shelter Island, NY: Manning Publications.

Jurafsky, D. and Martin, J.H. (2009). *Speech and Language Processing*, 2e. Upper Saddle River, NJ: Prentice Hall.

Lee, R.S. (2023). *Natural Language Processing: A Textbook with Python Implementation*. Singapore: Springer Nature.

Manning, C.D. and Schütze, H. (1999). *Foundations of Statistical Natural Language Processing*. Cambridge, MA: MIT Press.

Language Intelligence: Expanding Frontiers in Natural Language Processing, First Edition. Akshi Kumar.
© 2025 The Institute of Electrical and Electronics Engineers, Inc. Published 2025 by John Wiley & Sons, Inc.

Index

Note: Page numbers referring to figures are presented in *italics*, while those referring to tables are displayed in **bold**. This format is adopted to enable readers to quickly differentiate between visual elements and tabular data.

Language Intelligence: Expanding Frontiers in Natural Language Processing, First Edition. Akshi Kumar.
© 2025 The Institute of Electrical and Electronics Engineers, Inc. Published 2025 by John Wiley & Sons, Inc.

c

d

X

Z

Printed and bound by CPI Group (UK) Ltd, Croydon, CR0 4YY
17/09/2026
14964232-0007